The Rise and Fall of Human Rights

D0881847

Stanford Studies in Human Rights

The Rise and Fall of Human Rights

Cynicism and Politics in Occupied Palestine

Lori Allen

Stanford University Press
Stanford, California

Stanford University Press
Stanford, California

©2013 by the Board of Trustees of the Leland Stanford Junior University.

Printed in the United States of America on acid-free, archival-quality paper

Library of Congress Cataloging-in-Publication Data is available from the Library of Congress

ISBN 978-0-8047-8470-2 (cloth : alk. paper)--ISBN 978-0-8047-8471-9 (pbk. : alk. paper)
ISBN 978-0-8047-8551-8 (electronic)

To my parents, Betty and Joe Allen

This struggle may be a moral one, or it may be a physical one, and it may be both moral and physical, but it must be a struggle. Power concedes nothing without a demand. It never did and it never will. Find out just what any people will quietly submit to and you have found out the exact measure of injustice and wrong which will be imposed upon them, and these will continue till they are resisted with either words or blows, or with both. The limits of tyrants are prescribed by the endurance of those whom they oppress.

Frederick Douglass, 1857

We are not born equal; we become equal as members of a group on the strength of our decision to guarantee ourselves mutually equal rights. Our political life rests on the assumption that we can produce equality through organization, because man can act in and change and build a common world, together with his equals and only with his equals.

Hannah Arendt, 1994

Contents

Foreword

LORI ALLEN'S *The Rise and Fall of Human Rights* opens with a double-barreled epigraph. She first gives us the famous—and often misquoted—passage from the American abolitionist Frederick Douglass in which the world-historical catastrophe of American plantation slavery grounds a simple observation with monumental implications: that the physics of oppression can be countered only with an opposite and equal reaction, a struggle with "words or blows, or with both." These lines from Douglass have been used down through the decades as a reminder that structures of injustice do not just fade away; they must be confronted, witnessed, attacked, and if necessary burnt to the ground. Despite Douglass's careful inclusion of "words" as a potential tool of resistance, there can be no doubt that words alone will not make a sufficient "demand" on the ravages of power, as history has shown us time and time again. That it is Frederick Douglass from whom we learn this lesson and not, say, Karl Marx—whose theories of history, power, and conflict also lead to robust and, potentially, violent theories of action—is revealing. Like the victims of the Nazi regime, the generations of enslaved Africans—and the ideological and economic systems that justified such an abomination—have come to represent injustice itself, something absolute that does not admit of reasonable qualification. In other words, there are times, our troubled history teaches us, when the only thing left to do is fight and fight hard, when endurance of suffering is no longer noble but a form of complicity.

The second epigraph is from Hannah Arendt and, like the first, its import hangs over the book like a dark and ominous shadow. The legacy of Arendt's writings has troubled the life of human rights since the early postwar period, when human rights—as international law, as a form of politics, as a new transnational ethics—was deeply incipient, except for the coteries of international lawyers and diplomats who labored away within the United Nations to establish the rudiments of what would become the international human rights system. In 1951, however, with the Universal Declaration of Human Rights still hot off the presses, Arendt published her masterwork on the origins of totalitarianism. In one of its thirteen chapters, she levels a devastating critique against the "rights of man" as the doctrine had evolved through the first half of the twentieth century. One could hardly find a moment in history in which a politics and ethics based on the principle of human dignity would be more starkly contradicted in practice by the horrors of imperialism, militarism, and genocide. So, with the killing fields of World War I and the Holocaust in full view, it is not surprising that Arendt would look with some philosophical suspicion on *any* assertion of human equality that was anchored in the deontological ether.

As a solution to this yawning gap, Arendt argued that the neo-Enlightenment conception of human rights was not merely "nonsense on stilts," as Jeremy Bentham once put it, but something much worse: a dangerous discursive shell game that takes the place of the hard, and historically rare, work through which political institutions create the social conditions in which rights-bearing and citizenship can have any meaning at all. The idea and necessity of a prior "right to have rights" have, for some, kept the critical light shining on the broader political and social contexts in which human rights have become, especially after the end of the Cold War, such a compelling, inspirational, and even hegemonic geoethical presence.

Allen's remarkable study of the ways in which human rights has transformed a much older conflict between Israel and Palestinians living in the West Bank is profoundly shaped by the two categories of insights with which she begins the book. Given that the Palestinians will not achieve some form of self-recognized emancipation without winning a struggle that they are still losing, and given that the concept of human rights as a factor in the conflict has risen among a stateless people whose ability to create a meaningful political community—and thus legitimately ground a "right to have rights"—is as restricted as the sealed and divisive borders that continue to trap Palestinians in a geopolitical cage, what then? Allen's book is an answer to these questions and is rooted in years of close ethnographic attention to the lives of people who ultimately cannot deny their powerlessness and choked politics and yet must still establish and enact community on the terms they are given.

They do so, as she shows us with keen feeling tempered by a social scientist's equanimity, by finding meaning and cultural creativity in the performance of what Allen calls a "shared charade," the performance of the contested roles that have come to define the Israeli-Palestinian conflict in terms of human rights abuses, victims, perpetrators, activists, and institutions. A key to understanding the charade is the desire of many involved—the international donor community, the Palestinian Authority, opposition groups like Hamas—to look like a state. The examination of these cultural performances leads Allen onto an open, critical terrain on which human rights is only one among several key modes by which the conditions of domination are negotiated. Allen's book is a sobering reminder that the promises of human rights can appear to recede at the speed of light when they are taken seriously by those whose lived reality is defined by exclusion, deferred dreams, and what she calls the politics of "as if."

Mark Goodale
Series Editor
Stanford Studies in Human Rights

Acknowledgments

MY THANKS go first to the people of Palestine, who helped me, taught me, and shared so much about the joys, strengths, and sadnesses of their lives. Everywhere I went people were kind, generous, and eager to do whatever they could to help me understand something about life under occupation. I hope what I've written here does some justice to the injustices they live with every day. I offer special thanks to the staff of Defence for Children International–Palestine (DCI–Palestine) and numerous friends I made at that organization. Also in Palestine, Nidal and Nisreen al-Azzeh and family, Terry Boulatta, Catherine Cook and family, Adam Hanieh, Steph Khoury, Hanan El-Masu, Helen Pope, Diab Zayd, and families in Jenin, Ramallah, Daheisha, and Aida camps, in Bethlehem, and in al-Bireh have been sources of information, inspiration, and support for the research in this book since 2000. In different ways they all taught me about Palestine, and about what it takes to be a good and courageous human. My parents—Joseph and Betty Allen—and siblings—Jeff, Jari, Tom, Michele, Terry, Jim, and Tim Allen, and Vicki and Dave Benyo—and all their families in Kansas City and environs have been source, inspiration, and support for me since 1971; they have also taught me about good and courageous humanity.

Research for this book was supported by fellowships and grants from the British Academy (SG53934), the University of Cambridge Department of Middle Eastern Studies, the Harry Frank Guggenheim Foundation, the Isaac Newton Trust, the Palestinian American Research Center (twice), the Social Science Research Council's Program on Global Security and Cooperation and Program on the Middle East and North Africa, the United States Institute of Peace, the Wenner-Gren Foundation for Anthropological Research, and the Woodrow Wilson National Fellowship Foundation, and by a Charlotte W. Newcombe

Doctoral Dissertation Fellowship. The Center for Arabic Study Abroad provided language training. I gratefully acknowledge their support. The ideas and analyses expressed in this book are mine and do not necessarily reflect the views of these institutions.

Generous fellowships at the Pembroke Center for Teaching and Research on Women at Brown University and the Harvard Academy for International and Area Studies provided the precious time and space to write this book. At the Harvard Academy, the wonderfully helpful and attentive Jorge Dominguez, Kathleen Hoover, and Larry Winnie deserve special thanks for their always cheerful support of this project. A number of scholars were enormously generous in their participation at the author's conference that the Harvard Academy hosted, and the critical comments of Jane Cowan, Didier Fassin, Roger Owen, Sara Roy, Kimberly Theidon, and Richard A. Wilson provided me with key points of focus. Special thanks also go to Jane Cowan, reviewers, and editors at Stanford University Press.

Ajantha Subramanian kindly brought me into her writing group of stellar, smart women anthropologists in the Boston area, and I have a tremendous debt of gratitude to her for sharp, engaged feedback on so many of these pages, and for her open-hearted support, along with that of Elizabeth Ferry, Ann Marie Leskowich, Janet McIntosh, Heather Paxson, Smita Lahiri, and Chris Walley. Ajantha and Vince Brown and their two sparkling daughters, Zareen and Anisa, made a final write-up year at Harvard especially fun and sustaining.

Also very helpful was feedback offered by audiences at the University of Cambridge Centre of Governance and Human Rights, Duke University's Department of Cultural Anthropology, George Washington University's Institute for Middle East Studies, Harvard University's Middle East Anthropology Seminar, the Max Planck Institute for Social Anthropology, the University of Manchester, Reed College, SOAS (the University of London's School of Oriental and African Studies), the University of Sussex, the University of Chicago's Semiotics Workshop, the University of Illinois at Urbana–Champaign, the University of Vienna's Department of Anthropology, and the Institute for Social Anthropology in Vienna, especially by Director Andre Gingrich. The intelligent and honest comments of students in my 2010–2011 Human Rights in the Middle East course have improved Chapters 2 and 3. Thanks are also due for the research assistance of Miranda Margowsky, Hannah Trachtman, and Ghia Ghazi Zaatari at Harvard; and more thanks are owed to Valentina Azarov, Nidal al-Azraq, James Eastman, Fuad Musallam, and Doaa' al-Nakhala, who have been efficient, thorough, bright research assistants. Without all of their help I would still be working on this book. Jeff Allen's eagle-eyed editing was invaluable.

I appreciate the feedback of numerous friends and colleagues who read many versions of the manuscript, starting from the earliest versions that Nadia Abu El-Haj, Jean Comaroff, Rashid Khalidi, and William Mazzarella read with remarkable attentiveness and apparent interest. I still miss the University of Chicago mostly because of them. Their scholarship and mentorship have been truly astounding and inspirational.

Various parts of the book were written in the beautiful shelters provided by many friends. For the sleeping, writing, and contemplating spaces they offered I thank Vicki and Dave Benyo in Lee's Summit; Jessica Clark and Dan Cook in Chicago and Philadelphia; Cathy Cook and Mitri Karkar in Ramallah; Omar Dajani and Nafiz and Maggie Husseini and family in Kythera; Aylette Jenness in Cape Cod and Cambridge; Dimitris Livanios and Anna Mastrogianni in Athens; George Mehrabian and Natasha Terlexis in Tzia; Brigitte Steger in Vienna; Helen Pope in Rome; Alessandra Sanguinetti in New York; Jessica Winegar and Hamdi Attia in Philadelphia; and Yezid Sayigh in Cambridge, Beirut, and Paris.

I was very grateful to receive the encouraging words and useful comments on Chapter 2 that Joost Hiltermann, Jonathan Kuttab, Emma Playfair, Charles Shammas, and Raja Shehadeh were so kind to give. The brave optimism and calm conviction of their work are an inspiration, and I hope the pages based on their work and words convey something of that spirit.

Over the many years and stages of research and writing that have gone into this book, I have benefited enormously from the comments of Zerrin Özlem Biner, Sheila Carapico, Elliott Colla, Harri Englund, Khaled Furani, Steven Hibbard, Maimuna Huq, Laleh Khalili, Genevieve Lakier, Ellen Moodie, Glen Rangwala, Kirsten Scheid, Gregg Starrett, Winifred Tate, and Sharika Thiranagama. I continue to rely in many ways on all their insightful scholarship and encouraging words. I have exploited Toby Kelly's scholarly generosity excessively, and he has been an attentive and encouraging reader of many of these chapters.

Amahl Bishara, Lara Deeb, Ilana Feldman, and Jessica Winegar have read through so many incarnations of these various chapters over many years, they'll probably never read the final product (beyond these acknowledgments), and I wouldn't blame them! Suffice it to say, my research and writing have been enormously sharpened by their careful, critical engagement; and more important, I have been continuously buoyed by their friendship, motivated by their political conviction, and ever reminded what good academics can and should be. Amahl was an unceasingly bright spark throughout the final phases of writing in "the other Cambridge." She and Nidal al-Azraq have helped me think through a lot of ideas, and their merriment lifted me when it was most needed. Yezid Sayigh heroically and helpfully commented on the entire manuscript. His superb cooking, challenging conversation, forceful and engaging intellect, zany comedy, and Greek island retreats have nourished me, mind, body, and soul. In his warm kitchens and good company I remain grateful, cheered, and encouraged pretty much all the time.

Any scholarly endeavor is a long process of accumulated indecisions, visions, and revisions, to paraphrase T. S. Eliot, and I thank the many other people not mentioned here by name who have helped me to decide, see, and revise.

I N 2009, during a break in a human rights training workshop in the West Bank, I sat drinking tea with staff from the Palestinian Independent Commission for Human Rights (ICHR), the semi-state institution that monitors the human rights performance of the Palestinian Authority (PA). As one of its regular activities, the ICHR was running a training session for PA security personnel. The fieldworkers and legal researchers who had just been lecturing on the Convention Against Torture and Other Cruel, Inhuman or Degrading Treatment or Punishment[1] were explaining to me other aspects of their jobs, including inspections of PA prisons.

A young fieldworker laughed as he told a story about a visit to a prison in the northern West Bank. He was shown into a room where a bruised, bloody prisoner was sitting bound, an obvious victim of torture. The security staff had mistakenly thought that the fieldworker was a doctor and had brought him there to treat the injured man. On another occasion a guard escorted this same fieldworker to a room where a prisoner was bound in *shabeh*, a torture position in which the prisoner is tied in a painful manner and left for hours. Apparently the man had accidentally been forgotten. When the guard's superior arrived to talk to the fieldworker and saw what had happened, he cuffed his underling on the head in anger. The staff around the table chuckled at the clumsiness of these security personnel who were so incompetent they couldn't even hide their abuses. The others then offered more stories. They told of inspecting prisons where they knew the administration had prepared more carefully, because the visits were routine and arranged in advance. Still, they could see the traces of torture in the line of dirty smudges where the sweaty foreheads of men bound in standing *shabeh* had been pushed up against the walls. These experienced human rights workers laughed not from disbelief but at the farce of it all.

I, on the other hand, was surprised. It was by no means news to me that the PA was torturing Palestinians. Palestinian and international human rights organizations (HROs) have been documenting these practices almost since the PA was established in the occupied territory in 1995 (PCHR 2002; AI 1998).[2] Plenty of observers have remarked on the distressing irony of Palestinians using the same torture techniques on each other that Israelis have used against them. Nor was it surprising that the PA was inefficient in its efforts to hide its abusive practices. What stunned me was the collective recognition that came through these stories of human rights as a performance. They conveyed a sense that concern for human rights was a pretense, a facade that everyone recognized as such but was feigning to keep up nevertheless. This book is my effort to understand the genesis and effects of that shared charade, and the state of cynicism that unites Palestinian human rights defenders, abusers, victims, critics, and observers alike.

. . .

In September 2000 the second Palestinian intifada against Israeli occupation began. Throughout the uprising, competing claims of suffering and rights violations were exchanged between Palestinians and Israelis, repeating a theme that has characterized the conflict for more than six decades. It is in part on the basis of their victimhood and violated rights that Palestinians waged their struggle for national rights and legitimacy, called for international protection, and sought humanitarian aid. They engaged with the transnational human rights framework, with both its practices and its meanings, to define their place in a global order. They deployed the vocabulary of human rights to explain their position as a people living without justice, in need of international assistance, and deserving of independence.

The international human rights system comprises a conglomeration of organizations, ideologies, activists, discourses, and declarations. As this system has grown increasingly large since the 1980s, human rights language has come to infuse the ways in which Palestinians from all walks of life—from politicians and representatives of civil society to militants and random victims of violations—speak and relate to outsiders and to one another. Human rights institutions, workers, activities, and representational forms have informed how Palestinians see themselves, and how they provide nationalist pedagogy about who and what the Palestinian citizen and state should be. The calls, categories, rules, and principles of human rights appear prominently in everything from school children's textbooks to international governance projects encouraging PA judicial development and "security sector reform."[3] The cyber circulation of the Gaza Youth's Manifesto for Change in 2010 invoked human rights in its critical expression of frustration. It began, "We, the youth in Gaza, are so fed up with Israel, Hamas, the occupation, the violations of human rights and the indifference of the international community!" (Carbajosa 2011). The human rights categories in which Palestinians speak their claims for justice shape how they create solidarities and provide a language by which they project their aspirations internationally, just as human rights claims reverberate in the language by which political rivals debate and try to prove themselves worthy to the Palestinian citizenry at home.

Little of this, however, is happening in a way that could have been foreseen by the drafters of the Universal Declaration of Human Rights (UDHR), whose noble hopes for international understanding and world peace underwrote that first official United Nations human rights statement.[4] Nor is it building what the UN call for human rights education envisioned as "a universal culture of human rights" (UNESCO 2006). Neither have the primary effects of human rights projects accorded with the "funding priorities" outlined in Western donors' calls for proposals, which request projects that "focus on rebuilding mutual trust through reconciliation, building capacity for conflict resistance, empowering marginalized parties and launching joint development policies" (EC 2007).

The mushrooming of the human rights industry in the occupied Palestinian territory and the infusion of donor funds that has encouraged this have led to a professionalization of human rights work, but they have not resulted in any improvement in most Palestinians' political and social circumstances. Human rights violations continue at the hands of Israeli forces, settlers, and PA security services and, if anything, most Palestinians are worse off whereas the human rights industry thrives. This material success has come at a cost. Palestinian HRO expansion and dependence on foreign funding increased as the first intifada wound down in the early 1990s. Largely at the behest of EU and US funders, the human rights industry has been utilized more and more as a technocratic tool, as if "human rights" were a set of skills that could be taught and mastered, regardless of any change in political framework. Palestinians believe that this donor relationship that has bolstered the human rights industry has also disfigured the Palestinian nationalist moral and political economies, resulting in a general alienation of HROs from the local population. However, it is precisely that space of alienation, that critical distance opened up by a cynical stance, that has kept at least some Palestinians immune from the technocratic approach to development and state-building brought by foreign donors. Cynicism, along with recollections of an earlier period of nationalist populism, has kept them wary of how human rights discourse is used in the political conflict between Fateh and Hamas, and unconvinced by these parties' efforts to prove their liberal legitimacy. Yet many others still cling to human rights discourse as the way to express to "the outside" the effects of the occupation's violence and demand its cessation.

Human Rights and the Human Rights Industry

A conceptual distinction between "human rights" and the "human rights industry" must be registered from the outset, lest my argument be misunderstood as yet another iteration of the cultural relativism debate that has dogged scholarship about human rights, and that might portray "Palestinian culture" as being somehow incompatible with "human rights values" (cf. Cowan, Dembour, and Wilson 2001:4–5). As I use it here, the term *human rights* encompasses a set of principles broadly related to what the UDHR originally articulated (regarding, among other things, the dignity of the human, entailing rights to freedom of movement, freedom from torture, political assembly, and so on). The values embodied in human rights conventions and agreements, the principles upon which they are based, are not alien to Palestinians in the occupied territory. Every protest against occupation, every objection to the indignities it inflicts, every effort to free political prisoners, and every vote cast is an assertion of dignity and, in some way, a demand for human rights.

In contrast, the term *human rights industry* (or *regime, system,* or *structure*)[5] refers to the material and financial infrastructure that buttresses human rights work (see also Goodale 2009:97; Sewell 1996:842). Broadly, it is the complex of activities and institutions that function under the label *human rights,* including the professionals who work within those organizations, the formulas they have learned in order to write reports and grant applications, and the funding streams that this industry generates and depends on. It is the tainting of human rights by the human rights industry that so many in Palestine reject. Nevertheless, the industry grows, and different groups—including Palestinian ones—have taken its language and forms in novel directions in the pursuit not only of human rights but also of politics itself.

'Abed's Analysis

Many Palestinians from all social strata and political angles believe that the gap between human rights and the human rights industry is large. For them, human rights discourse has become all hot air, nothing more than so many "empty words" (*haki fadi*). A conversation I had with a Palestinian man named 'Abed gives a sense of this perspective.[6] His narrative helps to explain why Palestinian NGOs have come to be referred to as donor-driven "shops," and why popular consensus maintains that the goal of these "shops" is to pad their directors' pockets rather than to provide for their constituents' needs.[7] 'Abed's discussion also introduces the reader to key political events in Palestine, a crucial element of the context that is shaping these negative attitudes toward the human rights industry.

. . .

To celebrate Ramadan in the occupied Palestinian territory, the British consulate hosted an iftar dinner, the fast-breaking meal during the Muslim holy month, for select invited guests. It took place at Darna, one of the most expensive restaurants in Ramallah, the cultural capital of the West Bank. In 2009, Ramadan stretched through August and into September, and the early evening weather was humid and still full of summer. The men's suits looked hot and the women's hair was flatter than many probably wished. I was there as the guest of a young British man, one of many Westerners involved in "security sector reform" in the West Bank. He introduced me to some of his friends who were there from the PA, including the head of information technology at the Ministry of Interior (MoI) and that ministry's legal advisor, the head of the president's office, a presidential military advisor, and officers from the Preventive Security Force. Among the other invitees I also recognized people from numerous civil society organizations, including the director of the ICHR. A white-haired older gentleman in line at the buffet table introduced himself to me as a member of FIDA, a leftist faction one doesn't hear much about these days. A rather serious young man seated across from me said he was from a center for Islamic nonviolence in Nablus. These people were involved in a broad mix of activities and institutions funded by foreigners.

The dining room was crammed full. The entire length of one wall was set up with a rich buffet of meats, fishes, and salads, dished out by servers in smart white kitchen uniforms and tall chef's hats. The luxury of the meal was a clear indication of the high status of the host and guests. At one point the British

Consul-General gave a brief speech. (My field notes have no record of what he said.) Given the British government's heavy investment in Palestinian development (broadly construed), surely the salaries of many in the room were at least partially funded by that country.

After filling my plate and returning to my seat, I introduced myself to the Palestinian woman sitting next to me, who turned out to be the head of a Palestinian human rights NGO. I tried to make small talk (that is, conduct research), asking her what kind of work she was involved in. She was clearly more interested in her food and her friends than in my clumsy chatter, but she briefly obliged my inquiries. She told me she had given testimony to the Goldstone Commission that had investigated the Israeli attacks in Gaza in 2009. She also said she makes a report to the UN every year. I thought she might be talking about the UN Special Committee to Investigate Israeli Practices Affecting the Human Rights of the Palestinian People and Other Arabs of the Occupied Territories,[8] which has been issuing annual reports since 1971. I asked what her thoughts were about the usefulness of such reports, trying to prompt her with my opinion that this UN committee seemed to issue essentially the same report every year, calling for the cessation of Israeli abuses in the same ineffective way each time.

"Nothing changes," I commented, echoing the cynical, critical tone I had come to expect from most Palestinians in conversations about the UN and human rights.

"No," she said, "the things that happen over the year change. The Israeli violations are different."

"OK, maybe Israeli tactics change," I said, trying hard to extend the dialogue, "but the UN's suggestions and condemnations are all the same, year after year." Despite my efforts, she responded with a noncommittal nod and turned back to her friends. Her reluctance to go along with my critique of the human rights industry should not have been surprising, given her personal and professional dependence on it.

A few more awkward interchanges later, feeling my fieldwork efforts to have been distinctly foiled, I concentrated on finishing my food and left without dessert. I went straight to the house of 'Abed and Zeena, brother-in-law and sister of my friend Nida', who is from a refugee camp in the West Bank. They and a number of 'Abed and Zeena's children were sitting around and enjoying a lazy post-iftar dessert in front of the TV. Musa, a handsome eight-year-old boy, greeted me from the corner of the living room, where he sat crosswise in an overstuffed chair, his skinny legs dangling over one armrest, his knobbly torso bent up against the other one, a seemingly universal child's TV-watching position.

Over tea and sweets I told the family about my evening surrounded by PA people. "They're all Fateh," 'Abed muttered, practically spitting out the name of the predominant political faction, with which most people in the PA are affiliated. I think the family—seven children and two parents sharing a modest three-bedroom home—was a bit resentfully impressed by the lavishness of the gathering I described. Zeena extended a plate of her delectable *qatayif* toward me and I eagerly took up a couple of the stuffed dessert pancakes traditionally served during Ramadan. I told them about my attempt to get the woman from the human rights NGO to admit that there were only dubious results from all those human rights activities. 'Abed, a graphic artist also working on a master's degree in law, said, "Well, of course she wouldn't. That's her bread and butter. NGOs are all just *dakakin*," he asserted, employing the word that Palestinians use to describe NGOs as money-making corner shops. He offered an example, saying, "All human rights training courses are for nothing but making money! I have attended tons of these courses. On international humanitarian law, on other legal issues. There was nothing meaningful or new in any of them. The NGOs just ran them to make money," he complained. The fact that so many of these courses are available is itself indication of the material success of the human rights industry in Palestine, and 'Abed's dismissal of them indicates their lack of credibility.

He conveyed surprise at my easy agreement with his negative assessment of human rights work in Palestine. He thought that I, an American anthropologist in Palestine working on human rights, must be a staunch and probably naive believer in the human rights industry. This was an assumption I encountered often. Palestinians figure that most Westerners hold idealistic views of human rights as universal standards, and they expect Westerners to criticize Palestinians for not upholding them.

My expression of my own distrust of the system opened the door to 'Abed's well-considered critique. A course on human rights was the only one he had not liked during his studies toward a law degree, 'Abed told me. "Human rights is just something that the United States government uses to excuse its attacks. Look at it: the US government is the biggest human rights abuser, as you yourself know, Lori. Look at your own country, with poverty, homelessness, and moral degradation." I nodded. "So before you try to spread human rights in the world, why not go fix yourselves!" he yelled to a hypothetical American, assuring me he was angry at the US government, not directing these criticisms at me personally. Nida' and Zeena looked on, bemused, used to 'Abed's vigorous discussion style, and nodding in agreement at his points.

'Abed had gotten himself on a roll as he thought about the uselessness of human rights NGOs in his country. He continued. From the US and human rights he jumped to the first intifada, the Palestinian uprising against Israeli occupation that began in 1987. For him, the comparison was stark: NGOs and the human rights industry were a sign of today's bad times, whereas "the first intifada was *stupendous*—at the beginning." It was a time of social solidarity, of collective effort against the occupation, mostly consisting of unarmed forms of civil disobedience and protest. "But then it fell apart—and *everything* fell apart after Oslo," he said, referring to the Norwegian-mediated peace accords signed in 1993 that established the PA with limited autonomy in parts of the occupied territory. "And the Left lost any direction. They have all been sucked up into the human rights organizations." It is widely known that many HRO workers used to be activists in leftist parties. "The PFLP," he offered as an example, naming one of the more radical left factions, the Popular Front for the Liberation of Palestine. "They used to have a place, fighting the occupation, but Oslo killed the spirit of the revolutionary (*tha' ir*). The real revolutionary, the real nationalist, was one who fought against the occupation."

Zeena had observed a similar decline. She pointed to the graffiti painted on a wall across the street from their house, welcoming home a young man from the neighborhood as a "prisoner-hero." She explained that in reality this guy had been a good-for-nothing in the neighborhood, infamous for stealing cars and general thuggishness. The Israelis had arrested him for car theft, and now his buddies were trying to whiten his reputation with nationalist iconography. Shaking her head with an expression of knowing skepticism, Zeena lamented their situation, the Palestinians' situation, in which such a scoundrel could be praised as a national hero.

'Abed continued this theme, expressing heavy disappointment with his own people. His impromptu history moved to the second intifada, which began in September 2000. It was another uprising against the occupation, but it was also a reaction against the PA's failures. "The second intifada was not an example of social solidarity." It was all self-serving corruption. "Fateh used to distribute food right outside our house," he explained, referring again to the ruling political party. "We saw it. Everything went through Fateh. The food was distributed through Fateh and only to Fateh people—nothing for others. Rich people would come, in their Mercedes, take bags of flour that were being distributed, and then resell them in the market." There are those who say Hamas does the same thing. "Everything is politicized (*musayyas*)," 'Abed said, full of glum anger. He leaned back into the couch and brushed crumbs of qatayif from his T-shirt. Produced by his son's graphic design company, the shirt bore a logo supporting the boycott of Israeli goods. I wondered whether this artistic assertion of Palestinian independence perhaps marked a move back to popular politics, or even represented an alternative kind of rights work taking place outside the NGO world. Notable about this boycott campaign is the fact that the young people who produced the T-shirts were intentionally not making a profit, as 'Abed's son later told me, and were very self-consciously refusing to commoditize their politics. It was striking punctuation to my exchange with 'Abed, a visible reminder that some people were still acting for the sake of the national cause and nothing else, that political action was, despite it all, still possible, still happening.

'Abed's potted history swept grandly—from the optimistic heights of the first intifada to, by the end of the second intifada, the decline of social solidarity and widespread disbelief in human rights, politics, and almost everything and everyone associated with them. In the milieu he described at the beginning of his account, an ethic of care and selflessness predominated, and a vision of social and political liberation drove political activism and the human rights movement. By the end of the second intifada, however, everything had become politicized, as 'Abed said, by which he meant that it was all put in the service of narrow, material interests. Personal rather than collective benefit motivated everything from aid distribution that political parties organized to human rights training by NGOs. 'Abed described how the institutions and workers in the human rights world, as well as the language and activities of politicians, have all lost credibility among Palestinians in the occupied territory.

Many Palestinians, like 'Abed, sense that their national movement has disintegrated and feel that the values of solidarity and loyalty, while still touted, are enacted less and less. The human rights system is one critical structure that mediates contests over the dynamics of nationalism, the nature of the Palestinian state and what kind of citizen should build it, and the national struggle against occupation and what kind of subject should undertake it. Human rights language exists among a range of discourses and activities for stating a case, for making political claims that encapsulate ethical principles, for explaining a sense of injustice, and for insisting that specific understandings of correct social relations should determine how people and governing institutions ought to interact.

At stake in Palestinians' ethical debates is the question of what social values unite them and who should be the custodian of those values. Is the fight against Israeli occupation the first and only priority, regardless of its form or efficacy? Should it be led by an Islamist movement that places ethical standards and family values (of a religiously justified sort) at the center of its political project and state-building efforts? Is it a basically secular police-state that makes law and order (of an authoritarian and anti-Islamist sort) its focus? Must the traditional gender, age, and class hierarchies that were shaken during the first intifada's mass movement against occupation be finally overthrown in order to generate a people capable of making and willing to make the sacrifices necessary to end the occupation once and for all? Should the end result be one truly democratic state across all of Israel and the occupied territory? These are just some of the formulations that different groups in Palestine contemplate and contest.

These conflicting debates take place, through word and deed, in a context of changing nationalist dynamics. Palestinian nationalism is constituted within a normative argument, productive of—and dependent on—a shared but shifting notion of moral community and political ethics—the standards of behavior, rules, values, and injunctions—by which political actors and activities are judged and held to account, unofficially or otherwise. It is the interlocking of ethics and political consciousness, the consciously evaluative aspect of political discourse, that some theories of the state cannot account for but that ethnographically sensitive studies can address. It is this integral link that is brought to the fore in this book.[9]

Much anthropology on the topic of the state has focused on what Timothy Mitchell (1991) calls the "state-effect," the production of an image of the state as an entity separate from society. Many scholars also draw on Abrams' (1988 [1977]) observation that the state is a social construction—not a thing, but an ideological mask. Most ethnographies of state-making recognize that "the state" always entails some level of spectacle and violence (Geertz 1981; Fujitani 1998; Adams 2010), and states everywhere must perform their powers in order to convince their subjects (Piot 2010:19). In the Durkheimian view, the influence of which is still felt in some studies, the state is "above all, supremely, the organ of moral discipline," and state formation requires a "cultural revolution . . . in the way the world is made sense of" (Corrigan and Sayer 1985:5). In different ways, all of these theoretical approaches focus on the semiotic, ideological work that goes into producing "a state" as "a triumph of concealment" (Abrams 1988 [1977]:77). Observations from Palestine, where a contest of inconsistent moral disciplines is ongoing and the revolution may forever remain incomplete, bring into focus what happens when the tricks of concealment are clumsy, obvious, observed, and objected to. The fitness of individuals and organizations to lead, rule, advocate for, or represent the Palestinian people and their quest for independence is a question of enduring and public conversation. Many of the PA's members and their material interests are well-known and much discussed by the Palestinian public, so the ideological masking that theories of the state might predict is not functioning. The "state effect" that is projecting a false division between civil society and state is not having its effect. Also, because the PA and the people are under occupation, neither members of the PA nor any institution can be a "magnanimous sorcerer . . . with the power to replace reality with fabulous fictions," as Fernando Coronil (1997:2) described the effects of oil wealth in the consolidation of the Venezuelan state. Rather than being an aberration or exception, however, the human rights world in Palestine is especially revealing of the interplay between legitimation and domination, performance and physical power—on national and international levels—that characterizes the modern state.

In Palestine, the tensions between, on the one hand, nationalist ideals and populist ethics and, on the other hand, their dependence on international sources of funding and law together make it impossible to render invisible the artifice of state performances. The PA flaunts a garish face of the state as spectacle and font of physical force while a still-popular nationalism, with its system of political ethics, persists. Although that ideological mask of the state is unconvincing for many, for some, such as PA officials and security officers, it may be *only* the mask that they are after. Their performance of human rights is one dimension of this. These officials recognize sovereignty as flowing not just from their control of the means of violence, and not from the citizenry, but from the international community. If they have to pretend to respect human rights to get the cash, then pretend they will. It is the clashing views of the source of sovereignty that help sustain the state's unsettlement.

How can we make sense of state-building when mass cynicism makes unconvincing, unnecessary for some, and perhaps impossible the invisible tricks by which "politically organized subjection is simultaneously accomplished and concealed" (Corrigan and Sayer 1985:7)? It may be that "the state" in Palestine is somewhat exceptional, given the fact that there is no internationally recognized state, and given the conditions of military occupation that tie state-building to nationalist goals. Nevertheless, the situation in the occupied territory reveals much about the moral dimensions of state-building generally, about the role of global governance institutions in the production of sovereignty, and about the importance of popular understandings of legitimate power in the ideological workings of states (see also Blom Hansen and Stepputat 2006:305). Because Palestine has no state but the PA is trying to become one, the core dynamics of state-making are laid bare.

The local history of reliance on human rights as a language of political claim-making in conjunction with the deep dependency of the PA on international funding and recognition makes the Palestinian case at once representative and unique. As ʿAbed's narrative shows, the human rights system has become inextricably intertwined with Palestinian politics. The Palestine Liberation Organization (PLO) achieved observer status at the UN in 1974, but it was especially in the 1980s that Palestinians mobilized human rights language to condemn the Israeli occupation and its abuses.[10] Since then the language of human rights has extended beyond civil society's protests against occupation and become imbricated with the state-building efforts of Palestinian proto-governments in the West Bank and the Gaza Strip. Human rights performances produce a face of the state that is turned outward.[11] The World Bank as well as state development agencies have entwined Palestinian civil society with a set of practices and financial structures that produce results similar to the "NGOization" of political activism and the "professionalization" of human rights work evident in places throughout the globe that are afflicted by International Monetary Fund structural adjustment schemes (cf. Ishkanian 2003; Elyachar 2006). The putative universalism of human rights categories and the fundamental internationalism of the human rights system has made human rights the channel for making political claims for those in a protracted condition of statelessness. Human rights performances are a standard feature of most states today; they are part of the work that goes into producing an ideological mask to reify "the state" and legitimize it.[12]

Many features of the Palestinian human rights world will be familiar to observers of NGOs and HROs in other so-called least developed countries (LDCs). The ways that donor "conditionalities" threaten, and often destroy, NGOs' local legitimacy has been noticed and critiqued by many scholars, just as donors' ability to determine NGO and state priorities was something my Palestinian interlocutors often condemned. Cases in Latin America—in Mexico (Richard 2009), Bolivia (Gill 1997), and Guatemala (Wallace and Diamente 2005)—the West Indies (Alvarez 1999), Britain (Curtis 2010), and elsewhere have shown how the resources available through NGOization have altered what once were the radical social visions of former revolutionaries, even if some activists have managed to cling to prior collectivist ethics. As in Palestine, human rights performances are a means by which "developing nations" and "weak states" such as Guatemala, Colombia, and Turkey are evaluated (Moodie 2006; Tate 2007; Smith 2004) and seek to prove their legitimacy to current and potential donors and state-makers.

One of the most obvious comparisons to be made with the Palestinian situation might be the human rights system in Israel, with which Palestinian human rights groups interact. Israeli HROs—such as the Israeli Information Center for Human Rights in the Occupied Territories (B'Tselem), the Association for Civil Rights in Israel (ACRI), and the Legal Center for Arab Minority Rights in Israel (Adalah)—tackle many of the same issues as Palestinian NGOs, submit joint alternative reports to the UN, are supported by many of the same donors, reference one another's research in their reports, and share some of their fieldworkers. The challenges that Israeli groups face, however, are quite distinct from those faced by Palestinian groups. The crisis that civil society, and indeed democracy, in Israel has encountered emerges out of a different set of ideologies. As evidence, legal and human rights critics of the Israeli state point to the so-called anti-boycott law passed by Israel in 2011, which "creates tort liability for any Israeli individual or entity that calls for an economic, cultural, or academic boycott of Israel, its institutions, or 'an area under its control'" (ACRI 2011; see also Sheizaf 2011). The Knesset (the Israeli parliament) has also considered bills that would disallow foreign funding for Israeli human rights work. Israeli debates about human rights have a different set of reference points than those among Palestinians. In Israel, calls for such legislation to curb civil society are often couched in terms of concern for the safety of the Israeli army, an iconic institution in that country. How Israeli HROs try to prove their credibility is thus also very different from how Palestinian HROs try to prove theirs. These distinctions throw into relief the specificities of Palestinian society as a stateless one that has yet to "prove" to the world that it "deserves" an independent state.

Palestine is also unique in ways related to its symbolic significance internationally, most evident in the enduring international interest in solving, or at least interfering in, the Arab-Israeli conflict. The pride of place accorded "the question of Palestine" within the UN also distinguishes it: it has its own portal on the UN website (UNISPAL n.d.); the UN holds an annual International Day of Solidarity with the Palestinian People and other public forums, conducts seminars on the topic as well as international and regional meetings, has dedicated committees, supports an extensive agency devoted to the care of Palestinian refugees (the UN Relief and Works Agency, or UNRWA), and archives tens of thousands of documents related to the issue of Palestine.

Another element particular to the Palestinian situation is the degree of tension in popular Palestinian political thought between different concepts of the state. One approach envisions Palestine as an ideal (albeit vague) aspirational state, an independent nation-state rooted in the values of populism and, most central, a state free of Israeli controls; it is a notional state that is the symbol of the transformation of a people "from those who are acted upon to those who initiate action," as Palestinian Prime Minister Salam Fayyad expressed it in an interview (Farraj, Mansour, and Tamari 2009). Another approach sees Palestine as a bureaucratically driven "modern" state populated by "professionals" bound by a network of "transparent" procedures geared toward stability and economic development. A third, more explicitly negative idea of the state derives from Palestinian experience under occupation; in this conception the state is equated with repression masquerading as law, turning law into an ignorable farce; it is a state characterized by arbitrary rule and restrictions, spectacular violence, injustice, cynical politics, and the immoral exercise of excessive power.

Those in government, those aspiring to rule, and those outside of formal political structures translate these paradigmatic statehood types into practices that fall somewhere between these poles, creating a space in which new forms of personhood and political relations are being introduced. Chapter 3 shows, for example, that human rights training for security officers is framed by "the idea of a state as an impersonal regime of relations [and] the idea of an individual subject" (Kaviraj 2010:17), not unlike colonial dynamics elsewhere. In contrast, human rights training for refugee youth promotes a democratic state that is responsive to, and part of, "the people." The kinds of human rights activity in Palestine, Palestinians' attitudes toward it, and the effects of human rights on politics can be understood only in light of these shifting visions and enactments of the state-as-national-agent, the impersonal state, and the state-as-oppressor.

The history of meanings and experiences that have accrued to the concept of human rights and the human rights system must also be considered. In Palestine this history begins in 1979 with the establishment of Al-Haq, the first Palestinian HRO. The importance of its rights-monitoring activities became increasingly recognized locally and internationally especially after the outbreak of the first intifada against occupation in 1987, when Israeli reprisals for Palestinian rebellion became increasingly brutal (see Chapter 1). By then, Al-Haq's legalistic approach had brought credibility to the organization and, by extension, to human rights activism generally. It was during this period that human rights discourse took root as a meaningful way to speak out against the occupation. The human rights system continues to be a privileged arena of political practice and discourse in the occupied territory because protest against human rights violations mattered historically as a form of resistance.

More HROs appeared throughout the 1990s, and after the 1993 Oslo accords ushered in the establishment of the PA (formally instituted in 1994), changes in international donors' priorities created new forms of competition over resources, both among HROs and between HROs and the PA.[13] As Chapter 2 explains, seismic shifts in the Palestinian political architecture occasioned by the PA's arrival started the decline of NGOs' popular credibility within Palestinian society, because they came to be seen as more concerned with sustaining themselves institutionally and financially than with serving the people.

Since then, they have become tied to transnational institutions and their attendant structural constraints. The human rights industry has become a kind of treadmill, spinning and rolling out projects, representational forms, funds, and jobs; but they have not ended the occupation or its abuses, instigated effective international intervention to protect basic human rights, or produced an accountable Palestinian government. As a result, human rights has become the object and inspiration of cynicism for many Palestinians, the result of years of unfulfilled promises, unregistered claims, and unsuccessful battles for political change.

Many Palestinians recognize that the term *human rights* has become a label sewn on for show, easily affixed to an office, a workshop, a training course. They see that the human rights system encourages government officials, police officers, and NGO workers to perform roles that many, including those actors themselves, simply do not believe.[14] The specific ways in which the human rights system has developed in the occupied territory—as a source for political claim-making, as a means of critiquing the PA, as a language of political legitimation, as a way to make money—have produced inconsistent results.

Human rights claims and the practices of the human rights industry have helped produce performances of Palestinian statehood, partly because of this history of resistance and partly because of the international community's focus on human rights. These performances appear in security forces' attendance at human rights trainings (see Chapter 3), in the West Bank PA's interactions with the state human rights agency (see Chapter 4), and in Hamas's reports to the UN (see Chapter 5). Human rights activities produce notions of legitimate statehood; they have helped shape the language in which Palestinians debate what kind of state they are after. The human rights regime also sustains certain narratives about and practices of "the international"—however nebulous that realm may be. Political subjectivity, however, is not determined by a single regime of power. The ways in which political subjectivities and institutions are developing and debated in Palestine is a product of the asynchronous moralities—rooted in cultural, political, nationalist, and for some, religious foundations—that Palestinians bring to evaluations of state and human rights performances and institutions.

Another result has been the destruction of faith in the human rights system, and the creation of a broad cynicism—a stance, attitude, mode of expression, and value judgment—that has implications throughout society—in all its political, legal, economic, and religious dimensions. Rather than view this widespread cynicism as a lamentable condition, however, I consider it to be a mode of understanding, a location from which at least some people remain aloof from the power structures that are trying to sweep them up.[15] It may be the case, as Yael Navaro-Yashin (2002:4) argues (calling on Slavoj Zizek [1989]), that in many instances "the political endures and survives" the deconstruction and critique of the cynical, and that those who critique the state also reproduce it through their "fantasies" for it. In Palestine, however, cynicism can be a form of awareness and a motor of action by which subjection and subjectification are self-consciously resisted or at least creatively engaged—even though for others it does engender inaction or feed into structures of domination.

Despite such deep cynicism toward politics and the human rights system, it is this history that continues to allow human rights work to be a form of creative social action, an expression of Palestinian national identity, a sustaining force and method for assertion of Palestinians' national rights.[16] One of the core ideas of those who critique the current state of politics and the human rights system informs a central theme of this book: the human rights system can work according to actual human rights principles and actually further social justice only when that system is mobilized to further explicitly national projects.[17] There is an ideal of the state, and of politics generally, beyond the cynical recognition of its abuses that continues to animate forms of nationalism; cynicism toward the powerful newer forms of politics is part of what enables a continuing investment in a nationalist idea of "the Palestinian people" as in need of an ethically bound national state.

This book explores Palestinian nationalism as an ethical discourse, a framework of values, a system of political and social ethics in profound transition. In this moment of crisis, multiple value systems organized within frameworks of nationalism and human rights, anchored by notions of social solidarity and elements of a specific kind of moral economy, remain suspended in an uneasy and as yet unresolved tension. In the story I tell here about the human rights world, we see the tribulations of a form of nationalism that is struggling to keep its place in a context of state-building guided by "the principles of good governance, accountability and transparency" (PNA 2009:3). Nationalism and state-building are not usually contradictory forces, but they have become so, at least as Palestinians in the occupied territory understand these terms and values. A debate posed along similar lines is as old as the PLO's role as representative of the Palestinian people, since 1973, when the opposing options for political action were framed as a choice between revolutionary and statist approaches (Sayigh 1997:332–333). A distinctly neoliberal ethos, rather than a nationalist spirit built out of notions of collective care and solidarity, has come to define the West Bank PA's approach to building a state. According to a PA planning document from 2009, the Palestinian state is to be one in which "all citizens are entitled to be served by an economical and well-managed public sector organized to deliver high-quality social, justice and security services at a reasonable cost" (PNA 2009:14). This conceptualization of citizen-as-consumer and the practice of engaging with human rights as a market-driven industry clash with a Palestinian nationalist idiom that speaks first and foremost of collective liberation and solidarity.

The emergence of a neoliberal discourse of state-building underlines the need to unpack understandings of what the state is, or appears to be. How can we grasp conceptually the image of "the state" that different groups of Palestinians are trying to project? The work of Phillip Abrams ([1977] 1988) and Rogers Brubaker (1996) is useful for considering nationalism and state-building and the nature of their interaction. Following Abrams, many scholars have addressed the state theoretically as an idea that glosses the forces that dominate; it is the congeries of people, powers, and organizations that attempt to legitimize themselves by creating the illusion that there is an entity called "the state."[18] It is specifically the processual aspects in Abrams' definition that seem useful to the study of Palestine, a stateless society. Like Rogers Brubaker's concept of the "nation" as a category of practice that structures perception, informs thought and experience, and organizes discourse and political action (7), the state is a historically developed social construction (see also Gupta and Sharma 2006), part of the social imaginary that frames political community (Brubaker 1996:63), and that waxes and wanes in people's concerns. Abrams' approach raises questions about what goes into the making of a state as the struggle occurs, before any particular idea or institution becomes entrenched and believed. In Palestine, the ideological mask of the state has not been fully affixed and questions remain as to when, if ever, a believable illusion of a stable state form will be achieved.

The state is not merely the crystallization of powers of domination, nor simply the performative spectacle of power; neither is it a subjectless constellation of institutions and narratives by which power is self-authorized. The Palestinian case reveals the state also to be an ongoing negotiation, or argument through deed and word, among various groups and interests. While the approach to state formation adopted here resonates in places with the view of classic political anthropology that understood "politics as calculated instrumentality" (Spencer 2007:15) and recognizes political actors as acting with thoughtful (in the sense of considered but not necessarily kind) intentions, I also take into account cultural and ideological dimensions (see also Chalfin 2010), as well as the moralizing and personalizing reactions of those who are subject to, and suffer the effects of, those rational calculations. Even if Prime Minister Fayyad assures an international public that "we take fully into account that our people expect a government that provides them with security and basic services and fosters development in all spheres while respecting their rights and liberties" (PNA 2009:3–4), many of "our people" are not convinced. In Palestine, the disunited goings-on of government and power brokering are evident to the people, who still view those activities critically, through a distinctly moral, nationalist lens. That is part of what sustains aspirations for a more ideal state, one that is a truer expression of a popular will.

The tenuous nature of the PA's power, the fact that it is deeply engaged in a self-conscious state-building project while still under military occupation, and its utter dependence on international powers, shows more clearly the continuum of statehood. Some powers are more fixed, sovereign, in control, and convincing (if not totally legitimate) to local and international audiences; others are not. To be sure, all states are performative, and statehood never acquires an unqualified permanence that can be accomplished once and for all. However, the PA's imbrication within a field of overlapping sovereignties, caught between many states' interests and "subject to the vagaries of authoritarian politics" (Giacaman 1998:13), makes it a particularly instructive case in which to examine how the illusions of statehood work, precisely because in the eyes of many the performances and pretense are still so apparent. In contrast to theories of sovereignty that focus on "sites of abjection and disposability" (Piot 2010:12) where the state has withdrawn and NGOs and religion have stepped in (Sassen 1996), the Palestinian case demonstrates the role of the supranational in producing, rather than rolling back, the state.[19]

The Rise and Plateau of Human Rights

Human rights and political horizons in Palestine have not always been so bleak, the Palestinian public not always so pessimistic. Those who were involved in the early period of human rights activism were sincerely committed to the struggle against occupation, which they also undertook as part of fulfilling a broad vision of social and national liberation and building a justly governed state for Palestine. They believed in human rights law and saw it as a powerful tool for Palestinians seeking liberation from Israeli occupation, internal oppression, and international hypocrisy, especially during the first intifada.

Indeed, human rights activists and organizations—including a few Israeli ones—have successfully contributed to exposing the systematic rights abuses that are an everyday part of the Israeli occupation of the West Bank, East Jerusalem, and Gaza. In the early days of the first intifada, for example, they focused on, among other things, documenting and trying to stop collective punishment meted out by the Israeli army. The almost threefold increase in the rate of home demolitions in the West Bank within the first eight months of the first intifada's outbreak gives some indication of what they were up against (Hiltermann 1989a:110). Detailed legal analysis by human rights researchers has also brought to light the contradiction between the ideology of rights espoused by the international community and the inability—or unwillingness—of those same states that have signed on to human rights declarations to hold Israel accountable for its abuses. While Israel has continued building settlements and subsidizing the hundreds of thousands of exclusively Jewish citizens who live in them, actions illegal under international law, HROs continue to remind the 190 states that are party to the Fourth Geneva Convention that it is their obligation "to ensure respect for the present convention in all circumstances" (Shehadeh 2008:35–36).[20] During the second intifada, HROs documented a range of abuses, including deaths and injuries of Palestinian civilians caused by Israeli attacks.[21] Then, throughout the heavy bouts of internal fighting, primarily between the Palestinian factions Hamas and Fateh, and the subsequent split between the Gaza Strip and the West Bank, Palestinian HROs recorded the deadly effects of these violent episodes. They called attention to the repression of political and social freedoms (the freedom to organize political rallies or for women to smoke water pipes in public, for instance), and criticized the narrowing space for freedom of speech, opinion, and movement that the opposing Palestinian governments have imposed on their populations (Freed 2007; PCHR 2009a).

Despite all their labors, however, activists can name few human rights successes. When pressed, they can point to the occasional delayed demolition of a Palestinian home by Israeli bulldozers, or the very rare punishment of an individual Israeli soldier or PA security officer. There is clear recognition that what is actually required to end abuses are fundamental political changes, but there have been no real structural shifts in the conditions of occupation and statelessness that breed human rights violations. The question is not why the human rights system does not actually protect human rights. Most observers and anyone working within the system recognizes that rights are protectable only within authorized political structures that can enforce accountability. The question, rather, is how such a system that so obviously does not deliver on its promises continues to grow, functioning as if it could fulfill those ideals. The continuous flow of funds available to those in the system is part of the answer. Occasional legal successes also feed the faith that human rights activism can achieve results—such as the rerouting of Israel's separation wall to take up less Palestinian land (B'Tselem 2011b).[22] Although these successes are few and far between, human rights work gives people a sense that they are at least doing *something* to speak against oppression, even if they know that such work alone will not stop the abuses.

Yet the language and work of human rights continue to swell, and HROs issue daily reports cataloging Israeli abuses across the occupied territory. Even though their victories are few, Palestinian HROs diligently detail the ongoing violations inflicted by the occupation, from punitive and administrative home demolitions,[23] arbitrary arrests, and excessive use of force, to willful killing and injury. The UN Office of the High Commissioner for Human Rights has expanded its operations, opening new offices and increasing staff across the West Bank to produce more documentation of Israeli rights violations. Human rights work has also infiltrated deeply into internal Palestinian politics and institution-building. The PA has set up a human rights and democracy unit in the Interior Ministry, for example. Palestinian security services, including those branches accused most often of torturing Hamas detainees, take human rights training courses delivered by local NGOs. US Lieutenant General Keith Dayton, who oversaw US security assistance to the PA from 2005 to 2010, publicly lauded the attention to human rights displayed by Palestinian participants in his highly controversial security sector reform program.[24] Local youth centers offer human rights, civics, and democracy courses to teens, the citizens of a future Palestinian state.

Why do so many Palestinian and international organizations teach lists of rights and generate lists of abuses when their futility is so readily admitted by so many? My questions parallel those of Tania Li (2007), who has written about the development industry's stubborn and repeatedly thwarted "will to improve" social conditions through technical and "expert" means. Like Li and others before her (Cowan 2006; Ferguson 1994), I am curious about the "contingent and diverse" side effects (Li 2007:272) of such improvement projects and schemes. If human rights work does not protect people from violations (and evidently it does not), there is still the question of how the tremendous investment of time, money, and talk in a suspect set of practices carried out under the human rights label affects Palestinian politics, Palestinians' views of one another, and their relationship to the international community. How the PA in the West Bank and Gaza engages the human rights system reveals the role that human rights play in the production of sovereignty and, crucially, in its legitimacy and illegitimacy.

Diverging from studies of development such as Li's and Ferguson's (see also Smith 2008), I add to these questions the problem of history and the concept of cynicism. By taking into account the fact that people learn, that they get wise to the side effects of human rights schemes, that they adapt, maneuver within, and transform systems—intentionally and otherwise—we can better understand the human rights industry as a living organism, one that is always contested, changing, and multiple. This history is marked by the human rights system's long years of failure to protect Palestinians, the ongoing inability of the UN and unwillingness of the international community to stop Israel's military occupation, its human rights violations and most brutal excesses, its complicity in PA abuses, and the inability of global civil society to enable Palestinian freedom. In addition, this history of failed efforts is part of what has led to a generalized cynicism. It is, I argue, precisely in the space of cynicism—where the condition of lost faith flourishes, where people continue to participate as if what they were doing made a difference and despite their recognition that it mostly won't—that an attitude of disdain and disregard becomes a language of criticism and critique.

Historicizing Human Rights

By chronicling developments in the Palestinian human rights world, this book contributes to the growing number of human rights histories (see, for example, Cmiel 1999, 2004; Dubois 2004, 2006; Lauren 2003; Mazower 2009; Moyn 2010) and ethnographies (see, for example, Merry 2006; Postero 2007; Speed 2007) that examine the ways in which the universal claims of human rights are put to work in specific political and cultural settings. Anthropology that focuses on processes that render "human rights into social knowledge that shapes social action" (Goodale 2007:8) has increasingly attended to what *limits* the emancipatory "potential of human rights discourse" (20) in different contexts. Others rightly warn against too easily "pathologizing" NGOs as "nothing more than one power resource for elites" (Dorman 2005:57). Building on these studies, I suggest another set of questions about what happens when the emancipatory potential of human rights is unrelentingly foreclosed. Through the development of new signifying practices, changing political configurations, the accumulation of mostly disappointing experiences, and the varying emotions such experiences evoke through time, we can see how the dynamic of history opens the way for novel deployments of human rights discourse, human rights ideas, and the human rights system generally.

The history of human rights in Palestine also provides insight into the processes by which history unhinges from concepts their meanings and original force. In other words, we see the working out of a standard anthropological puzzle: how "externalities are indigenized, engaged in local configurations and become different from what they were" (Sahlins 1999:412), what in another context Sally Engle Merry (2006) has termed "vernacularization." Although it is useful to see how the "global" is made "local" in the snapshot of a "cultural system" (Sewell 1996:39), because the term *human rights* is "universal," universalizing, and a universally available idiom that circulates and becomes powerful within a global system, we must consider how what happens in one part of the structure ramifies across it, synchronically and diachronically. As Ajantha Subramanian (2009:18) has discussed, anthropological approaches to rights tend to view them as either "flowing from the West outward," where they are then "vernacularized," or as a "form of governmentality through which subjects are incorporated into a normative legal framework." Subramanian's work eloquently argues for a distinct form of analysis that considers "rights in more historical, processual terms . . . as a *structure of feeling* that is not simply of Western origin" (19). Her assessment of the assumptions underlying anthropology's standard approaches are incisive, and open up the way for analyzing the "dialogical relationship between claims and rights in which the practice of claim making is generative of new understandings and subjects of rights" (19). Although her concern is to understand rights (broadly conceived) as "a dynamic cultural formation that encodes understandings of justice and accountability" (19), Subramanian's insights are useful for thinking about *human* rights specifically as well.

Only by taking into account this dynamic history—in Palestine and elsewhere—can we understand how the concept of human rights has become encrusted with a symbolic load that makes it pervasive in political and social life while also being bitterly contested, and even rejected. Anger over and aversion to human rights hypocrisies similar to what I found in Palestine have developed over many decades in various contexts across the globe.[25] This, I would argue, makes cynicism a defining—but understudied—force in human rights dynamics today.

Cynicism and the Politics of "As If"

Many who have written on the dynamics of cynicism in modern Western politics narrate a unilinear movement of democracy-inspired hopes, through disappointment and cynicism to apathy and inertia. The Palestinian case reveals a more complicated, internally inconsistent terrain, showing how cynicism can develop out of and lead to much more varied results—even within the same person. In contrast to the contingencies and complications of the experiences and effects of cynicism that can be revealed through ethnography, one sociolegal approach to human rights defines cynicism as the practice of "using rights talk (or legal reasoning) as no more than a way to formulate demands" (Kennedy 2002a:190). In this analysis, cynicism is a negative evaluation. It points to the corruption of the fiction on which the power of human rights language depends: the idea that a "right" is "something that is outside and preexists legal reasoning" (186)—outside politics and outside opinion. Scholars from a variety of fields, including comparative literature, philosophy, and anthropology, have adumbrated the meaning and power of cynicism in diverse times and places. It has been described variously as a "sensibility" (Bewes 1997:24), a "kind of mass survival strategy" (Caldwell 2006:20), an "enlightened false consciousness" (Sloterdijk 1988), "the dominant operational mode of ideology" (Zizek 1989), something that renders people "perpetually aware of a certain conditionality" (Humphrey 1995:45), "face work" (in Goffman's [1955] sense), and "a rueful recognition of local sociality that defines communities of complicity" (Stein-müller 2010:547). Some critique the narrow use of cynicism that refers only to a "highly specific mode of consciousness [of] 'some yuppie stockbrokers'" (Eagleton 1991:39, quoted in Bewes 1997:25).

In most of these renderings, cynicism is linked with the character of the mocking faultfinder—one who does not believe in the sincere goodness of human motive. This has become the standard model, or base theory, of cynicism and its function in modernity, and according to Sloterdijk (1988), it is ingrained as a part of modern consciousness. It is a "natural strategy in the struggle to endure the numbing alienation, hopelessness, and powerlessness of the modern human condition . . . one of the approaches humans use to cope with the ambiguities of the moral wasteland that is the modern era" (Caldwell 2006:30). It stems "from the absence of widely available, meaningful political spaces" (Keenan 1998). What is the result? For Zizek (1989:42), because cynicism promotes inaction, it "remains a form of self-deception."[26]

Social scientists have brought these more philosophical conceptualizations into their analyses of ethnographic contexts to try to understand how dominating powers sustain themselves. Navaro-Yashin (2002), for one, has deployed the concept of cynicism in order to understand the role of affect in state power. In her study, cynicism is "a central structure of feeling of the production and regeneration of the political in Turkey's public life . . . a feeling of political existence . . . , a more common and ordinary way of managing existence in a realm of state power" (2002:5).[27] Her adaptation of Zizek's (1989:2) argument that "in contemporary societies people are aware of the falsity of ideology" is helpful in pointing to the gap between awareness and action that cynicism produces, or perhaps indexes. Navaro-Yashin elaborates the ways in which "through ideological pretension and consciously verbalized critique . . . [people] are conscious of the reality of social relations that underlie icons of reification. And yet . . . [they act] *as if* they did not know" (2002:159–160, emphasis added).

The political efficacy of people acting "as if" was also usefully demonstrated in Lisa Wedeen's (1998, 1999) study of Syria under the authoritarian regime of Hafez al-Asad, and her characterization of the politics of "as if" is helpful in making sense of cynicism in the human rights system as it has intertwined with Palestinian politics. Adopting arguments put forth by Havel (2010) and Zizek (1989), Wedeen sought to understand how the political power of a state is produced in the absence of belief or emotional commitment. She found that the cult of al-Asad—in which Syrians were continually forced to profess allegiance and false faith in their "great leader"—was a strategy of domination based on compliance rather than legitimacy. It generated a politics of public dissimulation in which citizens, who were compelled to display outward signs of obedience, acted "as if" they revered al-Asad (1999:6, 29). Wedeen's signal contribution was to elucidate the integrative power of the "shared condition of unbelief" (1999:121) in which ordinary Syrians participated, and which thereby made them complicit in perpetuating "the formulas that frame the terms of state dominance and national belonging" (73) and sustained the regime's fictions and its power. Navaro-Yashin (2002) also examined the ways in which cynicism and fantasy combined to reproduce a fraudulent state in Turkey. Cynicism there has helped sustain a state that keeps its citizens down, caught in a political vortex performed by "automatons," despite their consciousness that it is self-destructive (Navaro-Yashin 2002:5, 162).

Cynicism has many other culturally and historically specific guises and effects, however. In Palestine, cynicism is part of the process whereby human rights has come to be a frame of reference for people acting "as if"—that is, acting as if the human rights industry could stop abuses outside of real political, structural change. In Palestine there are also people going through the motions, taking part in a system of symbols and rhetoric that has not lived up to its liberatory claims. Just as Wedeen sought to explain the permanence of an authoritarian regime led by a despot, one of my goals is to understand the tenacity of the human rights system in Palestine, to make sense of the breadth and depth of its tentacles' reach. However, in contrast to how the collective practice of acting "as if" cemented the Syrian regime's power by entangling citizens "in self-enforcing relations of domination" (Wedeen 1999:84), the participation of Palestinians in human rights dissimulation has had more ambiguous effects and causes than Wedeen identified in Syria. Beyond the obvious differences between an authoritarian state such as al-Asad's Syria and an apparently noncoercive, international human rights system, a crucial point of distinction between the two situations derives from the nationalist context in Palestine.

The contradictory matrices of value and forms of action entailed within human rights principles, the human rights industry, and nationalist culture complicate the practice of acting "as if" in Palestine. A clutch of Palestinian values, including sincerity, self-sacrifice, and altruism, are the political principles that underlie the Palestinian nationalist narrative and constitute the qualities that many Palestinians view as necessary for pursuing nationalist goals and successfully resisting the occupation. These are also values that Palestinians point to as characteristics of a good person, someone who is upstanding and respectable. Since the Palestinian dispossession began, the goals of the Palestinian national movement have accorded with the core of human rights principles, including equality, justice, dignity, and freedom. However, developments within the human rights system have led to a context in which contrary values are enacted, empty rhetoric is the norm, and organizations within the system generate profit without producing positive social change. Neither sincerity nor self-sacrifice and altruism are seen as being promoted within the framework. Although it is by no means the case that all of those involved in the human rights industry are actually contradicting those values in intention or in practice, for many the term *human rights* has come to stand for a system that goes directly against Palestinian values and that is both a source and result of cynicism.

The concept requires further elaboration, because beyond the people acting "as if" through human rights activity, in Palestine cynicism is an emotion tied to political stasis, apathy, and hope, all uncomfortably combined and anchored in a political phase of perceived limbo. There is no good one-to-one Arabic translation of *cynicism*. The closest Arabic terms for *cynical* and *cynic* translate as pessimistic (*mutasha' im*), sarcastic (*sakhir*), scornful (*muhtaqir*), one who has lost faith (*faqed al-iman*), despair (*ya's*), scoffing (*yahza'a*), critical (*intiqady* or *tahakkumy*), fault-finder (*'ayab*), or one who doesn't believe in anything (*la yu'-min bi-shay'*)—none of which carry exactly the same sense as the English word. Cynicism is my characterization, which I use because its broadness contains something of all these other meanings. It is meant to evoke the sense of shared disappointment and "fed-upness" (*zahaq* in Arabic; see Allen 2008) that is anchored in the memory of and desire for better political conditions. Although *cynicism* does not accord with what anthropologists sometimes refer to as a folk concept that Palestinians use to describe themselves or their situation, it is a term that I think most people living in occupied Palestine today would recognize as capturing something important about how they have been feeling, thinking, and reacting to their political situation and its social consequences. I use the term to focus attention on how the changing place of human rights in Palestinian nationalist practice has produced and comes out of a sense—at once intellectual and emotional, critical, contemplative, and felt—that is simultaneously an expression of disappointment, frustration, and hope. Also, in contrast to some other researchers who have explored the dynamics of cynicism in politics and seen it functioning to maintain hegemonic systems of power, the Palestinian case shows that cynicism can be not only a way that power is reproduced and political stasis maintained, but also part of how people continue to critique and search, or at least hope, for something better.

Cynicism is linked to the ongoing, and seemingly unstoppable, Israeli colonization of Palestinian land and the indefatigably brutal occupation. This attitude has been the result of decades of what could be described as "noneventful" history. The Palestinian situation requires us to take seriously the transformative effect of the accumulation of aborted events and frustrated expectations, rather than see rupturing events as the key to understanding social change (Sewell 1996:843). Focusing away from eventful history may seem an unlikely approach to take to analyzing such an apparently dramatic place as Palestine, where so many violent confrontations and spectacularly lethal practices have become part of the international news media's palette of events. Indeed, neither Palestinians nor Israelis rest tranquilly amid the mix of suicide bombs, one-ton bombs, flesh-eating white phosphorous munitions, homemade bombs, and rockets exchanged between them—never mind the sound bombs, Molotov cocktails, rocks, and rubber-coated steel bullets that disrupt their air, their sleep, and their public demonstrations.[28] This is what the news shows to those who live in the West and elsewhere. It is instead the monotony of an unresolved conflict that I think especially requires analysis, because it is this that has led to a change in the nature of Palestinian politics and political emotion.

Cynicism is also an outcome of the multifarious failures of the Oslo accords that were supposed to have ended the occupation and fostered renewed hope for an independent Palestinian state. It was born of the harsh economic conditions that have left the vast majority of Palestinians in the West Bank, Gaza Strip, and East Jerusalem struggling while a thin layer of elite manage to profit and thrive. It has been exacerbated by the deterioration of the internal Palestinian political scene, in which two separate governing regimes took over in the West Bank and Gaza Strip, deepening the Israeli-enforced split between the two territories and between the people confined within them, and widening the corollary rift between Fateh and Hamas. This political disorder has left most Palestinians on the sidelines (Hammami and Tamari 2001) grumbling about politicians who want only to fight over the shreds of land and scraps of power that Israel lets dangle just out of their pawing reach. Although there are many studies that provide thorough and often damning critiques of the political effects of Oslo and the role of the international community in producing a corrupt PA (see, for example, Brown 2003; Jamal 2007) and in supporting authoritarian states, this book offers the reader a sense of how many Palestinians experienced all this, how they live with, engage in, see, and describe the spider web of cracks in the nationalist edifice and state-building project that has resulted.

Methods

As a social scientist, I am not necessarily looking for a more honorable human rights regime, a more effective nationalist movement, more sincere politics, or more efficient state-building. Nor do I pretend to offer more effective ways to defend the human rights of the people caught up in those current practices and structures. My job, as I see it, is to explain how and why Palestinians have come to perceive the inefficacy and even corruption in the human rights system, to reveal the political and social effects of those developments, and to show how they are entangled within the larger structures of power that continue to thwart Palestinian efforts at self-liberation. This book is concerned with the system of ideas, attitudes, feelings, and moral discourse on rights that underlie various human rights activities. Although some of this material was gathered while I conducted participant-observation in the daily lives of human rights workers and organizations, this book is not an ethnography of a single HRO or group of activists. Rather, it is an investigation of how and what Palestinians from a variety of backgrounds and political stances think about human rights values and the value of the human rights system, of how they are involved with human rights institutions, and of what they make of that involvement; and it is a book about the broader social and political dynamics that shape and are shaped by those interactions and attitudes.

To learn about these issues, I carried out field research in two phases (after conducting preliminary research in the West Bank in the summers of 1992 and 1997). The first period, from November 2000 to February 2003 and for an additional four weeks in September to October of 2003, overlapped with some of the most sustained violence of the second intifada. During most of this time I lived in a small stone house in Al-Bireh, a couple of blocks from Yasir Arafat's Ramallah compound, the *muqata'ah*, where he would live out the last years of his life, confined under Israeli siege. The majority of human rights NGOs have their offices in Ramallah, and some have satellite offices and researchers throughout the West Bank and Gaza. From my home base in Ramallah–Al-Bireh, I traveled throughout the West Bank, visiting Jenin and Bethlehem most often, while making occasional trips to Gaza City, Qalqilya, Hebron, Jerusalem, and villages in between. Nine months of this research time was split between Ramallah and a small refugee camp (with approximately 4,500 residents) near Rachel's Tomb in Bethlehem, where I lived with a large and bustling family.

I began my research as a participant-observer and volunteer at Defence for Children International–Palestine Section (DCI-Palestine). Although affiliated with an international human rights NGO, DCI-Palestine was a fully Palestinian-led organization. The board and most of the staff were from the Ramallah, Bethlehem, and Hebron areas. Volunteers and Palestinian fieldworkers operated in most of the governorates of the West Bank and Gaza, and at the time there were two foreign nationals in the organization's international relations unit. Much of my time with DCI-Palestine was spent working on the 2002 annual report on Israeli violations of Palestinian children's rights, a book entitled *A Generation Denied*. I was involved in every aspect of the report's production, including translating the documentation into English, collecting interviews that appeared in the text, picking out the illustrating photographs, and writing some sections of the book. It was a long process that afforded me the opportunity to observe how events become "violations" and to understand the NGO's goals in producing such a book—how they were thinking about the book's audience, how they wanted to reach them, and how local and foreign staff negotiated strategies for achieving these goals. DCI-Palestine also graciously arranged for me to accompany its fieldworkers to visit families, where I observed the fieldworkers' interactions with victims of rights violations and conducted my own interviews. The vast majority of formal interviews I conducted during my research (through DCI-Palestine and otherwise) were in Arabic and recorded on tape.

I volunteered for briefer periods with three other human rights NGOs, including LAW (Land and Water Establishment for Studies and Legal Services), one of the largest NGOs at the time, where I worked on reports and translation. I accompanied and interviewed fieldworkers from some of these organizations, as well as from other NGOs.[29] In addition to formal and informal interviews with staff and clients of these and other organizations, I collected their publications and monitored coverage of human rights in the local press and on television.

Later in my research I was fortunate to make the acquaintance of an extended family, the al-Kareems, some of whose members were running a cultural center for youth, where I volunteered in various capacities throughout my research. In addition to teaching an introductory anthropology class that transformed into an oral history project to a number of their young adult members, I accompanied the center's members on field trips, attended their performances, helped them apply for funding, interviewed them, and spent countless pleasurable hours socializing with the center's directors and volunteers and their families. By living with this family, I became familiar with life in a small, relatively poor refugee camp. When I first visited them in 2002, the first floor windows were sandbagged, and many of the upper floor windows and walls were cracked, for they were on one of the front lines of the intifada. It was here that I listened to people reminisce about the first intifada, watched children play and react to the often frightening events of the day, attended engagement parties, cleaned house with the sisters, celebrated news of new babies, and listened to teenagers complain about homework and covertly hope for a curfew that might allow them to stay home from school. It was with members of this family that I visited extended family in other refugee camps, heard countless tales of checkpoint crossings, and listened to the poetry and watched the plays written by the center's volunteers; it was with them that I worried about young men and boys from their family and circle of friends who had been arrested, with them that I felt depressed and hopeless at the news of more deaths or shellings in Gaza, and with them that I scanned the horizon trying to spot military helicopters and buzzing drones or stood motionless listening for tanks. It was also with them that I learned something about the meaning of *sumud*, about the political import of shared emotion and solidarity, and about the ability to continue working for social change even in the midst of sharp cynical awareness.

The second phase of my research involved several trips of one to three months in 2005, 2007, 2008, and 2009, when I was again based mainly in a refuge camp in Bethlehem and in Ramallah, and also traveled around the West Bank. Throughout those years, the conflict with Israel took on a different shape. The second intifada had waned and the violence was more sporadic, but Israeli army raids, arrests, air attacks, and home demolitions continued, as did Palestinian attacks against Israeli soldiers, settlers, and civilians. Checkpoints still disrupted Palestinian economic and social life with drastic effects, and the construction of Israel's separation barrier pressed farther around and through Palestinian neighborhoods, fields, and villages in the West Bank.[30] From 2007 on, the intensity of caustic competition between the main political party rivals, Hamas and Fateh, increased dramatically, and the repression of the Islamists in the West Bank made research into their activities and attitudes difficult. Peoples' wariness of speaking "as Hamas" was certainly understandable given the regular occurrence of political arrests, beatings, torture, and killing of Islamists in PA prisons.[31] I did, however, manage to talk with some Hamas sympathizers, a few of their parliamentary and municipal representatives, a number of released political prisoners, and some civil servants purged from their jobs because of suspected Hamas affiliation. Because Israel's siege on the Gaza Strip meant that I could not go there and was therefore unable to meet with people in the seat of Hamas power, my analysis of the Hamas movement and government relied heavily on publicly available statements, publications, and media. This discourse provides a lens into Hamas's uniquely critical perspective on and approach to human rights practices that challenge presumptions about the universal status of human rights. Their critique is linked to nationalistically infused notions of political ethics, and to ideas about the proper relationship between words and actions, ideals and realities, surface and content.

The ICHR was another institution I focused on. There I interviewed staff members and attended numerous human rights training sessions. Among PA officials I spoke with were employees of the Ministry of Interior in Ramallah, a prison director, and other members of the security agencies, including civilian police and General Security (*mukhabarat*), the (not always so secret) secret police. In our conversations, ICHR staff and trainees assessed the PA and their own work on the basis of assumptions about what the rights and obligations of authorities and citizens were or should be. These appraisals were just as much a part of the process by which authority is represented and rejected as were the physical performances of the security forces in the streets, prisons, and public squares that I observed.

Chapter 1

The First Human Rights NGO

Al-Haq's Faith in Evidence

I N 1979, twelve years into the occupation of the West Bank, Gaza Strip, and East Jerusalem, Israel was successfully pursuing its expansionist strategies (which are ongoing)—confiscating Palestinian land, building Jewish-only settlements, controlling the Palestinian economy, and denying Palestinians most of their political and civil rights. Unlike today, however, at that point Israel was still able to maintain a facade of "benevolent" occupier, despite the fact that human rights violations, from torture to detention without trial, were a daily occurrence.[1] For Palestinians, however, the occupation meant arbitrary rule by a foreign military, and lack of civil, political, and human rights. Then, as today, humiliations and harassment at the hands of Israeli soldiers were a feature of daily life, leaving people in a constant state of insecurity and uncertainty. Among the many abuses that underwrote Israel's occupation was the widespread use of torture against Palestinian political detainees in Israeli prisons, where inhumane conditions were the norm.[2] Excessive and sometimes lethal force was used to quell demonstrations (see, for example, UNGA 1971, 1976). Attacks by settlers were rarely investigated.[3] West Bank residents, including suspected political activists and city mayors, were deported, in contravention of the Fourth Geneva Convention (Kretzmer 2002:187), which "prohibits individual or mass forcible transfer within and beyond the borders of the occupied territory" (Article 49). Demolition of the homes of prisoners' and suspects' families was used as a form of collective punishment. In addition, a range of occupation policies inhibited Palestinian infrastructure and business development and tied the Palestinian economy to Israel's in conditions highly unfavorable to the former.[4]

Although some international organizations and Western government officials knew about Israel's abuses, and even though Palestinian newspapers consistently covered UN activities related to Palestine (Rangwala 2002), Israel's violations were not widely acknowledged in the West.[5] The occupation's humiliations, harassment, and brutalities were a daily experience for Palestinian residents of the occupied territory, but most Palestinians believed that the rest of the world did not care, believe, or even know about their situation, taking as truth Israel's claim to be "the only democracy in the Middle East" (see also Shehadeh 1984:viii). Indeed, Israel was for many outsiders still a "symbol of human decency," as the *New York Times* labeled the country as late as the mid-1980s (quoted in Chomsky 1999:79).[6]

It was frustration at the contradiction between Israel's self-representation and Palestinians' lived realities that brought three people together in 1979 to establish the first Palestinian human rights organization (HRO), Al-Haq.[7] Charles Shamas, a Lebanese-American graduate of Yale, was a behavioral scientist and business entrepreneur; Raja Shehadeh studied philosophy in Beirut and had trained in London as a lawyer; and Jonathan Kuttab, also a lawyer, had emigrated with his family to the United States from Jerusalem when he was a teenager. One thing that brought this innovative trinity together in an effort to reframe the terms of the debate over Israel's occupation was a shared respect for, and hope in, the power of law, logic, and rationality. They believed that law could expose the inconsistencies and disrupt the image of Israel as a law-abiding democracy. They also had an assertive faith in facts and logic, which fueled their earnest optimism that they could confront the occupation successfully through law.

In an interview, Kuttab said to me that he "had a tremendous interest in understanding how the Israelis could possibly claim and even believe that they were a democratic country; that they were progressive, modern, liberal, even Western; and at the same time they were carrying out really horrible, fascist policies toward the Palestinians that were as despotic as those of any Middle Eastern country."[8] Shehadeh described the mission of Al-Haq as "working for promotion of rule of law and keeping correct records of Israeli violations and addressing them." According to Joost Hiltermann, sociologist and early researcher at the organization, "there was a faith in the rule of law as something that would resonate with a wider public anywhere in the world."

Contrary to those who would condemn the human rights system for disabling collective action (W. Brown 2004:461), or dismiss it as "a false ideological universality, which masks and legitimizes a concrete politics of Western imperialism, military interventions and neo-colonialism" (Zizek n.d.), the concept of human rights helped motivate a novel form of collective action and became a constitutive element of Palestinian nationalist politics. Human rights and international humanitarian law were sources of creativity and even courage for some people living under occupation.

The problem of how to make themselves audible and visible has been a central stumbling block of Palestinian nationalism, which has always operated in a context of competition with Israelis, who have been involved in their own struggles for legitimacy. After the dispossession and dispersal effected by the war of 1947–1948 and the resulting transformation of Palestinians into a refugee population, Palestinians were without any territorial or institutional platform from which to express their national aspirations. Israel focused on stifling any expression of Palestinian identity (even banning the colors of the Palestinian flag and nationalist songs) and preventing the development of any infrastructure for the coalescing of collective organization, including among Palestinians who became citizens of the state. By scratching away at the occupation's whitewash that painted Israel's domination as beneficial to the colonized Palestinians, Al-Haq revealed the gritty truths of the occupier's brutalities.[9]

Al-Haq's approach was logical, orderly, and methodical, which the organization's founders perceived to be the way to put right a system of occupation that was built on illogical notions and arbitrary rule. With painstaking attention to fact-finding methodology and a deep faith in the language of reason and law, Al-Haq produced meticulous documentation of rights violations that would challenge the reigning Israeli narrative of their supposedly benevolent occupation. Al-Haq's founders established these principles that would continue to undergird the organization's work throughout the subsequent decades up to today.

Palestine's occupiers had fastidiously underwritten their structure of colonial domination and their powers of Palestinian dispossession with an edifice of military rules and an entire legal system (Hajjar 2005; Kretzmer 2002; Shamir 1990).[10] Palestinian human rights activists responded in the same language, a universal language that they perceived could be a source of neutral authority transcending national and political boundaries.

Although human rights activism is now a recognized sphere of activity both in Palestine and globally, when Al-Haq was established in 1979 its terms were obscure, its proponents mostly unknown. To be sure, human rights discourse was evident in certain elite spheres. For example, in his speech to the UN General Assembly in 1974, Yasir Arafat invoked the Universal Declaration of

Human Rights several times and mentioned Israeli violations of human rights and of the Geneva Conventions (UNGA 1974).[11] Israeli human rights lawyer Felicia Langer has been arguing Palestinian cases in the Israeli courts since the 1970s (see Langer 1995), but it was Al-Haq that helped establish human rights as a general discursive framework, an institutionalized form of activity, and a novel mode of political appeal in Palestine.

How were the lines around this arena of debate, these forms of knowledge claims, engraved? How did rights and their violations come to be newsworthy topics in the mainstream media, in Palestine and elsewhere, and with what consequence for the nature of political debate in the Palestinian-Israeli conflict?

The development of human rights as a field of knowledge production in Palestine was a contested process involving cultural assumptions about experts and expertise, about intention and motive. In seeking to produce information about rights violations that was credible in a highly charged political context, Al-Haq introduced into the Israeli-Palestinian conflict a specific methodology. Al-Haq's methods—collection of affidavits, production of a database of violations, eyewitness reporting, unemotional testimonials, forensic pathology— became part of the typical approach for Palestinian HROs that came after it.

Impressions into Proof, Truth, and Credibility

With all of these methods, Al-Haq was trying to argue, to Israel and eventually to the world, that Palestinians deserved the rights, protections, and respect that are supposed to follow from inhabiting the basic status of "human." Hannah Arendt's description of the stateless person, penned in the wake of two world wars, fits the Palestinian situation well: a "human being in general—without a profession, without a citizenship, without an opinion, without a deed by which to identify or specify himself—and different in general, representing nothing but his own absolutely unique individuality which, deprived of expression within and action upon a common world, loses all significance" (Arendt 1994:302). As a colonized people generally seen through a colonialist framework as irrational, Palestinians were compelled to go to the extremes of objectivity. The standards of objectivity at play in Al-Haq's human rights work was not the sort of rhetorical politics evident in formulations of journalistic "objectivity" that demand a supposed "balance between the two sides" (Bishara 2012), or the criteria adopted by Human Rights Watch (HRW) that requires reports condemning Palestinians and Israelis in a tit-for-tat cycle (Rabbani 2009a). Al-Haq's methodology involved multiple techniques for producing disinterested knowledge specifically and for revealing "objective evidence" by "rationalizing" both their information and themselves as subjects through the statistical and legalistic idioms of law and human rights.[12]

The structural problems that Palestinians faced shaped the particular way in which Al-Haq developed the practice of human rights advocacy. The founders' position as Palestinians struggling against occupation by a state that enjoyed considerable international credibility and sympathy was a key factor, but it was also a locally specific framework of nationalist values and the resonant social category of "nationalist activist" that allowed the human rights approach to flourish in Palestine.

All three of Al-Haq's founders were educated abroad and gravitated toward what they saw in law as an objective standard against which Israeli practices could be measured and, ultimately, condemned and stopped. Shehadeh thought their work "could reveal to the world the true nature of the occupation while promoting among Palestinian society an appreciation for the principles of the rule of law" (2002:138). Shehadeh had returned from his law studies in England in 1976, "brimming with ideas of how things should be, enthusiastic about advocating principles of fairness, justice, and human rights" (Shehadeh 2008:36), his self-described "blind faith in reason" already deeply ingrained (Shehadeh 1984:66). By holding Israel to its word, calling on it to live up to its obligations as a state that adhered to the rule of law and human rights standards, Al-Haq sought to reveal the violations and injustices that were inherent to Israel's occupation.

Shamas was inspired by the "Aristotelian tradition that thought you could put your finger on, reconstruct, or represent what the essence of something was, using rational discourse." Rather than making identity claims to "coerce our way to liberation," he saw their task as being one of "reasoning" with the international order according to its normative content, embodied in international humanitarian and human rights law. "Rationality" has long been a category used to justify colonial efforts to discredit and denigrate the colonized, whose supposed irrational passions required the civilizing discipline of the liberal West.[13] Al-Haq's goal was to subvert that colonial logic, and the long history of orientalism that has obscured and distorted the facts of the Palestinians' case.[14] Abiding by these principles of objective proof, and with the eventual help of international supporters, including jurists, American Civil Liberties Union activists, and human rights professionals from the United States, Israel, and Europe, Al-Haq came to be recognized as a credible source of human rights information in the occupied Palestinian territory (Hajjar 2005:65).

For Kuttab, who was a history major before studying law, the tools of historiography also came into play in Al-Haq's practices of information gathering and documentation. There was for him a confluence between "seeking truth" and working for rights. "Always present in my mind, and those of my colleagues," he said, "were the value of corroboration, declarations against interest, a skeptical perspective, a constant awareness of the perspectives and biases of witnesses as we labored to approach objectivity and seek truth in a murky political situation."

The three men also shared a keen awareness of how Israel itself had used the law to bolster its regime of control. Kuttab, who had studied Hebrew and had a Jerusalem identity card, became a member of the Israeli Bar Association and in the process learned how the law can be a mask, offering a procedural disguise for political projects (also Parker 2003:46; Shehadeh 1984:50).[15] Kuttab learned how Israel "uses law as an instrument of illegality" to expand and entrench the occupation by simply making new regulations in order to decree occupation practices legal and official (also Weill 2007:418–419; Hajjar 2001:23). This approach to law, Kuttab explained to me, was based in the "positivist school," meaning that "it doesn't necessarily have anything to do with justice or with fairness." In the positivist tradition, law is not necessarily that which upholds morality (Green 2003; Hart 1994:185–186), but rather is seen as possessing "an objective binding force" imposed by the state (Pollis 1987:588; see also Shestack 1998:209). An "ethic of 'illegalism'" is how Israeli political scientist Ehud Sprinzak characterized it (Gorenberg 2006:45).

Scrutiny of Israeli practices in light of international humanitarian law (IHL), which is meant to regulate military occupation, bears out Kuttab's observations.[16] Israel's Supreme Court, for example, ratified the sealing and destruction of Palestinian homes, thereby institutionalizing the practice and routinizing this exercise of legal power (Bisharat 1995:374). The government's practice of declaring Palestinian land to be "state land" has led to Israel's seizure of 16 percent of the West Bank (B'Tselem 2010). Another example is the Landau Commission report, issued by an official governmental commission appointed to examine interrogation methods. The Israeli government declared as permissible "moderate physical pressure," thereby redefining and legalizing what many experts would call torture or, as Human Rights Watch/Middle East referred to it, "the bureaucratization of torture" (1994:55). The Supreme Court thus lent its "symbolic capital to the military occupation" in order to legitimize the military's practices of control (Gordon 2008:32).

Al-Haq's first major publication, *The West Bank and the Rule of Law* (Kuttab and Shehadeh 1980), presented a detailed analysis of precisely how Israel established laws in the occupied territory of the West Bank to facilitate Jewish settlement there, which the book notes is a violation of international law (8).[17] One of the bases of Al-Haq's early argumentation was the contention that Israel was bound by international law, and specifically by the Fourth Geneva Convention, in its treatment of Palestinians in the occupied territory. (Israel has continued to argue otherwise.[18]) In responding to Israel in its own legalistic language, Al-Haq "represented the first organized effort to engage law as a form of resistance" in Palestine (Hajjar 2005:62). Shehadeh's memoirs from that period testify to the fear he had of Israeli recriminations for publishing their book (Shehadeh 1984:62–65). The legal system underpinning the military occupation had been unchallenged until then, and Shehadeh's anxiety points to how groundbreaking this kind of publication was at the time.

Among Al-Haq's first goals was to report on the impact and injustice of these laws and practices. In its early days, Al-Haq largely focused on IHL rather than on human rights, which is a distinct field with its own logic. The organization analyzed the evolution and production of a growing tangle of military orders that in effect created a new legal system, also in contravention of the laws of war embodied in the Geneva Conventions, as well as the Hague Conventions, which restrict an occupying power from altering local laws except "for reasons of security" (Al-Haq 1982a:3).[19] They demonstrated the deleterious effects of Israeli settlements on Palestinian access to water and of the military orders imposed to delimit Palestinian agriculture (Al-Haq 1982b). They also collected affidavits of Palestinians exposed to violence by settlers and soldiers, Palestinians denied freedom of movement, and students denied their right to education as a result of the repeated closure of universities by the occupation authorities (Al-Haq 1983). They assembled data on arrests and house demolitions, and collected depositions on human rights violations. Other issues that Al-Haq examined included residency rights in the West Bank and Israel's imposition of identity cards and their uses in controlling the occupied population.

Al-Haq launched its work with questions about how claims of violations could be authenticated as true—and actionable. They were clear from the beginning that styles of communication were extremely important; they knew that "a lot of emotion was not going to work," as Shehadeh said to me. Kuttab noted that, until then, only "generalized, exaggerated, and heartfelt but

inaccurate descriptions of the human rights situation" cloaked in "highly politicized and emotional tones" had been used to confront Israeli practices, a
style that could easily be dismissed, and indeed *was* dismissed by the Israeli
government and international bodies. They emphasized instead attention to
correct, detailed information with "objective and dispassionate appeal to internationally recognized principles" (Kuttab 1992:499). According to Shehadeh,
they allowed nothing to be published without first "going through it with the
assessment of a diplomat."

Al-Haq's activities, which initially focused on legal research and then on
human rights monitoring, emphasized universal standards of international law,
and although they were "acutely aware of the relevance of politics to human
rights," as Kuttab explained to me, they "were determined to actively downplay
it." Kuttab said they wanted to "give the discourse of human rights an opportunity to stand on its own in what was a supremely politicized situation, where
everything was so political. So we tried to de-emphasize and neutralize the 'politics,' but never denied its relevance." Kuttab described Al-Haq's insistence on
political independence as "revolutionary," because public activity opposing the
occupation at that time was highly factionalized. He explained that although
most of Al-Haq's employees had their own political affiliations, he assiduously
avoided knowing about them, because he believed that political affiliation was
irrelevant to human rights work.

This apolitical approach was also taken in order to avoid the accusation
of bias and inaccuracy that this early human rights work, which was inherently critical of Israel, was sure to provoke (Rabbani 1994; Hajjar 2001). Khaled
Batrawi (1999), a fieldwork coordinator at Al-Haq beginning in 1987, wrote
that "in all circumstances, [Palestinian HROs] maintained [their] belief in the
universality of human rights. . . . Human-rights organizations should avoid
bias, and examine the behavior of any power according to the relevant international criteria."

Avoidance of bias through strict reference to international law framed every
Al-Haq activity. In 1988, Emma Playfair, a British human rights lawyer working
as a researcher for Al-Haq, organized an international conference that brought
together preeminent international jurists to explore humanitarian law and to
develop understanding of the law on the administration of occupied territories.
Playfair explained to me that Al-Haq involved these international experts as
authoritative, unbiased people who were seen as such, in order to "be independent and create new knowledge."[20] Until Al-Haq's interventions, Israel's inter-

pretations of IHL had not been challenged in such a systematic and professional manner. Consistent reference to international law, perceived and portrayed as an objective system of standards, was what Al-Haq understood could ensure its own objectivity.

Staff members were also strictly enjoined to uphold this apolitical approach, which was seen as a key principle of objectivity. Unlike Al-Haq's founders, many of the first staff members fell into the work by chance. There was at that time no social or professional role of "human rights activist," and most members began as volunteers.[21] (Initially there were no paid positions and the organization ran entirely on volunteer effort; then, for some time the only salaried employee was a secretary.[22]) Although many of the employees were members of factions and were even rumored to be part of the Unified National Leadership of the Uprising, which led the first intifada, they separated those areas of their lives from their human rights work, and in their conversations with me, these early volunteers emphasized the shared humanist standards and values that had brought them together at Al-Haq.

This requirement of apoliticism—this refusal to allow local factional rivalries to sully the work—was as much a reaction to local political dynamics as it was a reflection of concerns about international opinion. "There was a clearly inward-directed Palestinian agenda that we also nurtured," Shamas said. He described their goals as "anti-corruption, anti-totalitarian, reformist." They believed, Kuttab said, that the "rule of law" was a very important concept to promote "among our people, who were not only living under occupation but who had known a string of regimes even before the Israelis, who ruled by arbitrary fiat and authority of power rather than rule of law. That was, and continues to be, part of our work at Al-Haq. Human rights, as an overarching system of rights, supposedly internationally guaranteed, is part of this rule of law, which we sought to promote."

Of Al-Haq's mission in general Shehadeh said, "I was in some way trying to substitute a sense of security through law, as opposed to a sense of security through political factions." The nationalist movement had been dominated by those who spoke a language that ranged in tone and message from radical leftist excoriation of Zionism as an outpost of Western imperialism, to calls for the recuperation of Palestine as a democracy that would ensure social justice for all sectors of society (Hudson 1972). The goal was the end of Zionist colonialism, and armed struggle was touted as the way to liberate Palestine (Y. Sayigh 1997:71–89).[23] Seeking accountability for Israeli violations through human rights work was a new form of protest and politics for Palestinians. "We aspired to challenge the prevailing internal political ethos and uncritical standards and self-serving dogmatism of the privileged elites of that time," Shamas recalled.

Credibility and Documentation

A combination of factors, including Israel's own fetishization of law, the unique political ideology of Al-Haq's founders, and the exigencies of the first intifada together contributed to the establishment of Al-Haq's credibility at home and abroad, as did shifts in the political scene in Israel and in the Palestine Liberation Organization (PLO). Al-Haq emerged at the moment when the Israeli settlement enterprise entered a new phase of accelerated expansion (under the Likud government that came to office in 1977).[24] Entrenching the occupation even further, this expansion set Israel on the path that has brought the number of Israeli settlements to more than 150, in addition to a hundred "outposts," and the number of Jewish settlers to more than half a million residing on more than 40 percent of the territory of the West Bank and East Jerusalem (OCHA 2012).[25] Beginning in 1969 and continuing into the 1970s, the PLO had serious internal debates in which a clear divergence emerged between those supporting more militancy and those, especially in Fateh, who advocated other forms of activity, including more anti-occupation activity in the occupied territory (Y. Sayigh 1997:345–349). Also in the 1970s, PLO discourse began to incorporate rights-based language and the organization began to engage with the UN, where it was granted observer status, making it the first liberation group to be so designated (Chamberlin 2011:26).[26] This development set the stage for Al-Haq's approach to be more effective.

Al-Haq never intended to establish human rights work as a better form of expressing political opposition to the occupation. As Kuttab pointed out, although the founders themselves were not engaged in armed struggle, "it is in fact sanctioned under international law, and we stated this in our publications. We always stated that human rights are only part of what Palestinians are entitled to, and that our political rights go beyond respect by the occupiers of our human rights and of the Geneva Convention."

Kuttab described Al-Haq's priority as documenting "very carefully, very objectively, the behavior of the Israelis, in courtroom-quality evidence. We wanted affidavits, we wanted pictures, we wanted medical reports. We wanted to take down statements of actual witnesses very skeptically and very critically. We did not want to be taken up with hyperbole or with hearsay or with politically charged positions" (see also LSM 1986:1).

"We thought we should let the facts speak for themselves," said an early Al-Haq lawyer and eventual director of the NGO. "Let's look at what happened: How was that house demolished? What time did it happen? The family was given how many minutes of prior notice? We published all these details. It shed a lot of light on the human consequences" of the occupation. Al-Haq would reveal those human consequences according to standards of evidence that would hold up in court, through scientifically verifiable data (LSM 1984).[27]

Like the nineteenth- and twentieth-century lawyers eager to carve out a field of "legal science" (Shapiro 1969:727), or like social theorists developing the new discipline of sociology (Calhoun 2007), these human rights actors elaborated a distinct form of reasoning and a technique of information production that would mark it out as impartial.[28] One of the first fieldworkers for al-Haq described in fine detail the way they went about collecting evidence and testimonials:

> The testimonial is the most important focus of documentation in HR, along with the questionnaire, photographing, interviews. The resulting report included extensive information on the person who was registering a violation (name, age, marital status, identification number, the location of the incident, when it happened, date, in addition to the appearance of the scene, noting the presence of eyewitnesses, soldiers, description of the body if there was one, its position). The report on what we called "the crime scene" had to be so clear and detailed that anybody anywhere could read it and understand.

The report would then go through extensive scrutiny by the fieldwork coordinator and then by the research coordinator, who would read for clarity, logic, and sufficiency of detail. This focus on methodology made Al-Haq a unique HRO for its time, internationally. Most HROs had not developed systematic, explicit fact-finding methodologies by the 1980s (Orentlicher 1990:85), nor did every HRO working at that time have the same concern for producing objective information about violations in this way. HROs in Canada and Australia, for example, relied on the stature of the personalities involved to boost the organization's credibility—as in a case involving the Canadian Civil Liberties Association, which enrolled a former provincial lieutenant governor as its president—or established their political neutrality by avoiding clearly partisan coalitions.[29] Al-Haq's trademark became its approach: precise and objective legal analysis applied to empirical information documented and corroborated in the field, and a professional tone free of the "politically charged language that was most common in Palestine at the time" (Azzam 2005:5).

The professionalization of human rights work took hold globally with a new model of human rights knowledge production in the 1990s that "was based on legal standards and focused on credibility: on making quantifiable and verifiable claims" (Tate 2007:118); it also included more explicit attention to NGOs' fact-finding methodology (Orentlicher 1990:92). Certainly there were other early human rights activists striving to adhere to high standards of evidence in their efforts to lobby on behalf of victims (Kates 1978), but Al Haq exhibited consistent dedication to the principle of objective fact-finding because the people who established the NGO were aware from the outset that the organization would face problems because it was a Palestinian organization. This was a context in which, as an early employee said, Palestinians "were generally held to be incapable of dispassionate investigation of anything concerning Israel." They were intervening in legal, political matters during a period in which Israel was perceived as innocent of any wrongdoing and Palestinians, as a people, were perceived as angry terrorists. Israel was not considered "a serious offender" of human rights, especially compared to other Middle Eastern regimes. Israel had attempted to "normalize the occupation" (Gordon 2008:1) and maintained that it was a moral army administering a benign occupation, a claim that had been left almost unchallenged until that point (Hajjar 2001; E. Said [1979] 1992:44).

Despite this dominant discourse, with its pristine methodology Al-Haq began to make waves internationally. Its publications were beginning to circulate widely. The advocacy director for Human Rights Watch at the time encouraged this by facilitating the distribution of Al-Haq's *Punishing a Nation* ([1988] 1990) in the United States (Al-Haq 1990). Established organizations like Amnesty International, Physicians for Human Rights, and the Lawyers Committee for Human Rights, based in New York, were also increasingly calling on Al-Haq for information and helping to circulate it.

As early as 1983, Al-Haq had also been using international law to address third-state conduct and responsibility. This was, as Shamas explained to me, "an instrument to engage self-proclaimed law-abiding actors and compel self-enforced modifications of their conduct (what we regarded as wrongful action or inaction on their part)." For instance, in one of their 1984 publications on an Israeli-proposed road plan in the West Bank, Al-Haq lawyers made the case that an International Court of Justice advisory opinion was in order because the road would violate international law (Shehadeh, Shehadeh, and Shehadeh 1984). As far as Shamas was aware, Al-Haq was "the first HRO to focus critical reflection and law-based normative debate on the actions of third states rather than just Israel."

Although the Israeli government would not admit to the veracity of Al-Haq's claims, they were forced to respond publicly to the Palestinian organization's legal arguments. One response came in *The Rule of Law in the Areas Administered by Israel*, which the Israel National Section of the International Commission of Jurists published in 1981. In a foreword that is liberally sprinkled with Latin phrases, Israeli military government lawyer Justice Haim Cohen asserts the book's credibility by referring to the authorities underwriting it: "erudite writers," "the opinions of courts of justice," and "the internationally recognized experts, whose books on the law of military occupation have been the vade mecum of the legal advisers of the military commanders throughout the years" (ix). Perhaps in a veiled reference to Al-Haq's work, the publication is presented "to the international legal community trusting that the discerning eye and the analytical mind of the lawyer, trained in the ascertainment and evaluation of facts, will easily differentiate between a *tractatus politicus* and a sober statement of law and fact" (xii). It was clear that within the first decade of its occupation, Israel was feeling the pressure of human rights scrutiny and sought to justify its actions. The Israeli leadership knew as early as September 1967 that settling Israelis in occupied Palestinian territory in the West Bank would violate international law (Gorenberg 2006:100). The Israeli Ministry of Justice and Ministry of Foreign Affairs both established human rights divisions in the late 1970s "to respond to foreign inquiries into human rights issues, primarily in the Occupied Territories" (Bisharat 1995:387). Additional volumes penned by lawyers in the Israeli military establishment were published in the 1980s and 1990s in an attempt to defend Israel in terms of international law (Bisharat 1995:388n157).

Such attempts only confirmed Al-Haq in emphasizing its methodology of verisimilitude, which was designed to extend and expand a witnessing public to include anyone who read its reports as a means of authenticating knowledge of the facts of violations (c.f. Shapin 1984:481–484). A collection of testimonies about torture that Al-Haq—then still called Law in the Service of Man (LSM)—published in 1985 stressed the methodology by which the affidavits were gathered:

> They were collected by trained field workers employed by LSM, who took great care to ensure accuracy and precision. In each instance, information was taken down as dictated by the affiant. Questions were asked on points of which he or she might have been unsure. The rule against hearsay was followed, as well as

other rules relating to evidence that are observed in judicial inquiries. Finally, the written version was read to the affiant, who was asked to sign it. [LSM 1986:5; see also Al-Haq n.d.]

Neither Abstractions nor Pitiful Victims

Testimony continued to be an important element of Al-Haq's field research. Niall MacDermot, an early Al-Haq supporter and secretary-general of the ICJ from 1970 to 1990,[30] encouraged the collection of these affidavits, and they were used as key documents in establishing the systematic practice of torture by Israel. MacDermot came up with the title for the LSM publication about conditions in a political prison, "Torture and Intimidation in the West Bank" (LSM 1986). "It was the first time that a credible organization used the term *torture* to describe what was going on in Palestine," according to an early Al-Haq lawyer. These testimonies also gave a human face and a name to Palestinians, who were often presented as an "abstract notion," she said.

The goal behind this humanizing effort was unlike the humanitarian testimony that privileges the "essential humanity" of "victim-witnesses" (Dembour and Haslam 2004:153), and psychological effects over recitation of facts and events (Fassin 2008). Al-Haq's lawyers were operating during an earlier era, within a legal framework; the human face presented in testimony was important for creating common cause that was ideological and principled, not emotional or sympathetic. "By emphasizing the human element, it provides the opportunity for a meeting of minds between people of differing political persuasions in a common concern for justice, dignity and respect for human rights" (Al-Haq 1983). They spoke as activists, not as vague "abstractions" or as victims in need of pity.

They were not, of course, the first to try to do this. In an interview with the BBC, Leila Khaled, a guerilla from the Popular Front for the Liberation of Palestine (PFLP) who became famous for her attempt to hijack an El Al flight from Amsterdam in 1970 described the motivation behind those who performed acts of spectacular violence in order to puncture the abstract view of Palestinians:

All the time we were being dealt with as refugees who only needed human aid. That was unjust. Nobody had heard our screams and suffering. All we got from the world was more tents and old clothes. After 1967 [when Israel occupied the West Bank, the Gaza Strip, and East Jerusalem], we were obliged to explain to the world that the Palestinians had a cause. . . . At the beginning of our revolution we had to create publicity for our struggle. I think that by using these tactics, we succeeded in putting our message in front of the whole world. [BBC 2001a]

Other factions engaged in armed attacks against Israel as well, launching border raids and airliner hijackings that brought Israeli reprisals. Al-Haq's methods, in contrast, were geared toward claiming respect and dignity as rational persons, specifically as political subjects with measured voices to be heard and reasonable demands to be recognized. Countering orientalist perceptions of Palestinians' supposed irrationality, Al-Haq affidavits were sterile in tone, relaying information about facts, including what violation had occurred, at precisely what time, what the Israeli guards did, how the detainee responded, and what the interrogators said. There was little subjective interpretation or emotive language clouding the text.[31] The report by Al-Haq (then called LSM) on al-Fara'a prison explains how the collection of testimony was gathered, emphasizing the measures taken to ensure the veracity of what the affiants said:

> Those who have been to al-Fara'a have given LSM detailed descriptions of their ordeals in statements under oath. LSM has considered it appropriate to describe the conditions at al-Fara'a using the statements under oath of those with first-hand experience. None of the affiants knew what had been said by the others, but the information given by each of those whose statements were taken supports that given by the others. In taking down these statements, LSM has taken great care to follow the rules of evidence observed by courts. [LSM 1986:1]

Just as some scholars have criticized forms of human rights testimonial that decontextualize violations or reduce them to isolated incidents (Wilson 2001:34–35; A. Feldman 2004), there was some dissatisfaction with Al-Haq's strategy among the organization's own staff. Mouin Rabbani, a volunteer at Al-Haq during the first intifada, contends that the organization's emphasis on strict human rights standards and an ideology of scientific objectivity "translated into an emphasis on micro-violations to the detriment of [conveying] the bigger picture or engaging with questions specifically of national rights" (1994). However, sociologist and early Al-Haq volunteer Joost Hiltermann (1989a:114) argued that this was part of Al-Haq's effort to contribute to a popular effort to "out-administer" the Israeli occupation and lay the foundations for independence via an institutional struggle. Al-Haq itself argued against portrayals of micro-violations, as is evident in their criticism of the US Report on Human Rights Practices in the Occupied Territories by Israel for 1982. Al-Haq described the report's coverage of the human rights situation in the occupied territory as "complacent in the extreme" and condemned its tone for implying "that the situation concerning human rights does not give grave cause for concern. Individual incidents are mentioned but the impression given is that these are isolated occurrences and are not part of an overall Israeli policy" (Hillier 1983:4).

Al-Haq's publications presented individual abuses in some detail, explicitly as illustrations of broad patterns, precisely to argue about the systematic violations of human rights that are inherent to occupation. The report on Al-Fara'a prison, for instance, describes it as an intimidation center, the overall purpose of which was to force detainees into confessing, usually to crimes they had not committed.

> The evidence demonstrates that al-Fara'a is intended to operate as an intimidation centre to which groups—mainly of young people—are taken for a certain period, given harsh treatment and later tried on the basis of confessions that appear in many cases to be extracted against their will, then released. This being the case, it is the function which al-Fara'a is intended to serve which constitutes the violation that must be stopped. [LSM 1986:2]

Their strategy, said one researcher, was to highlight general violation trends. "If Israelis uproot ten trees, no, we don't write about it. But if it became general, yes."[32] Only after collecting enough data to prove a pattern did Al-Haq publish it, analyzing it in light of IHL and international customary law. "Objectivity is accomplished by looking at patterns," the data manager at Al-Haq said, emphasizing the NGO's thorough and patient style. "That was true at Al-Haq. You discard the outlier affidavits as extraneous and go for the core and make an argument about that group."

They did not write that Israel practiced torture, for example, until they had collected dozens of affidavits from various geographical regions and researchers had investigated them. Torture is notoriously difficult to document and verify (Orentlicher 1990:94–95; Welsh 2000:5–10). In addition to employing computer software for building a database that would make it easier to identify patterns and policies (Hiltermann 1988), Al-Haq also enlisted the resources of medical science, a powerful authorizing discourse whose categories and methods could be borrowed for the creation and credibility of this new field of human rights. By 1987, Al-Haq had begun to incorporate the work of forensic pathologists to help investigate deaths in detention (Hiltermann 1990; Hiss, Kahana, and Arensburg 1997). Volunteer doctors from the United Kingdom and elsewhere offered their expertise and attended autopsies to determine cause of death. This testimony, which was both foreign and scientific, thus carried a particular weight, and Al-Haq's evidence was often called upon by journalists and UN members in wider public debate (see, for example, UNCAT 1997).

It was only a few years after its establishment that Al-Haq began to direct some of its efforts further outward, toward world public opinion. They did not consider public declarations and the performance of a political stance to be an effective tactic. From the beginning, Al-Haq's founders had intentionally not concerned themselves with making public declarations. Again, Hiltermann confirmed that in the early days of the first intifada Al-Haq communicated information about human rights violations "to organizations abroad, not as a matter of routine but with a specific purpose in mind: they are asked to take a particular type of action according to the circumstances" (Hiltermann 1988:9). Shehadeh contrasted this policy with the practices of other organizations that were "very into condemning Israeli actions, issuing releases saying, 'We condemn! We condemn!' But I told our group, we must never condemn. What's the point? Who are we? Our very existence is a condemnation of Israeli occupation. We were very careful about issuing press releases. We did not go public until we had tried every other way. In thirteen years we only issued fifty press releases. Now there's a press release every time something happens."

Al-Haq framed these arguments very consciously, driven by a faith that "producing information based on analysis and affidavits of factual accounts of what happened could persuade people," and that information would be "stronger if it was detached, first-person evidence" (Playfair 1992). They believed that the clarity and precision of detail was what could dent Israel's domination of the historical and political narrative. Firsthand testimonials and reporting by Al-Haq fieldworkers continues to be a point of pride for the organization. A fieldworker active during the 2002 Israeli invasion of Jenin that left the refugee camp partially destroyed spoke forcefully about the precise work of Al-Haq, one of the first organizations to enter the camp after the Israeli withdrawal. He told me they "take signed affidavits from eyewitnesses" and showed me the form on which they record relevant data: name, identification number, date, signature.

It was a specifically nationalist context that made establishing the credibility of the testimony takers just as important as that of the testimony. A former fieldwork coordinator, Khalil, recounted for me, and then again for a Palestinian audience to whom he was lecturing, the problem of sifting out honest affidavits from false and exaggerated reports. He told several stories of Palestinians who had called Al-Haq to the scene of an alleged Israeli violation that, upon investigation, was revealed to be false testimony that had been given in an effort to cover something up, such as a civil crime, an accident, a suicide, or a domestic fight. One instance was a man who was killed in Gaza and proclaimed a "martyr" (anyone killed as a result of the occupation, implying a good nationalist). "I doubted it," Khalil said. The facts did not seem to add up, so he put the case aside without filing it. Months later, he said, the Israelis found a video recording showing the victim sitting with a colleague. "They were holding guns. Only one of them had the safety on. It was the other guy who accidentally shot and killed him." There may have been a financial motive for the misrepresentation of this event given that the PLO gave stipends to "martyrs." Another fieldwork coordinator said, "We trained fieldworkers in taking statements under oath and documentation. We took a scientific approach." He talked about a field researcher who made a report about a family being forced out of their home with no time to retrieve their possessions before the house was demolished. Because it turned out that the report was based on incorrect testimony from neighbors rather than on the testimony of the victims themselves, the researcher was fired.

In telling such stories to me, a foreign observer, and to local audiences of Palestinian human rights trainees, Khalil and others demonstrated that the work of the organization was done in good faith. Although some Palestinians might consider Khalil's stories an unseemly or even dangerously unnationalist airing of dirty laundry better left hidden, Khalil underscored his willingness to buck nationalist protocol to attest to the rigor of his fact-finding. Like the authoritative scientist and other theorists of Robert Boyle's day "who recounted unsuccessful experiments" to show that the scientist was "a man whose objectivity was not distorted by his interests" (Shapin 1984:494), that he was an "unprejudiced observer" and "reasonable man" (Shapiro 1969:751), Khalil's willingness to publicly admit that some Palestinian claims were false illustrated his professionalism (as well as his canny reading of the evidence). Even more crucially, he was confirming his own trustworthiness.

It is particularly within a nationalist milieu that human rights activists, in their role as "translators" who "reframe local grievances in terms of global human rights principles" (Merry 2006:39), must carefully walk a line in order to establish their authority and credibility for audiences at home and abroad. Sally Merry has identified this necessity as the "paradox of making human rights in the vernacular." It involves the challenge of making human rights "resonant with the local cultural framework" while still according with a human rights ideology that emphasizes "individualism, autonomy, choice, bodily integrity, and equality"

(2006:49). For Palestinians, however, the challenge was not posed by these fundamental liberal principles. Rather, it was a matter of producing objective human rights knowledge and, in some sense, performing credibly to outsiders suspicious of, if not fully hostile to, their nationalist aspirations. However, they had to do this without at the same time calling into question their own national loyalties. When preservation of Palestinian unity and the nationalist cause was a priority vehemently upheld by most Palestinians, making public anything that might be useful to Israeli efforts at disqualifying Palestinian claims could be a dangerous, potentially treasonous act. It was within this context of multiple audiences of often clashing perspectives that Al-Haq had to plot its course.

In this entrance of human rights onto the Palestinian political scene, we see the double bind in which human rights workers have always been caught. In order for the international human rights movement, and the international community, to accept its work, and in order to deprive Israeli authorities of reasons to discredit its claims, Al-Haq had to maintain a pristinely apolitical face. Any claim made by a Palestinian *as* a Palestinian could be easily dismissed—as untrustworthy, partisan, and driven by a nationalist goal rather than by a genuine search for the truth. On the other side, Palestinian society also had to be convinced. To establish its credibility locally, Al-Haq had to bring a distinct set of criteria and practices into play. In this early period of human rights activism, it was a nationalist background and political activism—precisely what could discredit them abroad—that bestowed credibility on an individual or organization in Palestinian society.

Credibility at Home

The frames of meaning and motive of Al-Haq's staff, supporters, and constituency were not always complementary as Palestinian NGO activists tried "to navigate between their own professional and development requirements and Palestinian national aspirations for independence" (Hanafi and Tabar 2005:13). These tensions reveal the broad contradictions at the heart of the human rights regime in general. Competing allegiances to nationalist and humanist values, and to different standards of local and international credibility, have plagued the development of human rights activism in places such as Colombia (Tate 2007), Egypt (Abdelrahman 2007), and elsewhere (c.f. Wilson 2001:1). Such tensions have persisted in Palestine, albeit in different forms, from the time of Al-Haq's establishment through the first intifada in the late 1980s, and from the second intifada in late 2000 and up to today. There was friction between the demands of establishing the new discourse and methods of human rights in a way that was convincing to an international audience, and the nationalist demands of a society under occupation. Kuttab noted that although the new human rights framework they were establishing "ran squarely against the way many nationalists were then conducting their national struggle, nationalists eventually embraced this new discourse."

When the founders and staff of Al-Haq started their work, they faced challenges and suspicion from every quarter. One researcher, Ayman, who was a member of the Palestinian Communist Party when he began working with Al-Haq, said his faction was suspicious of his involvement there because few had heard of "human rights." He, however, never saw any contradiction between his political concerns and his human rights activism: "I felt that the struggle for human rights was part of the resistance to the occupation and this was my fundamental goal. As part of the communist party, we didn't believe in violence, but in peaceful resistance, and I felt that the principles of human rights were close to these ideas."

Some in Palestine thought that Al-Haq was an American organization working on behalf of the West and "that it was an effort to make the struggle against the occupation peaceful and not violent, which is what the Americans and Israelis wanted." A more long-lasting question has been whether Al-Haq's work challenged the occupation or reinforced it by recommending policies that would merely soften its features. Hiltermann called it "a perennial question that is not easily addressed." He described to me the pendulum of the problem: "If the conclusion of every inquiry into a pattern of human rights violations is that the occupation should be terminated, you lose your credibility as a human rights advocate; but if, on the other hand, you advocate an end to, for example, house demolitions, you are potentially advocating policies that would merely turn a nasty occupation into a somewhat more benevolent one, if such a thing is possible." Lawyers defending Palestinians in Israeli military courts wrangled with a similar dilemma, which led some to boycott the courts. Others continued offering legal representation, despite the fact that the courts were unfair, because their involvement meant they might be able to bargain for shorter sentences, and it at least allowed them the opportunity to visit detainees and offer moral support (Bisharat 1995).[33] Similar debates are periodically voiced about humanitarian aid and even about the existence of the PA, both of which, some argue, provide structures that enable the occupation to continue by softening Israel's blows and papering over the fact that the occupation is ongoing.

Among the other obstacles complicating the organization's work were some Palestinians' fears that the Israelis would seek retribution and punish them for providing information about abuses to Al-Haq. The PLO did not favor Al-Haq's approach either. Shehadeh characterized the Palestinian leadership's concern as political in that, "should the nonviolent ways of our organization gain popularity, Al-Haq might somehow challenge the jealously guarded supremacy of the sole representative of the Palestinian people, the PLO" (2008:37). Rumors that Al-Haq was working for the US Central Intelligence Agency circulated (and today some Palestinians still believe that most NGOs are in league with that agency), as did the belief that they were collaborators with the Israelis.

Ayman explained the early suspicion toward Al-Haq: "The founders were nationalists and good people, but they had no factional coverage or backing. They were not all from prominent families. No one knew them, and all three were Christian." He characterized the board of directors similarly, as "intellectuals, university professors, with no political affiliations, no ties to the people." What increased the credibility of this new NGO, according to Ayman, was the fact that most of the early Al-Haq fieldworkers, who were "the face of Al-Haq to the society," were political leaders or cadre. "We were the ones in communication with the people and gave human rights credibility. Without us, it might have taken another twenty years for the people to grasp what we were doing." Many came from leftist factions, including the Democratic Front for the Liberation of Palestine, the PFLP, and the Palestinian Communist Party (which became the Palestinian People's Party in 1991), and they worked throughout the occupied territory, traveling between the West Bank and Gaza Strip (until 1991, when Israel restricted free passage of Palestinians between the two areas). Indeed, members of all the factions of the PLO, and even Hamas, were on Al-Haq's staff, although this political range was not deliberate. As Hiltermann noted, this "was fortuitous, as no faction could find fault with Al-Haq as long as they felt their view was somehow represented." He found it interesting that this broad representation of factions was placating to the public, given that "people's political views never came up in internal discussions."

The First Intifada

A particular conjuncture of dramatic events led to the cementing of human rights and HROs as important political players in Palestinian politics. HROs and NGOs in general expanded considerably during the first intifada (Gordon and Berkovitch 2007; Hanafi and Tabar 2004:252), a major uprising against the occupation that began in December of 1987. After twenty years of military occupation, the intifada started with demonstrations in the Gaza Strip and quickly spread to the West Bank. This nationalist rebellion involved physical confrontation, civil disobedience, and revivified political organization. Palestinians' rejection of the occupation resulted in worldwide (if temporary and sporadic) recognition of their plight. Images of rock-throwing youth pitted against gun-toting Israeli soldiers became one of the intifada's preeminent symbols of the Palestinians' underdog role in this David and Goliath battle.

The uprising was met by Israel's harsh crackdown against the Palestinian population, which found its most vicious form in then Israeli Defense Minister Yitzhak Rabin's "Iron Fist" policy, which he announced in January of 1988 (UNGA 1988; Hiltermann 1989b:127; Gordon 2008). Beatings, deportations, and imprisonment of suspected political activists increased in rate and intensity. During the intifada, "the rate of incarceration in the territories was by far the highest known anywhere in the world: close to . . . one prisoner for every 100 persons" (Hajjar 1995:612; see also HRW 1991). One would be hardpressed to find a resident of the occupied territory who has not had a friend or relative in an Israeli jail at some point. Among other forms of collective punishment was the demolition or sealing of houses of the families of political detainees or suspects. The number of home demolition and sealing orders increased dramatically during the first intifada, and they were often imposed over and above any military court sentence passed on the accused (Al-Haq 1993:3, 6). Through curfews, roadblocks, checkpoints, and village closures, and by the countless required—but nearly impossible to obtain—"permits" for work and home construction, Israel tried to immobilize the Palestinians physically, economically, and politically.[34]

Writing after the first year of the intifada, Penny Johnson (1988), who was working in the public relations department of a major West Bank university at the time, described some of the turbulent events from the summer and autumn of 1988:

> As the 21st year of the occupation commenced, near midnight on June 6, Israeli settlers invaded the narrow alleys of Dheisheh refugee camp, breaking into houses, beating youths and terrorizing the population, in "retaliation" for stone-throwing on the nearby highway which leads to southern West Bank settlements. . . . Two waves of demonstrations and strikes swept the area, sparked by the Gaza killings and by an army sweep of Dheisheh [refugee] camp on October 26. . . . In the West Bank alone, 19 Palestinians have been killed and 100 wounded by army

bullets in 1986 and 1987 (as of November 11), over 80 percent in the course of demonstrations. Underlying both the tumultuous autumn and the somnolent summer is the steady erosion of individual Palestinian and collective rights. This has become a structural feature of the occupation. . . . The current phase, the "iron fist" policy introduced in August 1985, has brought a substantial increase in clear-cut human rights violations. One of the most striking features is this routinization of repression. [Johnson 1988][35]

The humiliations and brutalities have continued. A page from my field notes from January 2002 conveys something of the "routinized repression" that persists in Jerusalem and other areas where Israeli forces are present on the ground.

Last night in Jerusalem: Walking through the Old City on a Saturday night, most of the shops were closed or closing. As I approached the outer corridor to Damascus gate, up the steps from where the fruit sellers usually are, my friend and I saw a large number of Israeli soldiers, or maybe they were police. They were roughing up a number of Palestinian guys (who looked to be in their twenties). There were probably seven to ten soldiers (in greens) and maybe five or six Palestinians being searched. There were a number of shopkeepers standing around the perimeter, watching calmly. The soldiers were hitting one guy, a slappy punch here and there. At one point a soldier kicked his legs open wider as he was pushed up against a wall being searched. I saw one soldier try to calm down one of his colleagues who was roughing up one of the Palestinians.

My friend and I got up as close as possible to observe, in the (probably vain) hope that we could act as some kind of protective witnesses. One of the soldiers came up to me and instructed us, "Why don't you move on." I said, "Why?" He was surprised, I think, that I talked back, and said, "because you don't need to be here." We exchanged more acrimonious words. At one point a big blonde soldier who was being the roughest with the scrawniest Palestinian took the guy into the corner and I saw him make the guy drop his pants. They were searching them all and checking their identification cards.

I asked a Palestinian man sitting on the steps next to the commotion why these soldiers were doing this. "Who knows. They're just nervous ('asabiyin)." I asked whether the Palestinians hadn't done something. "No. The soldiers don't want anything. As you see, they're just tense (mu'asab)." I understood him to mean that these soldiers were looking for trouble. Some of the soldiers started kicking around garbage cans, spilling it onto the steps. They finally just let the guys go, and my friend and I walked away. I think foreigners during the first intifada did more. The problem is that everyone knows that a higher level of brutality is expected, accepted, and nobody outside cares.

Throughout the first intifada, the abusive techniques that the occupation authorities employed to quell the uprising increased coverage of the occupied territory by international media. The reports of HROs, including Al-Haq, also enhanced international attention to the Palestinians' cause, and provided another source of information for media professionals. This was the period when, as Palestinian social scientist George Giacaman contends, Palestinians "discovered" human rights as the ideal language with which to make their voices heard internationally. "We addressed the world from within the framework of human rights discourse as a common language that connects Palestinians to the world outside" (Giacaman 2000:10). Other Palestinian HROs were formed, facilitated by the increase in international funds as well as money from the PLO in Tunis, where it was based after being driven out of Lebanon. They used legal language to criticize the occupation and to assert what needed to change (Hajjar 2001:27). Even if law is always a form of politics, human rights law included, its practitioners do not always announce it as such. Through their clear political focus on critiquing Israel's violation of international law, Al-Haq and other NGOs politicized law itself and reframed the purpose of human rights (Hajjar 2001:25). They continued to argue that Israel was bound by international law, and specifically by the Fourth Geneva Convention, in their treatment of Palestinians in the occupied territory (while Israel continued to deny that they were so obliged).

In addition to the formal entrenchment of human rights language and activities in NGOs and other organizations, human rights was also popularized and became part of how Palestinians expressed their political demands (Hajjar 2001:27). For example, a leaflet issued by the Unified National Leadership, the intifada's underground coordinating body, referred to the Geneva Conventions and other international instruments. More Palestinian HROs were established, and international human rights groups like Amnesty International, and eventually Human Rights Watch, began to take more active interest in the occupied Palestinian territory as well. The expanding breach between international humanitarian and human rights standards and actual Israeli treatment of its occupied subjects was made more evident by the brutality with which Israel tried to quash the uprising (Hajjar 2001:26; Rabbani 1994).

The intensified levels of occupation violence increased Al-Haq's activities. Their interactions with the public became more frequent, as fieldworkers gathered data on the growing number of violations and the NGO's lawyers represented more and more clients in front of Israeli military court judges. Palestinian-run human rights NGOs became involved in a variety of projects. Their activities often centered on gathering statistical data and writing reports about human rights violations, offering workshops to instruct people about the rights that are their due according to human rights law, pressing foreign governments to implement the international humanitarian and human rights laws, and hosting journalists and foreign delegations, including state officials and representatives of international political and legal organizations. These activities and the greater need for HRO reporting and legal services raised public awareness and the credibility of Al-Haq and human rights work in general in Palestine.

Human rights consciousness continued to increase from that moment forward and came to infuse people's discourse at almost every level of Palestinian society, from religious leaders to political parties. Early in the second intifada, for example, a sheikh delivering a televised Friday sermon (*khutba*) to local viewers in Ramallah called out to "those looking for human rights, those looking for civilization in this century. What's happening with them?" he asked. "Where are those looking for human rights in Europe, America, Africa? They should come here, to see what's happening to the Palestinian people." Such vocabulary can now be heard in a variety of lobbying efforts. For example, at a demonstration on behalf of women political prisoners that I attended in 2001 outside the International Red Crescent headquarters in Ramallah, handwritten placards in English and Arabic declared, "Women Prisoners are victims of Israeli human rights violations," and although not precisely accurate, another sign insisted, "Arresting children is a violation of human rights." Most HROs also issue pamphlets and other educational materials, such as booklets explaining laws related to military courts. Education or "consciousness-raising" (*tathqif*) about human rights, a practice that was initiated with Al-Haq's *Know Your Rights* series, is a typical component of most HRO projects today.

Empowerment Through Law, Not Victimhood

At Al-Haq, human rights and the law in general were considered to be tools of empowerment. Shehadeh saw the law as an instrument of change and as a means by which people could stand up for themselves. The *Know Your Rights* pamphlets, originally published in the Arabic daily newspaper *Al-Quds*, "inculcated in those who read them the crucial notion that not only did they—Palestinians, victims, fighters, people—have fundamental rights, but they had a right to assert these rights, and the booklets showed them how they might begin to do so" (Hiltermann 2000; see also Hiltermann 1988:10). Al-Haq provided free legal aid as a "service to the people," Shehadeh said, because it should not be an expensive luxury available only to the privileged. It offered public assistance that could also "serve the political situation and have an impact on occupation." A former fieldworker believed that the widespread lack of legal knowledge contributed to the Palestinians' problems as a people. "The settlers were stealing our land and there was no one who believed that the law could be used to redress this. As a result, the settlers took half the West Bank. I believed that if the poor farmer knew he could challenge the settlers, the land would not have been taken." Legal aid is now a standard service provided by most HROs, who have lawyers on staff to represent Palestinian political prisoners in Israeli courts or, more often, to bargain with prosecutors for reduced jail terms.

Al-Haq's philosophy provides a distinct contrast to the portrayals by some scholars who are critical of human rights and decry its production of "a theater of roles, in which people are victims,' 'violators,' and 'bystanders'" (Kennedy 2002b:111). Al-Haq's documents, practices, and regnant beliefs did not figure "victims as passive and innocent, violators as deviant, and human rights professionals as heroic" (Kennedy 2002b:111), but rather activated human rights as a language in which Palestinians could speak for themselves. To be sure, the work of human rights advocates in Palestine eventually came to be the target of blame, for the way some human rights representations did figure Palestinians as victims, and for the overall system's corruption of meaningful political activity (see Chapter 2). It was well before such tendencies and criticisms became entrenched, however, that Al-Haq saw itself as an expression of Palestinian collective empowerment through law. The fact that the organization was run by Palestinians, with foreigners playing a role as assistants providing a channel to the West, was integral to its ethos. The organization's existence, and the work it did, "was about Palestinians taking their fate into their own hands," said one staff member. The people they served did come in to tell their stories of victimization, and "yes, people are victims," he said. "Horrible things happened and we wrote it all down, but we did not treat them as victims. We wanted to use these stories as a means for Palestinians to stand up for their rights." Moreover, the organization made conscious efforts to retain ownership of its work in the face of pressures from international human rights groups to bend to their distinct purposes and methodologies (Hiltermann 1988). My interviewees from Al-Haq emphasized their autonomy and the fact that Al-Haq prioritized its own agenda, in contrast to the complaints heard about donor-driven NGOs today.[36] I was told that Al-Haq always had a clear policy about how and why it communicated information about human rights violations to groups abroad. The reasons for circulating information were clear and strategized. When information was shared with international groups, it was always accompanied by a specific request to take a particular action in response to the events on which Al-Haq was reporting.

Successes

The people I spoke with considered Al-Haq's biggest achievements to be the gradual shifts in attitudes toward and awareness of the Palestinian condition they detected among outsiders, and the small, individual victories they observed at home. "A success was when a house was not demolished. I suppose there were a few such cases," one interlocutor responded somewhat listlessly. Home demolition orders were occasionally delayed, a few soldiers were tried for criminal abuses, and some of those cases resulted in compensation for the victims. As far back as 1990, Joost Hiltermann assessed that the Israeli authorities were responding to the embarrassment caused by increased media and human rights organizations' attention to the deaths of Palestinians in Israel (Hiltermann 1990). A former fieldworker also recalled Al-Haq's role in proving that a Palestinian detainee, Khaled Al-Sheikh, had died as a result of torture in an Israeli prison in 1989.[37] He offered this case as one small, rare example of triumph. Mouin Rabbani located Al-Haq's successes in an earlier period, when in the 1980s the organization revealed "the extent of secret and unpublished legislation" of the Israeli occupation, which prompted the military authorities to publicize new military orders, albeit in a disorganized fashion (1994). Kuttab, too, observed that Israel responded more quickly and positively to Palestinians whose cases were taken up by Al-Haq and made known to international organizations (1992:501).

Many with whom I spoke pointed to the very fact of helping to start a human rights movement as an accomplishment. One said, "We did this at a time when even the liberated nations of the Arab and Third World didn't have a human rights movement, but in the occupied territories we did. Al-Haq shared their experience across the Arab world and helped raise awareness and interest in HR concepts in Palestinian society." Al-Haq's work was also aimed at laying the infrastructure of a judicial system for an independent Palestinian state. "It has," as Hiltermann (1988:9) described it, "endeavored to prepare the population's collective consciousness for its future task of organizing Palestinian society in a just and equitable manner." Likewise, Jonathan Kuttab pointed positively to the "systematic inculcation into the whole population of the importance of accurate documentation—the belief in human rights as a universal value and not just a tool to fight occupation." As evidence, he noted as "a sign of great maturity that as soon as the PA was installed in the occupied territories in 1995, everyone expected them to abide by human rights standards. Any torture in PA prisons was immediately condemned by everyone. I remember people who were tortured by the Palestinian Authority, upon being released coming on local TV, talking to the newspapers, and telling their stories and pointing to the camera, saying 'I know you tortured me. I know who you are because we used to be colleagues. This is wrong. This is wrong.'" Although political detainees from Palestinian jails report being warned not to talk of their experiences, and if some do fear reprisals, the number of reports documenting PA abuses indicate that many speak out nevertheless.

The poor recording of Palestinians' earlier history contributed to human rights activists' belief that their documentation of events was an important service in and of itself. The need to record the Palestinian experience for the historical record and for future accountability has been a motivating concern for many human rights activists in Palestine. For them, human rights documentation is a form of history writing, and like other Palestinian historians, they work within a trajectory of dispersal and upheaval that has denied Palestinians a national archive or even much official documentation, leaving them to strain against others' portrayals, and against the treatment of the Palestinian national narrative as being merely an addendum to that of other nations (see Muslih 1987; Doumani 1992). They believed that older organizations, like the UN Relief and Works Agency, the UN agency responsible for refugees, had not done enough in this regard, leading to the lack of information on what happened to the refugees in 1948 and to the Palestinian villages destroyed during the war. Raja Shehadeh asked why he bothered to write down the stories of abuse and injustice, and answered himself with the assertion that letting others write one's history is "the ultimate capitulation" (1984:67–68).

A fieldworker described HRO revelations about Israeli violations, about the illegality and international illegitimacy of Israel's settlements, as political messages. These are assertions, he said, "that we have a right to be liberated from the occupation. When I defend the rights of an individual, when we show the brutality of occupation policies, we energize world public opinion around our issue."

"Just making things known was making a difference," Emma Playfair said. "Success is changing people's perspective. These were small steps." Al-Haq's human rights work "was part of a mass movement that was increasing the cost of occupation by throwing the laws back on the occupier," Hiltermann said (see also Hiltermann 1988). "This was also part of the process of building international solidarity." He went on, saying, "Yes, the victories were temporary and partial, and the violations continue, because Israel is a strong state with international influence. It is not easy to confront those policies, but that doesn't mean we stop this work."

In response to my question about Al-Haq's successes, a legal expert who was a consultant with the Palestinian Red Crescent Society pointed to the ways in which activists were mobilizing international law, including in the case of Salah Shehadeh (no relation to Al-Haq's Raja Shehadeh), a Hamas leader killed by the Israeli army in 2002, along with fourteen civilians, when they dropped a one-ton bomb in a densely populated Gaza neighborhood (Weill 2009). The possibility of prosecuting Israeli leaders for a war crime energized the use of universal jurisdiction, which allows a state to try suspects alleged to have committed crimes outside its borders, to seek redress for Palestinians and obtain Israeli accountability. Soon after the killing of Shehadeh, a Spanish judge opened an investigation of seven Israelis to determine whether they were responsible for the crime. Spain recognizes the principle of universal jurisdiction, but the Spanish court eventually shelved the case in response to international pressure (Mazzawi and Jamjoum 2009; PCHR 2010a). "Spain withdrew, but Israeli generals are afraid to travel," Ayman noted, referring to the threat of arrest that senior Israeli army officers and politicians face abroad (Tetta 2009:6; Mitnick 2009; McCarthy 2007:25; Hider 2009:35; Ynet News 2009). "No one's been arrested, but they've started thinking twice." Indeed, high-ranking Israeli officials began curbing visits to the United Kingdom, fearing arrest for war crimes under the law of universal jurisdiction, to such an extent that the British government started "looking urgently at ways in which the UK system might be changed to avoid this situation arising again" (McCarthy 2010). For Shehadeh, this constituted "a major leap and promising development" that emerged "perhaps as a natural or organic outcome" of earlier human rights work. Al-Haq's website announces other successes, such as the exclusion of a French multinational company, Veolia Environnement, from contracts in cities across Europe that object to its involvement in constructing the Jerusalem Light Rail system that links West Jerusalem to illegal Jewish settlements in occupied East Jerusalem and elsewhere in the West Bank (Al-Haq 2012). These gains, however small, help explain why those who are making human rights claims are still animated by a measure of hope.

Al-Haq's website also records, however, a range of ongoing abuses: settler attacks, mistreatment of Palestinian political prisoners, Palestinians' lack of water due to the occupation, and refugees' unfulfilled right of return. All with whom I spoke conceded that the struggle for human rights is ongoing. Of course the violations continue, said Kuttab: "You don't just win and that's it; you have to continuously fight for it"—and many have done just that. Several of Al-Haq's early volunteers and staff members continued in the human rights field as investigators with Human Rights Watch and other international, Israeli, and local NGOs, or with donors who fund human rights work. Some of those who have left remain active as consultants, training others in human rights throughout the Middle East, contributing to books on human rights fact-finding, and providing legal consultation. Joost Hiltermann, who went on from Al-Haq to work with international HROs, said, "You do make a difference. You build a body of work that is a totally reliable record, which cannot be undone. The Palestinians have such a strong case, but it has been diluted by bad politicians and people with guns." Raja Shehadeh became a legal advisor to the peace negotiations.[38] "Only a political process could have succeeded in getting Israel to concede that the Fourth Geneva Convention applied to their rule in the occupied territories," he said. Even so, he believes that "international law will save all of us. It's had a bad time, but it will get better." He continues to believe in "common humanity, which is an amazing thing," he said. "It's a wonderful thing that keeps people going. There's this species thing going on. You might not know a person, but you don't like that they are being treated badly."

Conclusion

Embedded in the stories of these groundbreaking human rights activists is a broader point about the importance of understanding how and why local groups actively define their human rights agendas in the ways they do. Individuals and groups across the globe utilize human rights institutions and legitimizing discourses in their strategic interactions with state agencies and international actors. It is only by appreciating the plans and motivations of the people who first wielded human rights tools, and the institutional and political context in which they did so, that we can understand how far later developments traveled away from those original aims. It is also only with this background that we can assess the relative weight of structure and intention, context and contingency, society and individual in the production of "rights consciousness" (cf. Merry 2003:344) and what that consciousness means and can mobilize for people in different places.

Since the early days of Al-Haq, tens of human rights NGOs have sprung up in the occupied territory, along with tens more development NGOs that dabble in human rights advocacy and training. As other NGOs developed, Al-Haq continued to grow. Throughout the first intifada, they published numerous reports on Israeli violations during the uprising, conducted research on Israeli home demolitions, and published legal analyses of Israeli demolition methods. They developed their website, which is now a widely cited research and information source, where they post select affidavits and publicize their field reports and documentation.

While the organization matured and expanded, new challenges came their way. Paradoxically, one of the most dramatic was the establishment of the Palestinian National Authority (PA), which was awarded partial autonomy in some areas of the West Bank after the 1993 Israel-PLO agreement in Oslo. During this period—generally referred to as "the Oslo period"—the PA had limited self-governance in areas from which Israeli forces had been redeployed. The major stumbling blocks of the conflict remained unresolved, with no final agreement over the status of Palestinian refugees, Jerusalem, water rights, or how much territory the Israelis would eventually cede.[39] Although some believed that this process should have led to an independent Palestinian state, many at the time suspected that the Oslo agreement constituted occupation by other means. The Israeli legal adviser to Israel's Ministry of Foreign Affairs said explicitly that the Palestinian entity formed by Oslo "'will not be independent or sovereign in nature, but rather will be legally subordinate to the authority of the military government' in the territories" (Usher 1995:44). Israel's multiple invasions of and attacks against "Area A," regions under full Palestinian sovereignty, are manifestations of the PA's actual subordinate position.[40]

During the Oslo period, Al-Haq's relationship with the PA grew increasingly antagonistic.[41] The truncated sovereignty of the PA and the pseudo-state's harsh measures against opposition members left some HROs uncertain about how to proceed. Some concluded that the PA should be left alone and that human rights monitoring should remain focused on Israeli occupation. Others contended that rights abuses had to be condemned, regardless of who committed them. The arguments about how to function in this new political terrain were rancorous. These debates, underwritten by nationalist political ethics that were still firmly entrenched, caused turmoil within Al-Haq, and within the human rights world in general. Those HROs that criticized the PA's use of torture and other repressive measures were countered by PA accusations that NGOs were serving foreign interests (N. Brown 2003). Al-Haq initially engaged the PA in "constructive dialogue" and offered human rights training rather than resort to public "shaming" in response to PA abuses (Azzam 2005:10). As patterns of human rights violations by the PA became clear, Al-Haq did issue reports on PA practices, such as attacks on freedom of assembly, unfair trials, and the establishment of the Palestinian State Security Court (Azzam 2005:11).

A third challenge for HROs was the shift in international funding trends when state funding agencies and other donors began to direct their large grants to PA ministries and infrastructural projects, as the next chapter details.[42] During the second intifada, the scale of violence and the concomitant renewed international support for human rights groups reinvigorated HROs with an increase in funding and activities. However, this rekindling did little to inspire renewed confidence in HROs among their "constituents," the Palestinian people. Nevertheless, Al-Haq is firmly established, with some forty members on staff and a regular stream of volunteers, as well as funders, who in 2010 provided more than $1.5 million in grants to the organization (Rizek and Sidoti 2010:37).

The use of law in political struggle has various consequences, often unintended and sometimes deleterious to the underdogs who engage it as a weapon against more powerful interests (Comaroff and Comaroff 2009). As time went on, human rights activity was transformed from a means of seeking justice and accountability into an idiom for public relations spin and a language for justifying state-making. However, just as it created the institutional infrastructure and financial pipelines for jobs and moneymaking ventures, it also sparked legal innovations, pioneering educational programs, new consciousness-raising tactics, and a medium for debating the nature of the Palestinian state and for defining what the future Palestinian citizen should be and do within it.

In moving the history of the Palestinian human rights world forward, the next chapter explains the role of international funders and of the peace process in the growth of the HRO industry after the Oslo peace accords.

Chapter 2

The Beginning of the Decline

International Aid and the Production of Bad Faith

I N THE EARLY YEARS of Al-Haq's existence and during the first intifada, human rights work elaborated a nationalist conception of rights and responsibilities. Al-Haq translated those concepts into a new political idiom and put them into action through a broad set of practices—spreading rights awareness among the general public; providing legal services, including advocacy for political prisoners in the Israeli military courts; recording the effects of occupation violence in people's lives; analyzing the occupation from a legal perspective; creating a database of violations with which to prove the systematic nature of Israel's violent practices; spreading information abroad; and working to lay the foundations for a functioning judiciary in Palestine. NGOs were appreciated not only for the services they provided, but also for the particular model of democracy they expressed and practiced, and for the democratic independent state they augured, for which many Palestinians hoped.

After the first uprising and the establishment of the PA, a new level of institutionalized politics was established, along with the professionalization of human rights activism and the battles for funding that were part of both systems. In the eyes of many Palestinians, these developments were accompanied by new, disturbing trends, especially the tendency among politicians and others to shirk social and national responsibilities in favor of private gain. This chapter traces how foreign funding and the establishment of the PA have shaped the human rights world in the occupied Palestinian territory since the 1990s. It charts the rise of the human rights industry and shows how it coincided with what many Palestinians perceive to be the demise of the nationalist ethos.

During the first intifada, Al-Haq and other NGOs were important sources of information about the uprising and rights violations that were occurring daily. Many in the Palestinian human rights world saw themselves as key players in a local movement for social justice, speaking out against the occupation's abuses and lobbying for more equitable political and social systems in Palestine. During the second intifada, by contrast, NGOs played a much less publicly recognized role. This was in part due to the nature of the second uprising, in which most of Palestinian society was much less actively engaged. Some local observers have attributed the decreased impact of NGOs to their lack of a grassroots base or of popular legitimacy, which was partly due to the competition among them (Hanafi and Tabar 2003). NGO workers expressed to me their disgust with the infighting that plagues their community. Nimr, for example, described a rivalry between the heads of two major HROs as being "all about personal competition." There was, in his opinion, no substance to the antagonism, no actual ideological difference or clash of vision. It was simply a base rivalry over funds, a competition for leadership of the Palestinian NGO Network (PNGO, a coordinating umbrella organization for NGOs), and "a struggle over who is more important," as Nimr summarized it. For many human rights workers and observers alike, the concept of human rights existed in an echo chamber. Omar, a college graduate who had been a field researcher for human rights and UN organizations, asserted that most people outside the human rights world do not actually pay much attention to human rights issues. "Maybe the intellectuals think about these things," he said, "but human rights people talk to themselves. It doesn't reach the rest of the people." He acknowledged the strong possibility that the field of human rights has no practical effects at all.

An even more forceful expression of dissatisfaction with the NGO world came from a friend, Ghassan, who works for a women's rights NGO. As we chatted by messenger on Skype in early 2011 about the demonstrations in Egypt that eventually saw the end of Hosni Mubarak's presidency, he described the PA's efforts to prevent a public demonstration in the West Bank in support of the Egyptian people:

> G: All regimes are afraid of people power, I guess. . . . Maybe this is why the Amin [security] here prevented demonstrations.
> L: Did you go out? To demonstrate?
> G: I was there and, unfortunately, no political party was there. All are NGOs
> L: That's interesting. Why do you think no political parties went out?

G: Do you remember when I told you that it is NGOs' time as alternatives to the political parties?

L: Yep. So do you think that NGOs taking the place of political parties is better than nothing? Good that *someone* is trying to organize people?

G: NGOs will never be alternatives to political parties, but I think the process is NGO-izing the Palestinian community

L: What do you mean by "NGO-izing"?

G: Making the Palestinian life NGO-only. It is transferring NGO into a verb

L: And NGOs can't create political change? Or social change?

G: NGOs work as long as funding is there and all the funds we get are international

L: And that's not dependable, I guess

G: It is not and will never be

L: But you're still good at getting the funds for your NGO! :)

G: I became expert in that, fuck such a position

L: Why are you negative about that job?

G: I hate it. I became a technical person expert in writing proposals and reporting about activities. I feel sick of that and I wish to change my career

Among rights workers there was widespread awareness of the systemic problems inherent in the human rights industry as it developed after Oslo. Simply knowing that they were caught in a structure built on crumbling, if not rotten, foundations, however, was not enough to cause many to flee it entirely. In the stories of human rights workers that I recount in this chapter, they describe their efforts to sidestep the debris as they figured out where to go next.

As the previous chapter noted, Al-Haq's legacy is mixed. It has paved the way not only for a new form of political language, but also for a new profession. In addition to this expanding career path, HROs also offer a range of activities that have surpassed Al-Haq's original focus on legal analysis and documentation. There are now Palestinian HROs dedicated specifically to the rights of workers, women, children, and prisoners, as well as to environmental issues, among others. Human rights work has also spread into areas as diverse as psychosocial crisis intervention, land mine awareness for children, and human rights education for security personnel. Such programs have come to be viewed by some, including human rights critics and HRO workers, as "cash cows," donor-driven projects taken on mainly to garner international funds rather than to serve the Palestinian people according to a locally relevant agenda of priorities. The human rights business in Palestine is now relatively lucrative, with most NGO workers making a salary well above that of a public school teacher. This "NGO elite" (Hanafi and Tabar 2005), whose members also enjoy a lifestyle replete with perks such as international travel and sometimes company cars, has garnered much criticism in Palestine and engendered among many Palestinians a cynical distrust of anything related to the human rights regime.

In fact, NGO salaries generally do not provide enough income to support a lavish lifestyle and are not excessive in comparison with those of successful business owners or senior-level employees of the PA (although this is a relatively high standard nonetheless). The way funding works, in Palestine as elsewhere, has been described by some as a form of soft colonialism and is mostly dictated by foreign donors and tied to the political goals of their countries. There is some critique by Palestinians of those structural constraints and the unequal donor-recipient relationship. However, the work of NGOs is comprehended through the grid of a particular moral economy—a system of social norms, values, and judgments about appropriate social and economic relations (Scott 1977; Thompson 1971). In Palestine, this moral economy is tied to a political economy and national history. Most Palestinians are struggling financially, with many reduced to poverty. Allocating donor funds to what are deemed to be private luxuries is perceived not only as extravagant, wasteful, and selfish, but also as antinationalist. Debates among Palestinians about donor money and NGO behavior are debates about the fundamental nature of the Palestinian nation.

The views of four HRO workers presented in this chapter illustrate some of the many experiences and attitudes that are common in the Palestinian HRO world. These people are ambivalent about the role of human rights work and disturbed by the corrupting power of international aid. Through their narratives we see how the extraction of human rights work from a nationalist program after the first intifada instigated the decline of faith in the human rights system.

Although aspects of this story may corroborate theories about the distorting influences of money and developmentalism on social movements (see, for example, Ferguson 1994; Li 2007; Shah 2010), my interlocutors' accounts also challenge the typical criticism of human rights as "depoliticizing." These human rights workers have analyzed in eloquent and poignant terms the political events that led to their conditions of uncertainty. Their critiques, and how they live their lives, are themselves deeply political, even though most of them have left the formal politics of factional membership. Such individual perspectives rooted in local conditions show how very much more complicated such large-scale dynamics as *NGO-ization*, *development*, and *depoliticization* really are on the ground. Ethnographic accounts reveal the extent to which such terms never capture the nuance of people's lives and beliefs. They also demonstrate that any effort to be apolitical or any characterization of a person or process as depoliticizing is, in and of itself, political. Such labels are politically salient evaluations, a way in which subjects are produced, a way in which the political field is bounded and certain issues are ignored or excluded from that field (Cruikshank 1999; Butler 1992; Comaroff 2010:530).

This chapter does something more, however, than "complexify" and disrupt theoretical generalizations. It is also meant to reveal what happens—to people, their aspirations, and their life trajectories; to politics in its institutionalized and ad hoc forms; and to ideas about the human rights system itself—when human rights work is disarticulated from a broader political vision and national project. The formalization of human rights and nationalist projects created situations that led many Palestinians watching HROs and the PA to criticize what they saw as the production of a "bad faith" society.

One reading of Sartre's concept of "bad faith" interprets it as the condition of "accepting and being complicit with our social roles . . . fully subscribing to a freedom-limiting mystification" (Coombes 2001; see also Catalano 1996). There are people working in the human rights system who have accommodated themselves to being "mystified," to not really believing that human rights work is going to curb rights violations but continuing in the field as if it could or might. They remain, in their own estimation, comfortable cogs in a self-perpetuating human rights system. There are also those who oppose such accommodations, however. These are people trying to recapture what they see as a sincere, more meaningful form of political engagement that will have longer-lasting effects throughout society and reinfuse the citizenry with the sense that they can make a political difference. They hark back to the days of the first intifada, before the dismantling of popular mobilization structures of student, worker, and women's groups, and before politics was institutionalized within the PA. Their theory, although stated only implicitly, is one of this book's central arguments: the human rights system can promote social justice only when it is understood in explicitly political terms and motivated by political goals.

The first intifada was inspired by, and is remembered for, its ideals of solidarity and the principles of kinship, cohesion, and self-sacrifice that have been central to the Palestinians' national struggle.[1] These ethical ideals were part of the social fabric through which Palestinians supported each other, which many say has been rent since the second intifada. Even if they turn up more often in the breach or materialize more as aspirations than as practices, these ideals are still held up as a moral measuring rod against which NGOs, individuals, and political parties are judged, and against which so many seem to have fallen short. The political life of nostalgia emerges in these comparative assessments of then and now, as it often does, painting pictures of the past in idealizing hues; but the cynicism in the dark background of these bright pictures has moral content. Through the stories and struggles of HRO workers, in their critiques of the human rights system and of NGOs, in their fond recounting of more hopeful moments of popular political mobilization, Palestinians I talked with asserted a certain ethical vision: it is obvious what life is not supposed to be, even if what it should be is not yet clear. Their arguments, analyses, and condemnations, and the principles by which they make their assessments, are elaborations of what I call a system of political ethics—the system of values that govern how politics (its agents, activities, and everything related to that sphere of life) are evaluated.

The Ideals of the First Intifada

Al-Haq's vision for human rights work and for Palestinian society was nuanced and complicated. At its base when it was founded was a dual concern with opposing the occupation and creating a new kind of Palestinian society. Raja Shehadeh, introduced in the preceding chapter as one of Al-Haq's founders, said "we wanted a state and wanted it to be a state that has a good judiciary and observes rule of law, but we knew we were not going to get it unless we all did our bit, and we went about it by going into a very disturbing internal democracy. Everyone had to discuss everything." Indeed, each person I interviewed about Al-Haq's beginnings recalled with fondness the marathon weekly meetings. "We worked as if we were a family, cooperating and with mutual understanding," said Ramzy, a researcher from those days. "The meetings went until late at night. The Israelis didn't let us have telephones back then, so I couldn't call my family and let them know where I was, but I stayed." Even if his wife might worry when he had not arrived home, he continued on well past regular work hours. "We considered this work our mission." Solidarity and cooperation are the values that formed the core principles that guided Al-Haq, and they could be heard in slogans that helped motivate the first intifada.

The metaphor of family and the significance of cooperation in Ramzy's recollections are important. The family is, in Palestine as elsewhere, ideally a font of loyal support and a source of refuge. Kin ties and the family model are part of how society was organized, and they still influence rituals of nationalist solidarity.[2] For example, each year, Muslims celebrate the holy month of Rama-dan with outings among friends and, especially, family. Relatives of martyrs, those considered to have sacrificed the most for the national cause, have long been incorporated into these visiting rounds, and neighbors and community organizations sometimes offer gifts and donations at this time as well.[3] These long-standing traditions were especially activated during the intifadas. When I visited the widow of a man killed by the Israeli army during the first uprising, she pointed out to me the many plaques and wall hangings she had received from various civil associations and political parties over the years: a decorative carpet printed with an image of Jerusalem's Dome of the Rock, small shields engraved with the name of her martyred husband and the organization that donated it, a framed image of the Qur'an. She said these tokens of honor and re-spect given to her during the holidays since her husband's assassination by Israel made her feel that the community cared, and that she was not alone. Although she complained that this support was too short-lived, and that she felt forgotten during the second intifada, the nation was, in the ideal, a community of care.

Haneen, a colleague at an HRO where I volunteered in 2001, explained the way she taught her son to value and care for the national collective:

> It's also the feeling. We also raise our children with the feeling of the group. I might say to my boy, "What a shame, our neighbor is poor. Maybe we need to help them. If someone asks you to help, then help." There is a group feeling (*hiss jama'y*). There is an education about the necessity of feeling for others. This is the people's issue (*qadiyat sha'b*), not the issue of one person.

According to Yaqoub, a twenty-three-year-old activist, this feeling of to-getherness with the people, of belonging (*intima'*), is why he, and young men like him, were going to the clashes to throw stones at the Israeli army check-points in Ramallah during the second intifada. "I go to be with the people. I can't watch others go and not go myself," he said. "It's what it means to be a good Palestinian."

For Al-Haq during the first intifada, these principles of care and solidarity were enacted through full-consensus decision making and by eschewing mate-rial gain. "We involved the people who were working at Al-Haq in everything, and it paid off completely," Shehadeh explained. He went on:

> We said, if you're going to be employed, even in an administrative capacity, you'll have to be involved in the work. We spared nobody. We made it clear that

we were not going to have directors doing anything in a mysterious fashion. I was director without pay. This was very critical. Everything was totally voluntary. [Some staff had paid employment elsewhere, others were unemployed.] For the first few years, the only person with a paid position was a secretary. Our headquarters had a tiny rent, which we could afford out of our pockets. We did things ourselves from beginning to end, including collating and stapling. It was important that we were doing it ourselves and not depending on anybody.

Another of Al-Haq's early members elaborated on the ways in which the ethic of volunteerism was crucial to achieving the group's goals, especially the goal of maintaining their independence. They contrasted themselves with political organizations that "wanted to get money and set up an NGO to be able to announce, 'We are doing this,' and deliver patronage." When I talked with him in 2009, this loquacious intellectual waxed eloquent about the creative sparks that were enhanced by voluntary work. Activism organized in this way has a better chance of being innovative, he told me, in contrast to the professional track of nonvoluntary NGO activity that is geared toward attracting donor money. "There is not the process of invention, or innovation, or reflection and critical thinking. They take a formula and say, 'Now we apply this formula and our professional techniques and best practices, which we get from foreign NGOs. They tell us how to do it, and here we are.'" In his assessment, perhaps a few NGOs go beyond that generic model today, but for most of them, NGO work "is just about financial security—a professional thing." Al-Haq was something different. It was motivated by passionate concern and guided by a critical, constantly thoughtful, and self-appraising attitude.

When Al-Haq's budget grew a little, in the beginning "salaries were tiny," Shehadeh said. Volunteerism was part of a moral economy that organized society throughout the first intifada. Al-Haq did not have much money, nor did its members want the public to think they were doing this job because it was profitable. Their vision of voluntary work was informed partly by a sense of economic justice that eschewed individual perks and personal luxuries in favor of a common good. It may be that today "good governance," "rule of law," "democracy," and "transparency" have become widely recognized, and criticized, as "taken-for-granted, hackneyed notions . . . the analytical stock and trade of neoliberal think tanks and organizations" who tend to use them in managing countries of the South (Spyer 2006:188). They were not always so, however. Al-Haq's work represented an effort to bring a form of democracy into practice. On a quest to realize "rule of law" and "transparency" in the organization and in the national polity, Al-Haq regulated itself according to a distinct moral vision of how a democratic Palestinian society would function. It was also grounded in a notion of political ethics that emphasized people's abilities to criticize and create better political, social, and economic relations. Volunteerism and independence, innovation and transparency, solidarity and cooperation were all real goals for Al-Haq, and were part of how the founders organized it.

During Al-Haq's early years, these principles were simultaneously also being cultivated and expressed in other kinds of organizations. Throughout the first intifada, effective, mass-based voluntary organizations that mobilized students, women, and workers provided part of the framework for the uprising (Hiltermann 1991). The work of these popular groups included community gardens and food production cooperatives to promote self-sufficiency. In addition, student and women's groups helped organize popular protest and civil disobedience campaigns (Hiltermann 1991). A Palestinian model of democracy was elaborated and lived out in the work of Al-Haq and other voluntary groups, and through the nationalist pedagogy of people like Haneen, quoted earlier. It was based not explicitly on the concept of individual rights, but more on facilitating and encouraging equal participation and mutual responsibility through social solidarity.

Corruption and Codes of Conduct

At each stage in their nationalist history, Palestinians have negotiated what would be the values and moral norms guiding their struggles for independence and social change—struggles and negotiations that were taking place as much within the NGOs as outside in the intifada's street protests and, after 1996, in the nascent legislature, the Palestinian Legislative Council (PLC)—and they have had to renegotiate them anew as different kinds of international players, funders, and methods of global governance have appeared to shape, manage, or promote "democracy and the rule of law" among them. By 2007, almost twenty years after Al-Haq was established with unwritten but well-considered standards of conduct, distrust of NGOs among Palestinians and concerns over NGO corruption among funders had become so widespread that in an effort to reform their practices and their image, more than five hundred NGOs signed the Code of Conduct on Transparency and Accountability for Palestinian NGOs (AMAN n.d.; see also NDC 2009a).[4] The Code aimed to "define and specify moral guidelines in general, and those relating to transparency and accountability in particular." It declared that "Palestinian NGOs find it necessary to commit to principles and values that are closely tied to good governance and democracy, and that are supported by competence, effectiveness and professionalism in performing their duties while using financial resources most efficiently," in order to "promote an anticorruption culture."

The demands of donors have also come to regulate and standardize the work of Palestinian NGOs more formally.[5] Palestinian NGOs are now required to submit annual reports and audited accounts to their funders. Such reports must list outputs and outcomes (causing much consternation among report writers as to their distinction), and tabulate numbers of beneficiaries (how many are served, determined by the number of audience members at workshops, for example), which are subdivided across categories (of gender, regional, and age-range distinctions) in spreadsheets and tables. Plans for sustainability must be assessed, and risks to achieving future objectives (not to be confused with goals) must be periodically reconsidered and recorded. Also, in the name of transparency and accountability, the names of people on the advisory boards and boards of directors must also be listed.[6]

As of 2000, with the passing of the Palestinian Law of Charitable Associations and Community Organizations (see Addameer 2011), the regulation of Palestinian NGOs took on new layers. Among other requirements, the law mandated that Palestinian NGOs must be registered with the Ministry of Interior, must establish bylaws and a board of directors, and must deposit minutes of meetings and records of revenues in their files. This law, which ended up being less repressive of NGOs than earlier drafts, is one result of many battles between the PA and civil society. PA-NGO relations have always been tense, as a result of competition for funding and the quasi-state's efforts to shore up its power. PA attempts to monitor and control Palestinian NGOs, both bureaucratically and by force, are ongoing.[7]

In 2008, another group of Palestinian NGOs came together as the Code of Conduct Coalition and issued a draft of a code similar to the one developed in 2007, declaring for itself a milestone by introducing ethical principles for Palestinian NGOs to follow (NDC 2009b:6, 9, 16–18). The signatories of this second document, however, proclaimed their "right to reject funding with politically conditioned strings, since that is bound to distort the development process and/or undermine the legitimate struggle for independence and self-determination according to UN principles" (Code of Conduct Coalition 2008:10). What prompted the distrust toward NGOs and donors that led to all these codes of conduct and ethical guidelines?

The Oslo Era

Two overlapping processes have emerged since the 1990s to produce a shifting political terrain in which the social role of the "human rights worker" as
a category of profession has flourished, and cynicism and distrust toward it
has grown. The first process was the simultaneous efflorescence of HROs and
the constriction on their activities by donors. Just over a third of Palestinian organizations were established in a mushrooming of NGOs during the
first half of the 1990s, when the Oslo process (which began a partial removal
of the Israeli occupation) was negotiated and the PLO established the PA
(Sidoti and Daibes-Murad 2004:26). International funding patterns, in conjunction with the establishment of the PA, guided the way these NGOs func-
tioned and how they set their priorities in accordance with funders' agendas
(Hanafi and Tabar 2005), which included projects focused on "democratization," "peace," and "development."[8] At the same time, most donors shifted the
bulk of their aid to the PA and away from the NGOs that had been providing
vital services like health and education (Sullivan 1996:94; Brynen 2000:187).
This meant greater competition among NGOs and their decreased ability to
decide which donor criteria fit their own missions. Foreign funding came
attached to conditions that were guided by these governments' own foreign
policy goals, such as "coexistence," combating incitement against Israel, and
documenting human rights violations by the PA (Pitner 2000:35).[9] Their priorities, largely in the realm of "development" and "democracy," became the
NGOs' priorities. The United States has "relied on foreign aid as a principal diplomatic tool in the quest for Arab-Israeli peace" for more than thirty
years (Lasensky and Grace 2006), just as it and other donor governments
have been using money to try and daub over the crumbling edifice of the
peace process since it was initiated.[10]

The corralling of NGOs in these ways—toward a particular vision of
"peace," which many Palestinians felt to be skewed away from achieving actual
freedom—contributed to these organizations' declining credibility in Palestinian society. It distanced them from the grassroots, while at the same time it
expanded career paths into NGO work. A refugee activist and human rights
worker criticized Al-Haq specifically for the way the organization's efforts at
being "objective" had led them to give up on national principles after Oslo.
They are "all about being 'objective' and won't talk about the right of return," he
said. "They want to say things that outsiders will accept. In this way they lose
their 'Palestinian-ness.' And this is bad."

The second process of the Oslo period was the arrival of the PA, the concomitant weakening of leftist parties, and Palestinians' dissociation from political parties and reduced political activism.[11] One such disaffected young man, Majd, described his situation by saying, "I parked and turned off the engine [*suffayt wa tuffayt*]," a colloquial expression communicating the general state of indifference suffered by a majority of the left's former activists. Resistance to occupation was to some degree removed from the hands of the people, as politics was formalized in a new way and commanded by the PA.

On the political left especially, HROs provided many formerly committed activists with a place to channel their now more half-hearted political energies. This too sullied the reputation of human rights organizations within the society, because they came to be seen under a harsh light as catchalls for the political dropouts, cop-outs, and sellouts who had nowhere else to go. It also deepened human rights workers' own apathy. The effects were widespread. Mudar Kassis, a professor at Birzeit University in the West Bank and one of the founders of the Human Rights and Democracy master's program at that university, explained to me the problems of Oslo's professionalization of politics.

> Suddenly politics became an extremely technical issue. You practically needed a PhD in negotiations to be able to think about the future of your own country. This is part of what led to people's alienation from politics. Research into public opinion at that time showed that there was a tripling of political apathy after Oslo, from about 1994 to 1999. There was enormous alienation. People wanted to get away from politics. People stopped caring.

A word is necessary about what the Oslo process was, what kinds of criticisms were leveled at it, and why NGO views about it might have been at odds with those of the donors. The Israel-PLO Declaration of Principles on Interim Self-Government Arrangements (DoP) in 1993 established an initial Israeli withdrawal from parts of the Gaza Strip and West Bank, where Palestinians had limited powers of self-governance. Further withdrawals were planned for what was supposed to be a five-year interim period. Although initially many in Palestine favored the deal (Rabbani 1996; Usher 1993), there was criticism of the DoP in various quarters from the outset, especially among Hamas and leftist groups, who believed that the half-finished deal, which left the fate of refugees, Jerusalem, water rights, and final boundaries undetermined, was worse than no deal at all. Among the many ways in which the DoP left Palestinians severely disadvantaged was the classification of only about 3 percent of the West Bank as "Area A," under nominal Palestinian Authority control; and almost 70 percent of the West Bank as "Area C," under complete Israeli control, including "water-rich areas, border regions, main roads, and most lands outside Palestinian municipal and village boundaries" and Jewish settlements, the expansion of which was left wholly unrestricted (Rabbani 1996). Deteriorating conditions while the interim period dragged on—including the expansion of Israeli settlements in occupied Palestinian territory, increasing unemployment, tighter restrictions on Palestinian movement, and an overall decline in Palestinians' economic situation (Lasensky 2004)—left many critics bitterly vindicated.

Haneen, a former women's activist with a leftist faction, explained to me in 2002 that, in her opinion,

> alienating the public was actually an intent of the so-called peacemakers, of the designers of the peace process. It was intended to be very elitist—a kind of process to avoid public participation because they felt that otherwise they could not maintain it. The Oslo agreements met the very least of the aspirations of the Palestinian street. Then came the PA. We said, "OK, we'll try the PA." Then the frustration increased further. Problems increased: unemployment; civil society was not present. It was a situation of political oppression, economic and social troubles. Our ability to move was curtailed by checkpoints and roadblocks. The aspiration was only for this little state? We didn't achieve anything, really, on the ground. . . . Every period of Oslo, the acceptance of Oslo, has been at root an acceptance of defeat.

Another common charge was that the PA was not actually on the road to becoming a sovereign state but was instead established as a security agent for the Israeli occupation, a lackey charged with protecting Israel's interests and repressing opposition. This opinion about the PA has held strong over time. During a conversation with Abu Wisam, an elderly patriarch in 'Aida refugee camp, and his daughter Nizar in 2009, they brought up a census that the UN Relief and Works Agency (UNRWA) had conducted in the camp to assess who was in need and who was not. As they explained, the census was taken as part of the UN's plan, which the United Kingdom encouraged (House of Commons 2004), in order to transfer responsibility for health care in the refugee camps to the PA. Abu Wisam, a man with a long history of ties to Fateh, doubted they would be able to do it. "Fifteen years of the PA and what have we got? Just more police oppressing the people. The PA take money for themselves, not for the people" (see also Sahiliyah 2004). I asked about what Prime Minister Fayyad (a political independent) might be able to accomplish, to which Abu Wisam replied, "He can't do it by himself. [President] Abu Mazen and his group are building the businesses just for themselves."

The Oslo accords were, in the view of many Palestinians and others, a nail in the coffin of Palestinian nationalist politics, a nail made rusty by the murky economic deals in which that process has fermented (see also Jamal 2007; E. Said 2001). Notions of social solidarity, generosity, and populist ideals that many believed had sustained and motivated the Palestinian nationalist move-ment were barely even a pretense of action for the political elite. Members of the PA were profiting as Israeli businesses began forging economic links with Palestinian elite. Some in the upper echelons of the PA consolidated monopo-lies over trade in various goods such as cement and tobacco. Palestinians saw that among their leadership, business interests had edged out any nationalist commitment to liberation.

Within a few years of the Oslo accords and the PA's tenuous grasp of au-tonomy in parts of the occupied territory, it became increasingly clear to ever more Palestinians that the imbalance of powers between the PA and Israel was structurally embedded within the DoP. An interpretation regnant among more critical members of civil society holds that the international donors poured in money to those organizations that were promoting "democracy" and development, thus creating a field of lucrative NGO work, and quieting the people who used to make "problems" through political activity by plying them with money. According to this theory, the "peace" of Oslo required and promoted the pacification of Palestinian national leaders, in order to create a stable ground in which business could grow. The financial and institutional growth of human rights organizations is seen by many to be causing a kind of desocialization and depoliticization. A rights worker and former political ac-tivist told me that one of the most difficult things for him to do was determine whether people he knows or knew are still loyal to their beliefs and affiliations. "I do not think that it is accurate to say any of the people at an NGO have a political identity," he remarked, adding that "this depoliticization of Palestin-ians is one result of Oslo."

International Donors Driving with Money

The occupied territory has seen the "highest levels of multilateral per capita foreign aid in the world at about US$300 per year" (Le More 2005:984; see also Lasensky and Grace 2006; World Bank 2004a). The Oslo period came with increased levels of donor involvement, with $2.4 billion pledged at a donor conference directly after the signing of the accords in October 1993 (House of Commons 2004). The infusion of international funds into the Palestinian government and, especially, development NGOs was a way of "buying consensus to Oslo," as one critic told me. These donor funds have come to be seen as morally dubious, directed by people with private political interests rather than Palestinian nationalist goals. This money has helped expand human rights organizations, but because of how it is viewed within the Palestinian political ethical system, it has also tainted their work.

Although the majority of that aid has gone to provide humanitarian and development assistance, a significant portion funds the approximately twenty-seven human rights organizations operating in the West Bank and Gaza Strip,[12] and the additional twenty-one organizations working on issues related to democracy and "good governance" (De Voir and Tartir 2009:36).[13] This is a sizable number for a population of about 3.5 million living in an area roughly the size of the U.S. state of Delaware or the UK county of Cumbria.[14] As of 2008, among Palestinian NGOs, rights-based organizations received the highest proportion of external aid at 30 percent (whereas Palestinian NGOs [PNGOs] that are focused on education make up more than one-fifth of the PNGO population but receive only 13.9 percent of external funds [De Voir and Tartir 2009:x, 38; see also Jamal 2007:69]). To take just one donor as an example, the Swiss government planned to give approximately $5.3 million to Palestinian projects in the category of "Human Rights and IHL" between 2010 and 2014 (SDC 2010:22). Although total annual figures are not available for Palestine as a whole, it is clear that donors dedicate significant amounts to HROs.

In order to benefit from such financial poultices, HROs had to be very careful about how they framed their research, reports, and criticisms. They had to be sure not to promote, or even imply, political positions to which Israel might object or that might be seen to threaten the peace process. In one instance, the Palestinian Society for the Protection of Human Rights and the Environment (LAW), a major human rights organization, organized a large conference to mark the fiftieth anniversary of the occupation. In an interview with a former LAW staff member in 2002, he told me that the heads of the NGO instructed staff to avoid discussing Palestinians living inside the Green Line, the 1967 border of Israel. They were also discouraged from even using the term *Green Line*, because, they claimed, it could have been interpreted as implying that Israel does not have a right to exist. Such donor-imposed strictures were not depoliticizing the work of HROs so much as circumscribing the range of political claims that could be made, or even hinted at.

While volunteering at Defence for Children International–Palestine (DCI-Palestine), I heard a lot about donors hewing to a narrow concept of the "peace process" and trying to impose it on their grantees. In one instance, DCI-Palestine had submitted a proposal to a Canadian nonprofit organization outlining a research project that would involve children in writing about the situation of child prisoners in Israeli jails. The Canadian organization rejected this project because it was "too political." Despite the fact that it was a rights-based plan that focused on children's empowerment and the rights of children deprived of their liberty—and thus accorded with the Canadian organization's mission—the problem of Palestinian child political prisoners was too awkward for this particular group. Carolyn, a member of the DCI-Palestine staff from the United States, said, "They didn't want to work on Palestinian child political prisoners' rights because the issue is too politically sensitive. Someone who advises their organization told them that if they addressed this topic they would likely face difficulty getting money for other projects they have." Other NGOs have reported similar problems when tackling issues perceived to be politically "sensitive," such as information campaigns related to settlement expansion. International donors effectively censor NGOs by refusing to fund such projects.

Talking with me in the spring of 2002, Carolyn described her frustration with the censorship and artifice of international organizations and their funding biases, which she had experienced firsthand at DCI-Palestine.

> There is all this money for infrastructure and development aid, but no one is touching the occupation. We bring rice, but no one is talking about why Palestinians are hungry. We talk about violations, but we're not going to talk about the occupation as a whole. An editor once said that my article for an NGO magazine was too angry. She cut my active use of the subject "Israeli" and changed the sentence to passive voice. She cut out my reference to Israeli occupation policies as "discriminatory." People can say that Palestinians are suffering, but not the reasons. Aid organizations are especially like this. They're there to give humanitarian aid, not deal with the political situation. This approach isn't appropriate. Palestine is not in the position of most developing countries. They're not suffering a lack of food because of lack of resources. None of the aid organizations except a few small ones talk about this. The UN won't talk about the real issues, and then USAID puts so much money into roads that the Israelis then dig up. They just go in and build the road again. The EU [European Union] is the same. None of it is sustainable.

Like Carolyn, most human rights workers I know are not at all "mystified" by the aid regime. They see how donors are acting in "bad faith," touting their financial aid as a way to curb human rights violations despite the stark reality that only systemic political solutions could do so. During my fieldwork HROs were struggling with their place in these dynamics, and staff constantly considered their options in the face of such constraints.

During a staff discussion about funders at DCI-Palestine, a general consensus emerged that staff did not like many of the foreign donors because they gave money for things without consulting the people who were implementing projects or being served by them. They criticized some donors for their lack of oversight and discretion, because they "just give money and the organizations they fund just spend and spend" on things that should not be prioritized. Moral opprobrium was leveled not only at the donors who made such slush funds available, but also at some HROs for their willingness to gulp from these poisoned wells. One staff member mentioned an organization's budgeting of more than US$40,000 for furniture, which she considered to be an excessive amount for the size of that group's operation. She described the incident as being *haram*, a term that in this particular context connoted something shameful, disgraceful, a pity, and morally wrong.

Despite the extensive flow of funds, the ways in which they were channeled left many NGOs trying to collect from these streams with teaspoons. Priority setting occurs in a top-down fashion, to local NGOs from donors, who "actually only pay lip service to local advocacy priorities" (Challand 2009:159–160). The vast majority of funding was disbursed on a project-by-project basis, leaving NGOs responding to donors' funding priorities and scrambling to sustain themselves institutionally by racking up multiple distinct projects, thereby creating heavy administrative burdens, with numerous reports required for each project. Donors' focus on quantifiable outcomes rather than on process left little room for Palestinians' input in determining their own priorities, and no coherent framework for long-term planning for economic development (Abdelnour 2010; Brynen 1996; S. Roy 1996).

This piecemeal funding has had further ramifications, including directly curbing political organizing and NGO efficacy. Although the problems are structural and rooted in donor tactics, within the dominant Palestinian nationalist ethos, the NGOs' deficiencies are often seen to be political and moral. Islah Jad, a scholar at Birzeit University, has discussed the relative political inefficacy of NGOs compared to the social movements that preceded them. Popular committees that were branches of political parties during the first intifada worked through and sustained mass bases of popular involvement (Jad 2004; see also Hiltermann 1991). Palestinian political factions were outlawed by the military occupation and much of their social development and recruitment activities were carried out through affiliated grassroots organizations. Informal structures facilitated more effective evasion of Israeli controls and mobilization of the population (Y. Sayigh 1997:609). They played what Palestinians considered to be an "honorable role" (Jamal 2007:51), but as the organizations have institutionalized, the rift between civil society organizations and the people they purport to serve has widened. In contrast to the popular committees, NGOs "cannot sustain and expand a constituency; or tackle issues related to social, political or economic rights on a macro or national level" due to the structural impediments caused by their financial dependence on Western donors (Jad 2004:39).[15] The suffusion of money has deepened the already existing division between the "elite" and the "street" (Allen 2002),[16] making both categories of actors less effectual while possibly hindering "the emergence and formation of effective parties since they splinter popular demands in a multiplicity of interests" (Middle East Report 2000; see also Hanafi and Tabar 2004).

The struggles of these human rights workers have emerged in the space of tension between transforming political economies and the accompanying changes in moral economies (cf. Shah 2010), and they are similar to what NGO actors confront across the global South. In Colombia, for example, NGO workers have faced similar pressures imposed by international donors whose demands for "professionalization" have resulted in the political co-optation of their social justice projects (Murdock 2008). Such demands have left Mexican NGO workers complaining that they have lost their shared sense of purpose and "moral commitment to solidarity," which they report has given way to enmity and competition (Richard 2009:182).

Strains such as these are apparent in any context in which people trying to work for social change according to distinct political ideologies are fully dependent on outside funders. In Palestine, the terms people used to explain how donor aid worked, and the effects of aid on society, illustrate the moral substrate of a specific nationalist ideology.

Moralizing the Politicization of Aid

One common observation was that NGO money promotes privilege and facilitates international travel for an elite strata of Palestinians under occupation, assuaging them with material comforts, giving them more, which means more to lose, and thus making riskier forms of political activism unattractive.[17] Some assign the blame for this alienation to Israel, which is thought to have had strategic reasons for allowing so much money to reach these organizations. Others point the finger at the UN. This view was once communicated to me by, among others, an HRO worker and former militant who saw himself as having succumbed to this subterfuge. He described what he considered to be the effects of the UN on Palestinian culture, especially among refugees. Having lived all his life in a refugee camp, where UNRWA provides education, health, and other basic provisions, he came to see the UN as an aid organization that had debilitating effects on his society. The UN had come to symbolize the oppressive power of the international community's charity. "People have become dependent on handouts. They want us to be dependent. They don't want us to be a strong player. The whole region, they try to keep us down. This is colonialism in the real meaning of the term," he said.

Whether as a result of intentional Israeli machinations or more diffuse international structural trends, by the early 1990s voluntary organizations that had been active during the first Palestinian uprising had, in the assessment of many, devolved into donor-driven NGO businesses. According to popular consensus, their goal has been to ply their directors with money rather than to provide services (Hammami 1995:55–56). As much as anyone, members of HROs held these beliefs about one another; and although some of this critical commentary could be attributed to internal competition between HROs, it is also the case that HRO workers knew more about one another's activities and attitudes, and developed their judgments from that inside perspective. Nationalist standards based in ideas about sacrifice, sincerity, and the common good underpinned such commentary. Abu Wisam, for one, blamed the donors for encouraging this moral deterioration. During a chat about my research he told me, "The EU is teaching people how to lie, how to make up all the details they ask for. People have learned to put democracy and human rights in a proposal to get money." The willingness of so many NGO workers to "learn how to lie" and adhere to such strictures, however financially coerced, reduced their credibility significantly among Palestinians.

An oft-cited example was the case of the director of LAW, who was reputed to have paid himself a salary that was twice that of a government minister. During the spring of 2003, a consortium of Western aid donors publicly announced a suspension of aid to LAW, which was one of the largest human rights organizations at the time, after discovering the NGO's misuse of an estimated 40 percent of the $10 million dollars it had received from Western donors.[18] The availability of aid money, and the way some people have misused it, has reduced the legitimacy of NGOs in general, a fact recorded by many researchers (see, for example, Challand 2009; Abdel Shafi 2004). When one considers the fact that in Palestine even a relatively small HRO (with a regular staff of fewer than twenty) might have an annual budget of $600,000 and up, providing monthly salaries of $700 to $1,500 (and more for lawyers and directors) while a teacher or policeman may make only $200 a month, it is not surprising that some Palestinians resent the affluence of the human rights community. It is not simply the perceived lack of justice in the distribution of wealth that makes these "morally marked moneys" (Maurer 2006:24), however. It is also the violation of other values—such as honesty, national solidarity, and self-sacrifice—violations that are perpetrated in their accrual and spending.

The following narratives of four human rights workers illustrate further the complex personal, political, and moral terrain laid down by the human rights industry and its financial foundations, and the distinct paths that individuals have forged in their attempts to navigate it. To be sure, some see human rights work as an acceptable line of employment simply because it is relatively profitable, which seemed to be the case with Mustafa, an HRO publicist. Others consider it to be an alternative, less sacrificing way to be political; or, as in the case of Nimr, a child rights advocate, they no longer care about national politics and derive satisfaction from making a living to support themselves while also providing social services to children in need. Others, such as Haneen, see many flaws in the human rights system but also appreciate the sincere convictions and hard work that so many put into it, still hoping that it will benefit their society and the national cause. There are also those like Dia' who combine employment in human rights organizations with other political work and agonize mightily about how to live life in a way that is meaningful and feasible personally while also benefiting the national cause, however vaguely defined that cause has become.

Mustafa: Human Rights on the Make?

Mustafa, a man in his early forties, was a student in the Human Rights and Democracy master's program at Birzeit University, where I met him and his girlfriend, Lamia. She was a lawyer not long out of school, and together they ran a private legal practice in Ramallah. They were both students in the human rights course I was attending, but they appeared in class only sporadically, pro-voking the ire of the professor when they did show up by whispering to each other during his lectures.

Mustafa worked for a prisoner rights HRO part-time, writing their press re-leases and publications. "I'm very good with language," he told me, handing me a small pile of the organization's pamphlets. The director was Mustafa's relative and although he was also prominent in a small leftist faction, the HRO did not have a very high profile, nor were its services for Palestinian political prisoners advertised on the Web. I was told by 'Ali, another human rights activist I had known for years, that this NGO was disreputable. It received money from the PA, did not offer much in the way of legal services or advocacy for prisoners, and its publications and press releases were without substance.

Over the course of the discussions I had with Mustafa and Lamia, I learned something of their attitudes toward the human rights world. Like many Pales-tinians, they were disparaging of HROs in general—except the one that Mus-tafa worked with. It became clear that their biggest complaint was about the political biases of NGOs, which they thought were too critical of the PA and not focused enough on the violations of Hamas. Mustafa's political leanings as a PA loyalist were clear. He told me up front that he used to be a member of the Preventive Security Force, an intelligence agency of the PA. He assured me that he was no longer involved in that work, because, he said, "human rights and in-telligence work is like marrying a Catholic to a follower of Bin Laden." Mustafa and Lamia also decried the way HROs make money off the backs of political prisoners. Prisoners' rights were turned into moneymaking projects, they said, which they thought was shameful, because prisoners had sacrificed so much for the national cause. Mustafa and Lamia spoke at length against HROs, blam-ing them for publishing meaningless reports while doing nothing practical for the cause of Palestinian rights.

I thought it peculiar that when I asked them what else HROs should be doing, they responded with suggestions like "organizing conferences" and "writing reports." Given their line of critique, I also found it strange when Mus-tafa suggested that I help them open up a new HRO. He could do the public relations and write the grant proposals, he said. "I'm an expert at grant writing and getting money," he boasted. I, on the other hand, the Cambridge University professor, would not have to do much, he assured me, adding cryptically that I could have a chair in their office. This was a particularly odd invitation, coming on the heels of Mustafa's repeated observation that one could run an HRO from any office, making up statistics and reports out of thin air while making money hand over fist. This was, perhaps not coincidentally, what 'Ali had said Mustafa's relative had done with the HRO he headed.

I didn't know what to make of these curious contradictions, so I asked 'Ali what he thought. He turned out to know Mustafa, and distrusted him utterly. Moreover, he believed that Mustafa was still part of the PA intelligence services. "Perhaps his human rights persona is his undercover assignment," he said. I wondered if Mustafa wanted to set up a ghost HRO, a virtual organization for attracting money. I was never to find out for sure, because I took 'Ali's advice and stayed well away from Mustafa after that.

I recount my interactions with Mustafa here even though they were brief and not representative of what I had come across in Palestine, and also more mysterious. His case is still important for what it reveals about the material opportunities that have been made possible within the human rights world, the opportunism of some people within it, and the kinds of distrust and suspicion they have provoked.[19]

People like Mustafa and cases of corruption such as occurred at LAW[20] have further cemented the negative reputation of NGO workers and what many have perceived to be their relative affluence (at least compared to the majority of people living on less than two dollars a day.)[21] As a result, it has become enough simply to be involved with an NGO for one to be rendered morally suspect in the eyes of one's community—or at least in the eyes of those looking for reasons to criticize. When Nasr, the founder of a small NGO in a West Bank refugee camp, added a room to his family's apartment after finally getting a job after a long stretch of unemployment, neighborhood enemies were suspicious and accused him of getting rich off the NGO's grants. Although his willingness to keep the NGO's accounting books open for anyone's inspection did little to deter the naysayers, he nevertheless persisted in his financial transparency. Among the Palestinians I talked with there was a strong sense of the wrongness of having inappropriate amounts of money spent for non-nationalist ends. At the core of the moral economy and political ethical system that frame the words of and about Mustafa and Nasr is a notion of money as corrupting, a concern driving the actions of Dia', another human rights worker.

Dia': Avoiding *Inhiyar*

Like Nasr, Dia' was similarly concerned about the effects of perceived ill-gotten donor gains on his personal reputation, but more so than Nasr he felt his worries acutely within a nationalist framework. The struggles of Dia' reflect another aspect of the tensions that human rights activists have experienced, pulled between an ongoing commitment to the collectivist values that were predominant during an earlier period of nationalism and growing trends toward the primacy of the individual over society, a focus on individual comforts over nationalist sacrifices. A young man who was very active with one of the leftist factions during the first intifada, Dia' had recently quit his job as a project coordinator at an NGO when I met him in 2002. The mission of the NGO was to help Palestinians access medical care abroad, but when Dia' discovered that the organization's leadership—including its foreign director—had been involved in misusing funds, he resigned. As Dia' reported, they had been taking on social work cases with ill patients that they could not handle, "and it turns out this was just to get donations," Dia' told me with disgust. "The people at this organization are more concerned about making money than helping our clients. The counselor they have makes US$5,000 a month!" This was an outrageous sum, in his mind. He resigned because he was unwilling to work with people he thought were corrupt.

Dia' ended up being unemployed for nearly a year as a result. Given the high levels of unemployment in the West Bank, he knew this would be a strong possibility when he quit. Despite the negative economic consequences entailed by following his principles, he was not willing to remain involved with a shady organization. In his opinion, this group, like most NGOs, was primarily a "money-making venture, all dependent on foreign funding. When the funding dries up, they are left in the dust. None of the organizations do anything to become self-sustaining." He believed it is the occupation that is behind this funding of NGOs and that keeps them dependent and chaotic. "Maybe it's not direct," he explained, "but the occupation does not want Palestinian society to pull itself together and be self-sufficient," a comment that echoed other criticisms I had heard of the UN-promoted culture of dependency.

Like most NGO workers, Dia' was college educated. With a degree in English literature, he was a perfect candidate to become my transcriptionist. Dia' also became my guide, friend, and personal political commentator early on in my fieldwork. After a year of odd jobs translating from Arabic into English for a range of organizations and transcribing my interview tapes, Dia' found employment with a women's rights NGO. He has become an expert at writing successful grant applications, bringing in millions of dollars to fund women's empowerment projects.

For many years the Israeli government refused to issue Dia' a permit to leave the country. He attributed their refusal to what happened to him during the first intifada. Dia' had been shot by an Israeli soldier and bore the effects of his injury in a permanent limp and partial paralysis. Eventually, in need of medical treatment for long-term side effects of these injuries, he managed to obtain permission and has been traveling abroad for his NGO work frequently since. When he isn't traveling, he is usually working fifteen hours a day, and I easily found him at his office during a visit to Ramallah in 2009.

He greeted me with a joke that as one of the very few men working at this big NGO full of women, he was so lucky to be in his position. Normally ready with a sardonic comment about current politics, which he often described as *tafih* (superficial, silly), or about life in general, I was surprised by his positive descriptions of some of the projects for which he had raised money. One he called "therapy for poor people," which entailed "helping people learn how to cope with difficult situations." Although the women's center where he worked could not, he said, provide material support for these people's daily needs, the project "helps them cope to prevent *inhiyar* (breakdown)." "The problem," Dia' told me, "is that there is no care for the individual in our society. We have to create strong individuals to create a strong society. The problem is that if the individual falls, the whole society falls." Speaking in the language of a grant application, he told me that "the direct beneficiaries of this project are women, while men and children are the indirect beneficiaries."

One comment about the central value of "the individual" does not a neoliberal lackey make,[22] but it did make me wonder whether Dia' might or might not reengage in politics and active resistance should circumstances change in Palestine. Over the years I have known Dia', he has always been a committed nationalist, intent on seeing the liberation of Palestine from occupation, even if he has also gone through phases of national disaffection, describing himself with the colloquialism *suffayt wa tuffayt*," which means (as noted earlier) "I parked and switched off the engine." "I'm moving," he told me on several occasions. "Many organizations abroad want to hire me." For more than a year he was telling me that his move to Tunis was imminent. He was sick of Palestine, disgusted at the apolitical, blasé nature of the bourgeois crowds in Ramallah, which had become the de facto political and cultural capital of the West Bank. Since there was no hope, he may as well move.

However, each time I return to Palestine, I find Dia' still there, working hard, not only at the women's NGO but also writing novels and translating for other

NGOs. Along with friends outside of Palestine, he is also organizing a "virtual Palestinian state" on the Internet, a website for collecting and preserving various forms of Palestinian heritage and cultural expression. He saw this as a way to "re-enliven the national question" for Palestinians, who, he complained, were becoming more and more concerned with individual gain and conspicuous consumption. The bankers are giving loans and spreading credit cards, he said, "in order to make people care about daily issues and forget about the national question." According to Dia', the material lures of a consumerist economy, of which NGOs are as much a part as debt-inducing banking practices, were hard for many to resist. All his friends were after loans to pay for new cars and other large items, he said with more than a hint of scorn. Dia' explained his unwillingness to get swept up in this new consumerism by pointing to his nationalist past.

In 2010, Dia' wrote an e-mail from Palestine updating me on his news, saying, "I am traveling a lot and each time I leave I feel more and more attached to this country." His moods and plans are unstable, just as his personal and political quandaries are ongoing. As he has told me more than once, "there is nothing certain in Palestine except the certainty that things are going to change."

Nimr: The Apathy of a New Bourgeoisie

Similar to Abu Wisam, who complained that donors are teaching Palestinians to lie, Hiba, the feisty director of a research center in Ramallah asserted to me in 2009 that "people do human rights just because there is money. It's just a trend. International funders set the agendas. The problem is that the resistance is now all working in NGOs. But what else could they do? What other opportunities are there? It's a problem." Not only does human rights work offer the educated, often formerly active leftists a place to focus their energies in the absence of any organized and appealing political venues, but through their cosmopolitan networks, relatively high salaries, and opportunities for international travel, the NGO system also promotes individualistic bourgeois values and interests that are inconsistent with nationalist politics. Mirroring trends across the Middle East and the global South, NGOs in Palestine have become "natural havens for disaffected party cadre" (Hammami 2000:17).[23]

Haitham, an HRO worker with definite Marxist views, explained what foreign funding and the growth of large NGOs has done to Palestinian politics:

> It has taken away a large section of people who were active or considered part of the grassroots intellectuals of the West Bank and Gaza Strip. It's like cutting the head off a popular movement. It does provide a temptation, and once you get

into the milieu, it removes you from that kind of [political] activity. It institutionalizes your political activity, and gives you benefits which are quite immense compared to the rest of the society, and that change in your social existence changes your consciousness as well. That's one of the reasons I think people are demoralized. Their social existence has changed. In a way it's a conscious attempt of imperialism to intervene in the Third World, take these people who should be leaders or have been leaders, and move them somewhere else.

Haitham's observations correlated closely with Nimr's story. I met Nimr when I volunteered at DCI-Palestine from 2000 to 2001. He was a man in his early thirties from a refugee camp in the southern West Bank. Married with a baby daughter when I met him, his situation exemplifies the case that many scholars have made about the relationship between human rights and depoliticization. In contrast to narratives of nationalist fortitude like that of Dia', Nimr felt that he had succumbed. His case illustrates further the correlation between moral and political economies, and shows how a loss of nationalist dedication is considered to be a moral failure linked to individualistic material desires.

A college graduate, Nimr had been a social worker at a human rights organization since the early 1990s. Throughout his youth he had been involved with a leftist faction. He was imprisoned, the first time at age fourteen, and tortured several times. He once described to me a particularly excruciating form of torture he had experienced. His Israeli interrogators hung him from the ceiling by his wrists, then kicked out from under him the stool on which he was standing, leaving all of his body weight pulling down from his shoulders. He said he felt like they would come apart. The look on his face as he described the experience made me wince; just the memory caused him evident distress.

Like many in his position, his formal political involvement ended after the PA came to power and his former party lost whatever effectiveness or popularity it once had enjoyed. The failures of the first intifada, which was unable to secure for the long term that uprising's social, political, and organizational gains, also contributed to the decline not only of leftist parties but also of trade unions, women's groups, and student organizations. Nimr told me how his attitude toward politics transformed over time:

I was active, but now I hate politics. Sure, I keep up on the news, but I hate politics. I'm fed up. I've seen a better life, and being active wasn't easy. I'm tired of that. I made this decision to leave politics in a snap during college—even before getting married. Che Guevara said, "marriage is the death of a revolutionary."

My wife joked that since I quit politics before she and I met, surely there must have been some woman in my life before her . . . but no, I just saw that there were better things, and now all of my friends are like this. We have lives outside of politics, because of the problems within the parties. There are lots of internal problems: they have no alternative vision, they're against the Oslo accords but they have no other suggestions, and they're against the Israeli policies, which really did wear people out. People are just too tired. We were all taught that the USSR was God. We read all about communism in prison, the paradise that was the USSR. But then, when it fell, it was like in a moment our dreams were gone. We realized it was all a lie. . . .

"Or," he added quietly, "maybe I'm a coward."

The growth of Palestinian NGOs, in both their number and their scope of operations, has been accompanied by a concomitant decline of the leftist parties and a rise in general political apathy that has led many party activists out of politics.[24] When the Soviet Union fell, leftists everywhere were stranded without material support, ideological base, or political focus (Browers 2004). In Palestine, leftist groups were also hit by the shift in support to Islamic parties from the Arab Gulf countries and away from the PLO (Hilal 1995:11). The Popular Front for the Liberation of Palestine, a leftist faction that Nimr presented as an example, "are not moderates; they are considered dangerous, but they have no political vision or goal." I heard many like Nimr complain of the left's lack of innovation and initiative (see also Hilal 2003:168). According to one opinion poll, support for secular left-wing groups dropped from an already paltry 5 percent at the beginning of the second intifada in September 2000 to 3.3 percent at the beginning of June 2001 (Hilal 2003:167).

Nimr recognized the place of human rights work in the imbrication of local and global politics, and he was negative and despondent about the personal and social consequences of his place in the system. Whenever I talked to him throughout 2001 and 2002, he said he wanted to leave his work, maybe even the country. He repeatedly told me "I hate Palestine." He thought that the idealizing tones of nationalist propaganda about the "beauty of Palestine" were farcical. "It's not beautiful. It's ugly." He complained that he felt himself to be submerged in apathy. Like many, he had become fed up with the violence and with the political limbo and sense of suffocation that the occupation and the second intifada had imposed (see also Allen 2008). Although he wanted to leave, the lack of other employment opportunities kept him tied to this job. He did his work at the HRO competently but halfheartedly. Although he had a conviction that the services they provided—legal defense and "fun days" to entertain traumatized children affected by the fighting during the intifada—were beneficial to the society, he was mostly hopeless about his country's situation. He worked there because it was a good job and his friend was the director. He knew he had become part of a new bourgeoisie, and he was ready to rest comfortably in that category. He was no longer willing to make the deep sacrifices required of a resistance fighter.

This cynicism toward human rights work was not always the dominant ethos, however, and as it took root, it did not do so for everyone in Palestine. Even for those who described themselves as apathetic and cynical, that was never all they were. Nor was the disaffection that is so common among former activists and current human rights workers singularly attributable to the institutionalization processes and the corrupting influence of money. Family circumstances, personal challenges, and political allegiances also come into it.

By 2008, Nimr had moved with his family to England and his best friend had also moved away from Palestine to work with a UN agency in the region as a "child protection specialist." Haitham and those with similar critiques of the NGO world might blame Nimr's situation on the global human rights industry. He was a former activist turned family man, no longer interested in politics, confined to being a passive observer and resentful victim, well-traveled and globally connected through his position at an expanding NGO, less and less connected to the homeland or to ideas about national liberation. Nimr's situation was actually the result of many factors: the simultaneous realization that party politics were faulty, that the new institutions of government did not truly carry the ideals for which he had fought, and a sense that he had been duped by politics and politicians. Together they led to his changing attitudes about what personal sacrifice should be for, which coincided with a life-stage transition toward a focus on family.

It is impossible to say that it is the structural and material effects of international aid that have produced another dispossessed Palestinian and lured Nimr abroad, or that it was primarily stable employment for the workaholic Dia' that dampened his nationalist fervor and focused his energies on raising money for psychotherapy for the poor. To be sure, international funding has produced specific channels of global travel and immigration for people like Nimr and sustained an industry of NGO professionals like Dia', but it is not so obvious how, or whether, human rights has become "instrumental in governmentality," creating ways for people to "participate in governing both themselves and others" (Englund 2006:37). Unlike the human rights activists in Malawi whom

Englund describes as haughtily believing in a "universal subjectivity that they alone can redeem . . . [and who were] propelled to act by the abstract victimhood of the downtrodden" (118), Palestinians I encountered were wary of what HROs could offer as money-making venture, vocation, or service provider. How that suspicion led them to act varied.

At least one small NGO has made conscious efforts to resist some of these corrupting trends. The prisoner-support HRO Addameer is led and staffed mostly by leftists, some of whom are still involved in organized secular politics. These are people with a well-developed critique of late capitalism and the negative effects of neoliberalism on southern countries. They have made a decision to "not create an artificial empire" and to resist the perquisites usually available to those who can access international funding. Although it is not unusual for the directors of even small HROs to receive a monthly salary of $2,000 or more, Addameer's director in 2001 received only $500. Although the human rights system has an effect on the nature of politics and on forms of sociality, Palestinians, like human rights workers elsewhere, engage with human rights work not simply as passive recipients; they and their culture are not overwhelmed by the "predatory globalizing 'western' discourses" (Speed 2007:32).

They are also not passive receivers of Western analyses. When I discussed my ideas with people in the West Bank, many agreed with my characterizations of the human rights system in Palestine, but others objected to such negative renderings of HROs and human rights workers. Although the critiques might apply to NGOs in general, which generally have a bad reputation, some insisted that the criticisms should be tempered when it comes to HROs, because they offer real services, such as legal aid, which people need and demand.

Haneen: Retaining Hope

The story of Haneen, who worked in the administration of DCI-Palestine, adds another angle to that moderate view. She was both critical of and engaged in human rights work. She explained why some Palestinians still harbored hope that the international community, the UN, and human rights law might help them achieve justice, despite the evident biases in their dealings with the Palestinian-Israeli conflict. I asked her, if so many people working in human rights are so critical of the UN and the human rights system, why do they persist? She replied,

> The EU does not work practically for rights. Human rights in meetings and conferences sound like something wonderful, but come see the facts on the ground. Look at how decisions are made by the UN, who they benefit and who they go

against. Even the EU has decided to hit Iraq. They're not thinking with the logic of human rights. Hit the civil society, even the schools, and hospitals. They're hitting all the infrastructure. Is this a response to the nuclear threat in Iraq? No. It's an intervention into another state in order to maintain power. I don't consider the EU to be innocent. They are part of the balance of power, but the oppressed people will always retain hope to achieve something in the end. We continue holding on to the UN as an international body whose agenda is in line with our aspirations. The aspirations of all people to live in freedom, to be secure, have a stable economy. Everything. So that's why we hold on to the UN.

During this conversation, which I had with her in 2002 as the second intifada raged, Haneen described the work at DCI-Palestine during this critical time. Despite her complaints about the hierarchies of power and income at the organization, which she thought were unfair, she still believed in the organization's work and praised her colleagues for their sincere engagement.

The nicest thing is the staff, which is highly committed to the rights of children, to the implementation of the CRC [Convention on the Rights of the Child] on the ground. They do more than just work for their work but are motivated by conviction. That always gives a person hope in the future—that there's a readiness for change. Like our crisis intervention program, which was necessary from the second week of the intifada—that was an amazing innovation. We were the first to work on the effects of shock on children from the Israeli occupation practices. We're talking about the anxiety that encompassed the whole society, including the children. When the mother herself is in a situation of anxiety, watching the news, there was relative neglect of children, a neglect of the psychological effects. I think that program was really important.

Most of us here have political background, so we can't be silent. We believe in our work. I can tell you, if we thought we're just workers and nothing else, we wouldn't work the way we have been here at DCI. At the beginning of the intifada, look what happened. If there were new challenges, a problem on the ground, I might have said, "What business is it of mine? I just work on my own program." But everyone said, "No, there are new situations, so let's think together about what to do." Everyone was working day and night, until 6:00 or 8:00 p.m., writing press releases and so on. A regular worker would say, "I work from 8:00 until 4:00 and that's it. Don't ask more of me." During the recent invasion [of Israeli forces into the West Bank], the staff took initiative. The director was traveling, but we called him and said, "We have to react." We were at home [stuck under curfew], but we said, "We have to do something. We have to document, work on case studies, work with people, get information about violations from people." We were thinking, we're in an invasion, let's see what's happening on the ground. This was a staff initiative, not the board or director—and we're still working this way.

By the time I left Palestine in 2003, the second intifada was winding down and the sense of emergency that had brought the organization's members together had dissipated. Haneen finally got fed up with what she saw as the lack of democracy within the organization. Although there was, for a time, *sidq bil 'amal*, a belief in and sincerity of purpose in this work, as Haneen repeatedly told me, different perspectives on how the organization should be run and how donor money should be used made some of the staff less convinced about their work. Haneen had been a political activist and fighter for women's rights during the first intifada, and she retained her political commitments and beliefs. During both intifadas, she could put those beliefs into action and focused on meeting the immediate challenges that arose during times of national emergency. However, when that intensity dissolved, broader questions of moral principle, and the inequity she herself faced at work, came to the fore. Haneen left her job at DCI-Palestine for better paying work at an international NGO, as did many of the other staff members I knew.

In Haneen's story, we can see the consistency of moral, national values that drove her. From how she raised her son to "feel with the people," her distrust of Oslo and her condemnation of the decline in national solidarity that she believed it had caused (see Chapter One), and her excitement about and appreciation of the nationalist dedication that recongealed that sense of solidarity among her human rights colleagues, to her disappointment and sense of dissatisfaction at the lack of democracy in her workplace.

Conclusion

A strong system of nationalist values and its attendant moral economy runs against the grain of the structural constraints of the human rights industry and the narrowing of possibilities for political engagement. Palestinian human rights workers have grappled with the political and economic conditions that emerged after the first intifada, the establishment of the PA, and the availability of new channels of donor funding. The ways in which Palestinians debate the meaning and morals of human rights work, the struggles between those who try to sustain it as a form of political pressure and liberation strategy, those keen to exploit its material benefits, and those just trying to make a living re-

flect the broader dilemmas that have confronted the Palestinian national movement since the establishment of the PA, as people are left trying to manage
multiple, and at times contradictory, moralities and desires. As Samuli Schielke
(2009:161) has pointed out, it is a "general feature of human subjectivity" that
"moral ideals, actions and expectations for life" are inconsistent. These uncer-
tainties and incongruities have troubled Palestinian human rights workers particularly acutely.

In the frustrations of these human rights workers we see the inevitable end
result of the inherent impotence built into the intertwined structures of the
human rights system and the PA. The human rights system could never enforce
its rules, never prevent abuses or punish violators, in Palestine as elsewhere.
As historians of the UN, its predecessor, the League of Nations, and the Universal Declaration of Human Rights have shown, such weaknesses are partly
due to the fact that these structures and declarations were never intended to
be enforceable (Mazower 2004, 2009). They represented the lowest common
denominator of compromises among sovereign states unwilling to devolve
meaningful power into the hands of others. Likewise, the PA, a quasi-state and
hobbled government, continues to fail. It is unable to end the Israeli occupation, consolidate sovereign power in a contiguous territory and guarantee security, or create a self-sustaining economy. It was constructed through the DoP,
which "formalized the fragmentation of the occupied territories into zones of
Palestinian and Jewish settlement and the atomization of Palestinian society"
(Rabbani 1996) and turned the PA into a mediating security force for the occupying power (Jamal 2007:11). As such, it has been unable to gain full legitimacy
from the people it is meant to govern.

The Oslo accords ushered in an era of international funding for a specifically defined notion of "development" that entailed macropolitical and economic effects and, as Palestinians experienced it, neocolonial impacts. Through
efforts like the Code of Conduct for NGOs, Palestinians were to become "re-
sponsibilized" citizens (N. Rose 1999) who would concern themselves with "accountability." They were meant to fit within "a new global economy" (Goldman
2005:13) in which Palestinian lands and workers would be transformed into
industrial free trade zones (Bahour 2010). HROs were subjects and agents of
these transformations, touting democracy and liberal values within a political
system that was a dependent pseudo-state for a population still under occupation, and inherently incapable of delivering on those liberal promises. Human
rights organizations became a refuge for former activists who, in the critics'

accounts quoted here (including those of self-critics), were not to remain nationalists and resistance fighters.

There are remarkable parallels here with transformations in human rights
and civil society NGOs throughout the world. Discontent with the "machinations" of NGOs focused on international funding but neglecting the needs of
the community is widespread (Elyachar 2006:422). Although the Palestinian
case is distinct, marked by the changes heralded by the Israeli-Palestinian accords of 1993, many of the same donor-propelled dynamics that are evident in
places afflicted by International Monetary Fund structural adjustment schemes
have plagued Palestinian civil society organizations as well. The NGOization
of political activism and the professionalization of human rights work have
caught activists and HRO staff in impossible binds, trying to balance the pragmatic need for employment with the desire to lead meaningful, politically
principled lives. The story of civil society in all these places—everywhere from
Mexico (Speed 2007) and Colombia (Murdock 2008; Tate 2007) to Egypt (Abdelrahman 2005; Elyachar 2006), Russia, Ukraine (Phillips 2008), and Armenia
(Ishkanian 2003)—features NGOs as part of a broader phenomenon in which
sincere and committed struggles for social justice are replaced by the "business" of development, individualistic self-promotion, and political apathy.

Unlike in these other places, however, no recognized, independent state exists in Palestine. The fact that processes and institutions of global governance
are so deeply imbricated within Palestinian society and political dynamics at
this formative stage may allow for greater impact from their interventions. Palestinians observe these effects as negative transformations in social relations;
they are distressed by the new kinds of avaricious, individualistic political subjects being formed.

That Palestinians concur, albeit obliquely, that the international system has
undercut social values indicates that principles of an ethical system still reign.
Populist priorities and concerns over the corrupting influence of money pre-
dominate within these critiques. If the infusion of donor aid has produced new
problems and kinds of social relations, popular opinion nevertheless remains a
powerful force for sustaining an ethical horizon against which these corrupting
influences and resulting problematic social relations are judged.

The fact that most Palestinians would not have a hard time believing that
Mustafa (the possible intelligence agent and lackadaisical student) worked for
an HRO that existed mainly on paper indicates just how entrenched the cynicism toward the NGO world has become. Nevertheless, the perceptions of and

interactions among donors, NGOs, human rights workers, and the people they are meant to serve are mediated by a network of ethical principles, social values, reputations, and expectations that have built up over time. If donors have played a significant role, however unwittingly or unintentionally, in producing the conditions of possibility for a bad-faith society in Palestine, Palestinians retain a horizon of different possibilities kept in view by memories of a different sort of past. Of the human rights workers I knew, some did consider themselves to have become depoliticized, and none took part in the fighting of the second intifada. Others, however, were searching for new ways to be political. Whether by offering cultural enrichment opportunities for neighborhood youth, teaching them about the range and value of different forms of nationalist involvement, including the importance of a free press and women's rights; by raising their children to have a national feeling of belonging and concern for others; or simply by staying in Palestine, they continued in their efforts to serve their society, support the national cause, and sustain the national values of volunteerism, solidarity, and sincerity. Palestinians' own trenchant critiques of the human rights industry have left open a space in which they produce their own meanings and political projects. The activities and effects of the human rights system in Palestine are multiple, complicated, and sometimes contradictory, but never completely defined by that system.

The next chapter features a group of Palestinians who tried to impart those values through human rights education to all sectors of Palestinian society. Although EU states may view human rights training as a key component in "supporting stability and economic development, which in turn creates a solid foundation for business and investment" (Almbladh n.d.), the organizations I have profiled have decidedly less interest in the market value of human rights. Instead, they pursue rights training as a form of nationalist consciousness raising.

Chapter 3

Teaching Human Rights

Citizens and Security Men in Training

TODAY, most people in the occupied territory know something about human rights. General awareness has increased as a result of campaigns like the *Know Your Rights* pamphlets that Al-Haq circulated (and other HROs have replicated) to help regular people understand their rights and the international standards meant to protect them. Human rights cases are reported in the media, local HROs advertise their activities in news dailies, and frequently the reports of Human Rights Watch and Amnesty International are debated by Israeli and Palestinian publics. Beyond such media circulation and awareness-raising activities, many kinds of Palestinian organizations offer human rights education. Local NGOs have produced textbooks for teaching preschool students about rights, responsibilities, and how to relate to authority; they also put on workshops for refugee youth instructing them in the ways and means of democracy and civic engagement. They provide human rights training courses for Palestinian security services in which officers are encouraged to review the Palestinian Basic Law (which provides a constitutional structure to the PA [Brown 2000]), discuss capital punishment or correct arrest procedures, and receive pamphlets explaining the Geneva Conventions to place in their uniform pockets for quick reference in the field. As an indication of how central this type of activity has become, in 2006, NGOs allocated a third of their budgets to awareness-raising activities, of which rights training was a part.[1]

The causes and effects of human rights education have changed dramatically since Al-Haq's early attempts to use human rights as a tool of popular empowerment. Human rights education is now a means by which different groups, from the PA and international donors to academics and civil society activists, try to create a Palestinian state and shape the political subjects they think are most appropriate to it. Human rights courses impart social values and political teachings about proper social relations; about democracy, tolerance, and the prestige of "modern" statehood; about the practical and symbolic significance of human rights; and about the appropriate relationships that must obtain among rights-bearing citizens and state representatives. As a subset of "technologies of government" (Miller and Rose 1989), these "technologies of citizenship" are designed to cultivate certain dispositions (Cruikshank 1999:4) among subjects who are disciplined and brought into being to inhabit the roles of "citizen" and "security."[2] These technologies, however, have not fixed these social categories into place; they have not fixed the problem of state-making. If the "security man" (*al-rajul al-amni*)[3] is being taught to contribute to creating an image of the state that is openly acknowledged as being an image, a staged performance, for those teaching students and youth, meaningful citizenship and human rights entail a constantly critical attitude toward the people trying to claim the mantle of the state.

In the ideals of the human rights system pronounced in international covenants like the Universal Declaration of Human Rights and the Convention on the Rights of the Child, and those espoused by the international donors who promote these courses, security forces and the state are to be constrained for the protection of individuals' rights, and if only human rights prescriptions were followed, the theory goes, then the right sort of state actors and respectful relations of governance would result. Although the same declarations and standards of human rights form the basis of all these courses, and although the human rights industry provides the money, materials, and idioms by which such trainings are formulated, the tenor and focus of these debates are variable, dependent on the goals and assumptions of the participants. The human rights system mediates but does not motivate or determine what human rights training produces. The structures of global governance that mistake shape-shifting political problems as round pegs to be forced into the square holes of formulaic solutions, and the pretense of donor governments to be able to resolve the il-logics inherent in the problematic of building a state under foreign belligerent military occupation through human rights education, are belied by what is actually happening through human rights training.

The sensibilities being inculcated and debated are distinctive, and sometimes clashing, as communitarian and liberal formulations (Isin and Turner 2002:3–4) vie for primacy in the competing designs for citizenship that appear in these courses. In the eyes of some who are involved in these courses, the Palestinian citizen should be a civically engaged person who critically evaluates and works to change unjust social and political structures; however, for PA officials, the citizen is someone to be both disciplined and coddled by the "security man," and the citizenry is perceived as an obstacle to social order that must be gotten around. In comparing "the learning of political agency" (Lazar 2010:182) that happens in human rights training for university students, security officers, and refugee youth, it becomes clear that ideas about the rights and obligations of state, citizen, and nation, and their right relations, are still under construction, the processes of "subject-ification" (Ong 1996:737) as yet incomplete.

It is in these concerted efforts to articulate, teach, and dictate new state-society relationships and to mold Palestinians into new forms of personhood that the power of cynicism becomes clear. Cynicism enables the continuance of contentious debates about the rights of citizens (to, for example, resist occupation, refuse arbitrary arrest by the PA, and expect a secure future), and it prevents security actors from assuming that coercive and oppressive powers can be wielded without pushback. Cynicism sustains the state's unsettlement, despite the international donors' efforts to create the "rights" kind of Palestinian citizen, and despite the PA's efforts to impose its own vision of proper, professional, modern statehood and obedient citizenry. Antagonisms between "the security man" and the citizen are not initiated by human rights training, but these courses do provide another arena in which the distinctions and antipathies are reinscribed, the unresolved tug-of-war of the Palestinian state kept taut.

Although cynicism may sustain critical consciousness about the state-making process, it also casts a shadow over the lessons provided in some human rights courses. Instead of ingraining legal principles into the attitudes and practices of security officers, because of the cynicism with which most of them regard the human rights industry and the structure of the courses themselves, human rights training for security officers reiterates the superficiality of the PA's commitment to human rights. It instills in officer trainees an understanding of the PA as an entity that must perform a falsely prettified face to the international community, encouraging them to act as if human rights matter while embedding the shared and open recognition that they are only acting "as if." In these courses, Palestinians not only articulate but also embody conflicting notions of what it means to be a good citizen. While these Palestinians go through the motions of human rights training, performing their participation in a state that is recognized as a performance, students in other courses enact an active, critical citizenship through discussions about human rights as they relate to current events, tolerant engagement with opposing opinions, and the organization of protest campaigns.

Proliferating Human Rights Education in Palestine

International developments encouraged the development of greater numbers and kinds of human rights education programs throughout the 1990s, when most development assistance agencies placed democracy promotion on their agenda for the Arab world. They encouraged NGOs to promote reform and a liberal agenda through the creation of educational projects, workshops, and master's programs (Carapico 2002:380–386). The foreign aid that Western funders poured into the occupied territory after the signing of the Oslo accords, "mainly motivated by a desire to sustain the peace process" (Le More 2008:8), also provided money for democracy promotion, including human rights education.[4] In addition, the UN declared 1995 to 2004 the Decade for Human Rights Education, followed in 2005 by the World Programme for Human Rights Education, which is ongoing and which the UN proclaimed in order "to advance the implementation of human rights education programmes in all sectors" (OHCHR 2004). The fact that the UN Educational, Scientific and Cultural Organization (UNESCO) has published six updated editions, most more than three hundred pages long, of the *World Directory of Human Rights Research and Training Institutions* (UNESCO 2003) suggests that attention to human rights education is growing globally. Other UN agencies, such as UNICEF and UNRWA, charged with the care of children and Palestinian refugees respectively, have also implemented tens of human rights education programs in Palestinian public schools (Democracy and Human Rights Program 2006). Amnesty International provided human rights training to school children as early as 1997, and many more institutions, such as the Palestinian Ministry of Education and Higher Education, the Palestinian Academic Society for the Study of International Affairs, and other local NGOs have since joined the human rights training trend, targeting a variety of social sectors, including security officers, children, journalists, lawyers, judges, young professionals, refugee youth, and women. In 1998, human rights and civic education became part of the new Palestinian school curriculum as well, emphasizing "democracy, citizenship, rights and obligations, and peaceful coexistence as aims of education" (Democracy and Human Rights Program 2006:14).

An innovation in human rights education in Palestine was the master's program in Democracy and Human Rights established at Birzeit University in the early 1990s. The educators involved in setting up that program had intended it to be a means of nurturing tolerant, democratic citizens in a newly forming Palestinian state. In their estimation, this program and other human rights education courses support human rights professionalism as much as they foster a democratic citizenry. For some, though, human rights is still a tool of "empowerment" for the Palestinian people, even while the question of what they are being empowered to do continues to be debated.

People participate in these programs, as trainers or students, for their own complicated reasons. Ra'id, a staff member of DCI-Palestine, was working toward his degree in the program despite the fact that he was himself dubious about the benefits of the human rights system. In a class discussion about the effects of human rights in which the term was being used in a broad and vague way, as it often is, he responded negatively to his professor's question about whether human rights indicated or could prompt moral progress among humans. He exclaimed, "No! There's no progress. There is regression." Arguing vehemently to his classmates, he explained his position by saying, "Human rights is just a political tool! And power rules."

Although many like Ra'id have negative opinions about the human rights system, and believe that human rights education is a waste of time or just a pragmatic exercise to be tolerated for the sake of achieving other, personal goals, they are sometimes self-contradictory as well. Later in that same class, he answered my question about why he was studying human rights by insisting that "the Palestinian issue is a human rights issue!" Ra'id, similar to many HRO workers, was a former activist who had spent many years in Israeli prison for his anti-occupation activities. He saw human rights advocacy as a method, however flawed, that he could employ against his oppressors. To be sure, there are those who just want to advance their careers and make some money. Some consider themselves to be pragmatists and appreciate human rights as an internationally recognized reference point for making political claims, which is something better than nothing. They work in human rights advocacy for a lack of other modalities of political engagement. There are also those who prefer the nonviolent, universalist nature of human rights activism to the corruption and militancy of party politics. Still others have their own ideas about how to work for social change, and although their visions for Palestinian society may overlap with the basic values expressed in human rights standards, they engage the human rights system primarily as a means of obtaining resources so that they can implement their own plans—plans that have emerged out of their own very particular political pasts.

Birzeit University Masters Program in Democracy and Human Rights: Civic Engagement and Certificates

Let's not forget that working to establish the rule of law in a country where its own people are not sovereign involves a certain futility. Therefore working to establish rule of law cannot acquire meaning except as part of a vision of the future. But if this vision is itself blurred and unclear, and if those who hold this vision are unable to explore it, unlock its riddle, then any such action will lack cohesion and coherence, and be ungoverned by logic or wisdom. . . . The flocking of students to a program on democracy and human rights is itself an indicator that even the pessimists, in their hearts, are persuaded of a promising future.

Mudar Kassis, cofounder of the Birzeit University
master's program in Democracy and Human Rights

The Birzeit University master's program in Democracy and Human Rights was one of the earliest institutionalized programs for human rights education in Palestine, and since it was established program staff have grappled with many of the very same inconsistencies that this book argues are inherent to the human rights system itself.[5] Instructors and students alike expressed a critical awareness of the ways in which the human rights system has failed to foster a just society and liberated state in Palestine, or elsewhere, and has become a superficial label to legitimize ineffective activities. The program thus exemplifies a situation in which people do in fact see well past "the fictions of neoliberal governance" (Tsing 2005:40), but find only a narrow horizon of possibility beyond them.

Each year the program admits twenty-five to thirty students, so approximately eighty-five students are enrolled in a given year, taking classes with professors in philosophy, law, political science, and education. The program has come to be one hub for the reproduction of what some describe as a semi-elite NGO class, producing graduates with degrees that can make them better placed to become well-paid NGO staff. What prompted the program's development, however, were the political and national motivations of Palestinian intellectuals who wanted to build something that was "politically and socially vital to the process of democratic state building in Palestine" and to provide knowledge resources for the formation of citizens and officials within the context of the newly forming PA (BMDHR 1999). With their plan to "graduate an aware national cadre, working in the public sector, especially in education, civil society and public order apparatuses," as Mudar Kassis (2006:9), one of the program's founders, wrote, the goal was "to make of them people engaged in the political life of the country from their feelings of responsibility to public issues . . . from their conviction that it is important for the rule of law to take root."

Discussions with students and professors in this program provided just the kind of "ethnographic access point . . . for the study of nationalism in action" (and likewise, state formation in action) to which Boyer and Lomnitz (2005:105) have drawn attention.[6] These Palestinian academics were "transformative intellectuals" promoting the development of "critical citizenship" (see also Lazar 2010:183), and they have articulated in broad terms one proposal for what kind of Palestinian state should emerge and what kind of people its citizens should be.

George Giacaman, a politics professor at Birzeit University and another of the program's founders, told me about the questions that he and his colleagues contemplated as the PA was coming into being:

> It was clear that a new set of issues would arrive: principally what kind of government would it be? Even if it was going to be limited, it would have some kind of authority over Palestinians in the West Bank and Gaza. Would it be accountable? Would there be elections? Would it be corrupt? Observe human rights? Would the Palestinian Authority be democratic, or just another security-operated, authoritarian regime similar to what exists in most Arab countries? These concerns were part of the impetus behind establishing the master's program.

Giacaman also helped establish Muwatin, the Palestinian Institute for the Study of Democracy, a research center based in Ramallah that publishes extensively on questions of democracy and civil society, topics on which he lectures to students at Birzeit as well. He described what he saw as the dual importance of human rights for Palestine. In the first place, there was hope that human rights "might provide some protection against the occupation." Second, human rights awareness could also have an impact on social issues in what he described as the "Palestinian-Arab context, where the idea of the equality of human rights found some resistance in relation to personal status laws, and regarding men and women." In fact, most of the professors with whom I spoke emphasized the local relevance of human rights education, highlighting its significance for the development of Palestinian society and the shaping of the PA, and not just for the struggle against occupation.

Recognizing the problems arising from substantial gaps in the distribution of wealth in his society and more generally, Kassis noted that "human rights practitioners have no serious social justice agenda." The only way to explain that, he said, "is that the human rights movement, no matter how great it is, is actually a colonial product." Wary of this legacy, he said they developed the master's program with a concept of human rights as a "progressive" force that could encourage democratization and the idea of equality of citizenship.

If Giacaman and Kassis referred to human rights as an obvious, if fragile, vessel by which to carry forward progressive politics and national pedagogy, it should also be kept in mind that this program was developed at a time when the possibilities of the Oslo period remained an open question and the fate of leftist politics appeared bleak. As already noted, leftist parties had lost their popular base by the early 1990s, and many from the opposition had turned to NGOs as an alternative framework for civil society activity (Giacaman 1998:8; Hammami 1995; Hilal 2003:166). As their political parties crumbled, the doors of HROs and other NGOs were opening. They turned to human rights work partly because the basic democratic values underlying human rights standards broadly accorded with the political ideologies of the Palestinian left.

The specificities of the Palestinian context factored heavily in Kassis's thinking. He spoke to me of the "need to counterbalance the different superficial approaches to issues of democratization, democracy, and human rights that were emerging with the aid that flowed into Palestine to support the peace process." He described the sense of foreboding at the time:

> Human rights was only equated with freedom of expression, democracy, elections—that's about it. We had a growing feeling that these concepts were going to backfire. Eventually we might have elections and be able to voice our concerns in the streets, or in the newspaper, or whatever, but living standards will not get any better, and there will not be real participatory decision making. I also worried that human rights might be highjacked by international law and human rights law and not be conceptualized in a broader sense that could be less technical and hence more accessible to the public. Out of this fear of the technical-legal approach to human rights, I saw the need to develop a society that respects human rights rather than a society that can sue for human rights violations. This was also a time when the US was bombing Yugoslavia. There was this notion of protecting human rights by killing people, which raised serious questions; and we had to see how to reflect on the abuse of the human rights concept in international politics, while avoiding the risk of allowing it to turn into propaganda.

The program's concept document stressed the careful balance the university sought to achieve by creating a course of study that reflected an understanding of "social science [that] is always part of society, and should not be in the ivory tower." The program would "increase the values of freedom and independence of thought" while being "neither just academic and objective, nor a call to a particular political or philosophical position" (BMDHR 1999). Human rights would be promoted "at the level of sensitization, values, and information," as Giacaman put it. In addition to courses in the history and critique of democracy, and democracy in Islamic and Arab thought, the curriculum also covers questions about the "cultural specificity versus the universal character of human rights." Keen to keep social and economic rights central to democracy's definition, it also includes a course on democracy and social justice; and bespeaking the program's emphasis on social change, at least one syllabus assigned Paulo Freire's revolutionary *Pedagogy of the Oppressed* ([1970] 1996).

Although the program's goals were far-reaching, Helga Baumgarten, a German political scientist, long-term resident of Palestine, and a director of the program, suggested that she and her colleagues were more "realistic than idealistic," aware that ultimately they could contribute "very little." She said, "What we would hope for is that people learn to define the challenges that Palestinian society is facing—on the NGO level, or on the level of the PA—and that we help them to cope better on the basis of Palestinians' interests, not imported, Western political, ideological interests." Kassis told me that in a study he conducted on the program's effects, he found that its "graduates are fully adopting the full sense of values that are related to human rights, and they have them as personal values.[7] Nonetheless, they are not so involved in making this happen on the political level" because they believe the occupation must first be dismantled. A Birzeit law professor who lectures on human rights and Palestinian law reported that many student papers explore the difference between PA law and what happens in practice, and in their papers and in class discussions "most students express their skepticism of human rights."

As an example of the small successes she has witnessed, however, Baumgarten described the role of students from the program in staging a protest against the 2008–2009 war in Gaza. They demonstrated on campus in solidarity with the Islamic University of Gaza, which had been bombed. They wanted to send a letter to President Mahmoud Abbas, and she encouraged them to consider the EU countries' role as well. "They wrote a letter to the general representative's office expressing shock about official German policy. They became

active; they did something. We had to push them a little bit, but they did it."
In her assessment, these actions were coming out of the students' "awareness
that human rights and international law were being offended on every possible
level. It was a feeling of civic engagement—that you have to become engaged."

Instructors emphasized the importance of practicing human rights in the
classes themselves. They considered critical thinking and tolerance in the class-
room, along with less hierarchical, rigid teaching methods, to be central principles for human rights pedagogy, moving it from an intellectual terrain to one
that is practiced in the everyday, on an individual level (see also Abdul Hadi
2006; Lazar 2010). Baumgarten expressed her delight at the student's willingness to discuss with one another in a respectful way, and even become friends.
She was especially impressed and pleased "when a student who was a Hamas
guy put his arm around the student who was a nun and asked the other students to photograph them."

Despite the politically oriented framework in which the program was
formed, and what Kassis called the "activist agenda" of the instructors, the professors with whom I spoke acknowledged that students do not uniformly share
in those aspirations. A law professor put it bluntly: "Many students come to
the human rights master's program because they think it's the easiest and they
want a title and they want to raise their salary." Although, as Kassis rightly
pointed out, "you can observe this type of thing in any graduate program in
the world, it being a natural part of the market economy," he and his colleagues
worried continuously about this situation, because "it contradicted the nature
of the project."

Students I spoke with expressed a variety of motivations. Some said they
were there for personal development, out of interest inspired by recognition of
the gap between the theory and claims of the human rights system and their
reality on the ground. A number worked for NGOs, a couple wanted to pursue
a PhD in a related field, and at least one member of the Palestinian Legislative
Council obtained her master's degree there. Numerous security officers have
also passed through the course. The academics running and teaching in the
program have tried, in their own intellectual work, to contribute to the production of a democratic Palestinian nation-state in which citizens, especially NGO
and PA workers, have the critical analytical faculties and information necessary
for participating in it. Notable is their focus on offering human rights education that would encourage scrutiny of the Palestinian governmental system
(and not only, or even primarily, Israeli abuses).

However, in targeting PA and NGO workers because they are the most likely to influence state-society relations in Palestine, the program implicitly conceives of state-building as an elite affair. This may be pragmatic, but it has led at least some local leftists to criticize it for being out of touch, too narrowly and theoretically focused. Kassis (2006) also noted some of the structural impediments to realizing the program's stated progressive goals:

> The program fills a need of civil society organizations which require workers, and public sector organizations and schools, which are looking to implement human rights, because democracy has become marketable for international donors. . . . Maybe the program has been too focused on elite theory and has less effect on political parties. It is presenting ideas about human rights that are not attractive to a wider audience.

Moreover, the program's location within the most prestigious university in the West Bank, which has relatively high entrance requirements, including some level of English language ability, and which charges considerable tuition, means that the program is not itself fully democratic. As at any elite university, this program contributes to the (re)production of class distinctions, allowing those who can already afford this school's tuition to climb the human rights ladder farther up the socioeconomic hierarchy.

The program has become successful for the university, and despite the fact that some professors wish they could accept fewer people and weed out the less serious applicants, the administration encourages the enrollment of paying students. The availability of an advanced educational degree in human rights has contributed to the increasing professionalization of the HRO sector, potentially restricting access to the field to those who can afford to obtain a degree that will designate them as "experts." Despite the political-ethical goals of the program's instigators, its bestowal of an official "qualification" for human rights work has added another layer to the human rights system, contributing to the hegemony of a particular form of marketable human rights work that does not always support political activism or engagement.

The "Security Man," the "Citizen," and the "Modern State"

Even if the progressive character of Palestinian collective identity, national belonging, and social order that Birzeit's intellectuals have outlined followed broad, liberal-democratic and human rights principles, the increasing institutionalization of human rights has made the system accessible to a state-building project that encourages the formalism of rights. This is most obvious in the articulation of goals that were pursued in the human rights training sessions for security forces that I attended. These courses articulated a vision of "modern" statehood policed by "professional security" in which the concept of human rights is wielded as a utilitarian tool that must be deployed to create the perception of professional people and organizations that "deserve" a state. Officers are being taught to contribute to producing a fantasy of the state, an illusion of a professional, modern, human-rights-respecting state in which they play a role that is understood to be a performance for specific audiences.[8]

A former field research coordinator for Al-Haq told me he was the first to give human rights training to the PA shortly after it was established—something he did alone and on his own initiative. His colleagues objected, he said, because they were afraid that HROs would be held responsible for the human rights violations committed by PA officials. Attitudes changed, however, and international agencies and local NGOs have been offering human rights training in growing numbers since 1996, when the Independent Commission for Human Rights (ICHR; then still called the Palestinian Independent Commission for Citizens' Rights, or PICCR) began doing so. The UN Office of the High Commissioner for Human Rights also opened an office in the Gaza Strip to provide human rights training for security forces and technical support for the newly established PA in an effort to ensure that Palestinian law accorded with international standards.

The training courses I attended in 2009 occurred at a time when many Palestinian human rights activists and others were renewing a belief that was common during the first years of the PA, that they were "headed towards a police state," as Rula told me.[9] This soft-spoken but tough HRO director in the West Bank said that abuse of power "has become part of the culture. It's widespread—not just among one security agency or an officer of a certain rank, but even among the lowliest who makes the initial arrest and takes you from your house" (see also DCAF 2008, 2009; Oxfam 2008). In 2009, a spate of articles on the role of then US security coordinator Lieutenant General Keith Dayton and his team of international security consultants in building up an abusive Palestinian security apparatus sparked additional attention and criticism.[10] Local and international human rights groups have scrutinized the PA's security institutions since their formation, reporting regularly on the abuses they have perpetrated, including mass arbitrary arrests and the torture and killing of detainees, which the Israeli HRO B'Tselem (1996:17) predicted was "in danger of becoming systematic" as early as 1996.[11] Since the split between Gaza and the West Bank in 2007 and the renewed crackdown on Hamas, HROs have reported an upsurge in politically motivated abuses in both territories.[12]

While the HROs continued to issue reports, the PA pushed back by launching investigations into the legal status of numerous HROs, harassing their lawyers and preventing their visits to clients in detention. Rula explained what happened when PA security detained a lawyer who worked at her HRO. When they called her with complaints about this lawyer's investigations into PA torture and ill-treatment, she said, "What are we supposed to do? Just come and say 'Hi' to our clients and 'your family sends their greetings'? We're supposed to do legal work! It looks like they're not happy that we were not intimidated by them," she surmised. This ebb and flow of protests and objections created the choppy waters in which security officers attended HR training (see PCHR 2010b). The tense conditions provoked defensiveness among some of the officer participants and colored the tone of the courses.

Perhaps hoping to allay such apprehensions, trainers presented themselves as "partners" with the security forces who were not there to "monitor" them. Conceding that the security forces exist in a "sensitive situation," they also acknowledged that human rights was a "sensitive label." One trainer chummily agreed with his audience of officers that NGOs are "annoying" and confirmed the problem of "excessive propaganda" that unjustly blames security services for abuses.[13] Recognizing that the participants might feel antagonistic toward human rights workers, the trainers tried to create a sense of shared identity, insisting that they and the officers—variously addressed as "brothers" and "guys" (*ya ikhwan*, *ya shebab*)—must "continue together as one people" with goals and benefits in common.

Human rights groups stage training sessions, usually lasting three days, at hotels or NGOs in conference rooms big enough to accommodate approximately twenty officers, the average number of participants, who hail from all of the security services—civilian police, National Security Forces (NSF), Preventive Security, and General Intelligence (*mukhabarat*). The civilian police are charged with day-to-day law and order, the NSF act as a sort of *gendarmerie*, and the others are domestic intelligence. The fact that all of these agencies send officers to human rights training underscores both the top-level concern with looking like they care about human rights, and the broad-based incentive structure in which all types of security officers see a personal benefit in attending.

Participants in the courses I attended had either volunteered or been or-dered to attend, and most were men from the lower ranks, along with a few women, including officers and administrative staff. (Higher ranking officers also received human rights training in other venues, such as the senior lead-ership course offered by Dayton's team.) Their roles and duties were varied, including purely administrative positions, which made dubious the usefulness of the majority of their training that focused on investigative procedures. The lecturers, all of whom were Palestinian in the courses I attended, were lawyers, former or current human rights workers, or staff from the Ministry of Interior (MoI). As at any long departmental or conference meeting, a steady stream of coffee and cookies was available to sustain the energy and attention of the participants, which nevertheless wavered consistently, evident in their slumped postures, bored expressions, side conversations, and fiddling with cell phones.

In the materials handed out, anodyne terms described such workshop goals as, among others, "to enhance the role of relevant parties in protecting rights of the Palestinian citizen during the conducting of their duties." Along with being given writing pads and pens, the participants in some sessions I attended also received sturdy folders and canvas conference bags announcing the gen-erous source of the loot.[14] Printed schedules (also emblazoned with the logos and names of the hosting NGO and funding institutions) outlined session top-ics. The course outline of one ICHR training program included a word about ICHR, citizen's rights during questioning, interrogation, minimum standards of treatment of prisoners, protection of women's and young people's rights in line with international agreements and local law, the ICHR's role in protecting children and youth, the death penalty according to international and regional agreements, open fire regulations, and opposing torture according to interna-tional and regional agreements, ending with the "certificate party." After sign-ing an attendance sheet and being instructed in the rules of session behavior, including turning off cell phones and prompt attendance, lectures and learning exercises commenced.

The content of these activities was the least significant aspect of such courses. It was, rather, their form that imparted the most important lesson: human rights are practically irrelevant. The abstraction, if not inconsequence, of rights and their distance from the officers' reality was continually reinforced in the interactions between trainers and trainees. Despite what the trainers told me was their focus—delivering "practical training" through "practical exam-ples"—most sessions were lectures, consisting mainly of a brief review of elements of international human rights agreements and the Palestinian Basic Law, and highlighting "the letter of the law" as such. Several trainers simply read out sections of the Palestinian Basic Law, delivering their points in dry, text-heavy, PowerPoint presentations. One of the more interactive instructors had the participants stand up and huddle together around him in an awkward circle. One by one they were asked to pick a slip of paper out of a bowl full of scraps on which was the text of various civil and political rights. The officer would then have to discuss whether the statement was true or false, and once veracity was established, the bowl was presented to the next participant, with no further discussion of the importance or potential ambiguities of the issues raised.

When I mentioned to one young lawyer that his PowerPoint lecture was rather heavy and hard for me to follow, he replied firmly, "The law is the law. You just have to understand it. You can't make it lighter." The slouching attitude of the men around the table indicated that I was not the only one struggling with the material. One of the most active participants in this session, an inquisitive, philosophically inclined thirty-something officer from the Preventive Security Force, raised his hand. He objected to the fact that the lecturer was presenting this deluge of information about the rules and regulations required of him and his colleagues "as if the security infrastructure is complete." He asked what they were supposed to do when they are allotted only twenty-four hours to charge a detainee but the judges "are all on vacation, or no general prosecutor is available." He challenged the lawyer with honest observations, stating that "the judicial system is not functioning, which makes it difficult for an officer to actually follow the rules and guarantee security. There are real situations we have to deal with." Blatantly ignoring the officer's comments, the lawyer went on lecturing about how many haircuts and blankets a detainee is entitled to according to Palestinian law. The disconnect between ideals and reality is being reenacted in microcosm in human rights training sessions, hardened through the style of training and the formalism with which rights are discussed. During another session on torture, an officer asked a question about a recent event in Palestine and the lecturer replied, "First we'll talk about the law, and then the situation here." (For reasons unclear to me, he never did so.) In these interactions and others like them, human and civil rights are portrayed and enacted as abstract rules and regulations that constrain political discussion and claims. No doubt contrary to the funders' intentions, some trainees told me they thought the benefit of these sessions went only to the host organization, which gets money for conducting the workshops. "The officers feel like they're just here so the project can happen, not to actually gain anything," an instructor observed. The point here is not that human rights training was boring or ineffective, but that the training reinforced the idea that human rights are notional and part of a money-making system, rather than practically relevant.

There is an obvious breach between, on the one hand, the theory of human rights and the ideals and values that the human rights system represents and, on the other hand, the exigencies of a nonstate entity being instructed to function like a state before the infrastructure (and almost everything else) is actually in place. Local observers note the gap between the human rights training that security personnel receive and the security forces' actual practices. Contributing factors include the very weak system of accountability and the US and Israeli demands on the PA to move against Hamas, along with Fateh's own struggling attempts to hold on to the threads of power in the West Bank, which together fuel the abuses (Y. Sayigh 2009:25, 2011). Israel, moreover, remains the actual sovereign over the occupied territory. Human rights training can do little if it is not conducted in tandem with the amelioration of related issues of accountability, the judiciary, infrastructure, and a political resolution domestically and with Israel. One experienced trainer and former ICHR staff member pointed out that "it has to be tied to a whole system: respect for the law, clear designation of responsibilities, and reform. Without everything tied together, there's no point." A scholar at a research center described rights training as a "virtual reality disconnected from what's happening on the ground. Rights training is pointless without a political structure." Remarking on the lack of field-based training, one lecturer with several years of experience conducting training sessions in Palestine and elsewhere in the region was critical of the theoretical approach of most courses, which presented human rights conventions but offered little practical application. "If I was an officer, I might enjoy the lectures and the lunches, but I wouldn't gain skills this way. It doesn't affect behavior. Why not just send them the text of the Convention Against Torture over the Internet and tell them to read it?" he asked with more than a hint of exasperation. To be sure, some trainers were convinced that what they were doing was important, took solace in the fact that protection of human rights "happens slowly," and believed themselves to be narrowing that gap between theory and practice by using "real-life examples." However, most officers just heard more theory.

None of the organizations I observed had developed an evaluation mechanism that tracked whether human rights training affects the behavior of security personnel or whether incidents of abuse are reduced as a result of these courses. The very superficial forms of training evaluation, which depend largely on students' individual reactions to the trainers, also suggest that human rights are taught not as a set of beliefs, values, or rules of behavior, but as a form of performance, the only real result being photographs of the trainees for their reports and websites. A Western aid worker claimed that since the late 1990s, donor governments have funded human rights training simply as a way to exhaust their budgets because they are "an easy way to spend money." A trainer concluded, "If you compare how much money goes into training versus what actual effect these workshops have on behavior, it's a failure." The fact that so many recognize the opportunism and see that it has become a core dynamic of human rights education has contributed to cynicism about the human rights system in general.

The structure and practices of training sessions communicate a particular ideology and ethics of state and national community as well. For example, the emphasis on etiquette and rules in the courses I observed called on participants to practice their "professionalism," a value that the training sessions taught and embodied in mimetic fashion. Little things like prompt and polite attendance, quiet attentiveness, and tolerant respect for others' opinions were behaviors that participants did not always exhibit but that instructors repeatedly held up as expectations. Post-session assessments by trainers included such evaluations as "Participants were active in the discussion and mastered the topics of discussion" and "Trainees were committed to the timing and were highly disciplined," indicating something of the Foucauldian nature of what the trainers believed was at stake in these sessions. The trainees were people being trained into not only representing but enacting "the state" as certain kinds of disciplined, civil subjects. Some instructors did endeavor to inculcate a specifically human rights habitus too. After a particularly heated discussion about the death penalty in which participants voiced firmly held and opposing views, a trainer told me that the goal of this exercise was to practice civil debate, "how to be tolerant and listen to each other." The real emphasis, however, was generally on the individual—and individualist—relevance of following human rights regulations.

Professional behavior, officers were to understand, entailed following the law and respecting human rights, and should be upheld toward three related goals: careerism, self-protection, and founding a modern state. In the first instance, officers were reminded that they should follow legal procedure, for their own professional records. A UN trainer explained his teaching method: "The security people complain that they don't have sufficient technology and equipment, like lie detectors and fingerprinting [machines] that they need for investigations. When they say this leads them to use force or torture to get results, we tell them that the case will get thrown out of court." Legal infractions can not only lead to the "bad guys" getting away, officers were told, but also obstruct the progress of the officers' careers.

Instructors also summoned a horizon of punishment. They warned officers to be careful because "there will come a time when human rights violations will not go unpunished." Lectures contained messages that activated the logics of rational calculation and concern for individual benefit. Officers learned that in a situation where torture is a possibility, they should not in fact consider human rights or think about the person suffering in front of them but instead simply worry about their own skin. "If you torture and get caught, you will get punished, not your commander" was the maxim summing up this lesson. To emphasize how dangerous the crime of torture is, and drawing on an understanding of the "security man" as someone who is "concerned with the laws, not issues of sentiment," lecturers drew attention to the fact that any act of torture is still punishable, even after someone has left his or her job.

In such discussions, trainers generally referred to nothing other than the rules of the profession and to Palestinian and international law to buttress the standards of behavior they were promoting. Explicitly nationalist and humanist values were absent from the discourse. The broader goal they did invoke was the building of a professional security service, which was understood to be a necessary element within the assumed teleology of creating a "modern state." Another compulsory feature of a modern state, trainers explained, was respect for human rights. A training coordinator expounded in front of an audience of young officers, "In order for this to be a lawful state, a state that is consistent with human rights treaties, it has to be a modern state (*dowlah hadithah*) with contemporary laws (*qawanin mu'asirah*) that is in line with international laws. A modern state is not a state in which somebody hits someone and then someone else hits him in return. We have a lot that is missing in this regard. Why? Because the PA doesn't have good tools." For her, progress on this front meant changing the hardheaded "mentality" of the security services, especially when it came to women's rights, but also to human rights in general. She made it clear that these principles were important to her personally. Another trainer explained to his audience the significance of human rights to professionalism in more global terms: "We have had to convince the international community that we are ready for a state, but to have a state, this requires a high level of professionalism. One of the most important guarantees of our existence as a people is to protect the human rights of the citizen—even the human rights of spies." One instructor rhetorically challenged the participants to name one civilized, developed country that does not respect human rights. Dismissing a chuckle-inducing insouciant response of "China" shouted from the back of the audience, he stated, "We are going towards a state in which the rule of law reigns, and human rights is part of that." "States of a higher level try to present themselves as respecting human rights and are considered among the elevated states (*al-duwal al-raqiyah*)," an instructor explained, reflecting the notion that respecting human rights is a mark of prestige.

This equation of modern statehood with human rights standards was echoed by the head of the MoI's Democracy and Human Rights Unit. Before meeting with this unit director, I spoke to human rights workers, other members of the PA, and one foreign consultant to the MoI. None had heard of the unit or knew its director (although I subsequently learned that she was a locally known Fateh activist). The low profile of the position indicated to most of them just how little significance the PA actually accorded to the Democracy and Human Rights Unit. Sitting in a small office full of paper piles, furnished with chairs still wrapped in their shipping plastic, the director of this one-person unit said, "Although it is true that the nature of any governmental authority is to impose the law, security, and stability, which entails a certain amount of power over people, the PA is intent on deepening the concepts of a modern state, built on the principles of democracy, pluralism, respect of freedoms, and human rights." Whether or not she thought that an office for receiving citizens' complaints would protect her compatriots from the state's excesses and brutalities, or even that all of them should be so protected, she added her voice, and her official MoI presence, to the chorus of officials acting "as if" they do (cf. Wedeen 1999).

That path into the elite and toward a modern state requires a specific kind of subject to inhabit the role of "security man." The security subjectivity being sketched out in these sessions featured a rationalized, individualized professional with restrained emotion.

Palestinians often refer to themselves as an "emotional" (*'atifi*) people who sometimes make unwise, hotheaded decisions as a result. I heard this most often when I asked people to help me understand the behavior of militants during the second intifada who engaged in what I, and many in Palestine and beyond, believed was foolhardy and ineffective activity (such as shooting at Israeli tanks with rifles). In this case, it was the hot blood of youth, the bravado of men, the desperation of the occupied, and especially the passions of nationalists that the people I talked with invoked to explain, although not justify, such behavior. In this new phase of state-building, however, according to these human rights workshops, emotions should be quelled. A bureaucratically rule-bound "security man" should be swayed neither by family ties nor by human sympathies. Tribal law must be set aside. In a discussion about torture, an officer raised his hand and made the straightforward remark that if a suspect is someone who is accused of a particularly heinous crime, like killing or abusing a child, and refuses to talk or give straight answers to an interrogator, "You might want to hit him." The lecturer responded, "Yes, of course everyone has feelings, and every person is different, but professionalism has to restrain you." A participant volunteered: "When I am an officer, I am no longer Mahmud," to emphasize the suppressing of individual personality that this restraint demands, symbolized in the loss of his name.

It is just this bureaucratized attitude that is being inculcated in the security services that critics of the PA with whom I talked found objectionable. To them it indicated the pseudo-state's dangerously denationalized approach to the public and to the state-building project. A Hamas animated cartoon portrayed the betrayal of family and nationalist ethics that is now being required of PA forces. It told the story of a sinister PA soldier who co-opted an unsuspecting boy and convinced him to inform on a relative who had been engaged in anti-occupation activity, fighting Israeli soldiers. Although it was a partisan message against the Fateh-dominated PA—Hamas's rival—it expressed an outrage I heard from West Bankers with no ties to Hamas. It was appalling to many Palestinians that PA security personnel would be expected not only to repress militant resistance to occupation—what most Palestinians believe is their right as guaranteed by international law—but also to arrest their own father if so ordered. "This is the first time we have a trained army, but they are not nationalist. They are just there to protect Israel. Imagine!" Nasser told me. Critics such as Nasser were troubled at what they saw as the fraying of fundamental social ties and of the senses of obligation to nation and family.

It was well known in the MoI, in institutions working in security sector reform, and among security personnel themselves that they were the object of disdain, fear, and suspicion. Palestinians made it known not only discursively but also in their interactions—from the violent to the dismissive—with security personnel. Security personnel have been stoned and attacked, thrown from windows, and denied romantic engagements because of their profession. Nadia, a grade school teacher, told me of a brief Internet exchange she had with a young man, someone she had "bumped into" virtually through a social networking site. When she found out he was a member of a security agency, she automatically took this to mean he was engaged in unsavory activities—if not torture, then at the very least he was repressing his own people. He did not deny the charge, and she ceased the flirtation immediately. Her brother shared with me what he knew of the harsh training that security personnel undergo, and how they are subject to all manner of abuse in order to inure them to any inciting emotions. When I suggested that this was probably standard military-boot-camp-style instruction, he objected: "Maybe this is how training for the marines should be, preparing for battle; but this is an internal security service!" Regardless of the appropriateness of such training from a technical or security perspective, cultural and national(ist) sensibilities were being offended, increasing the gap between security officer and citizen. To be sure, discriminatory application of the law, cronyism, and corruption in the PA have long been features of the government and a focus of Palestinian complaints, just as more transparency and less patronage are part of what they call for. But for many, the way the security services were going about the process of professionalization was causing betrayal on multiple levels.

Professionalization, as taught in these workshops, entailed the reformulation of social and interpersonal dealings, demanding of state representatives an objectifying attitude, formalizing relations between them and the citizens in a way that seemed to many not only foreign but also morally wrong. Another element of professionalization outlined for course participants was the proper treatment of citizens. In a handout prepared for a workshop by the strategic planning department of the MoI, the highest priority of the "security man" was identified as being the development of

> a good relationship built upon mutual respect and cooperation between security organizations and the individuals of society, in order to win their support to accomplish security goals. It is easy to notice that the relation between the security man and the citizen is much better now than it was, but it is not as it should be. Many citizens recoil from cooperation with the security services, and the security man commits mistakes which reflect badly on the image of security work in the citizens' minds. . . . [There is a] lack of understanding and confidence between citizen and security. In Palestine, some look at the security man with

suspicion, even with a level of animosity. . . . So the security man needs education [*tathqif*] into his role, how to behave in different situations and deal with
the citizens in a way that breaks the ice, abolishing the barriers between them.

The problem, as construed here, is not what kind of person the officer has to
be, nor what kind of system (which exists under occupation and lacks a fully
functioning judiciary, parliament, and constitutionally legitimate government)
he or she must function within. The issue, rather, is a lack of understanding, a
problem that education, communication, and sensitivity training can fix. According to the MoI plan, radio programs and other media, summer camps and
school presentations, and more songs about the security services were some
of the means by which this greater awareness could develop. Use of the media
was complicated, however, by "globalization and the proliferation of media and
satellite channels," which meant that "no state is able to govern and control the
policy of its media like before." Greater cooperation with the media was necessary so that journalists "can present information that does not infringe on security but helps knowledge of reality without rumor, which can harm much more
than truthful information can." The priorities of this human rights session were
the pragmatic goals of the security apparatus, a group presumed to be distinct
from, if not opposed to, citizens and the media. The security man himself was
not included in the category of citizen, nor was the citizen considered to be a
rights-bearing co-national whom the officer was bound to "protect and serve."
Neither the handout nor the workshop participants discussed the public's right
to information or their involvement in civic life. The citizen was the object of
spin, someone who had to be handled, managed, perhaps even placated so that
the security man could get on with his job.

   In a lecture on the relationship between the Palestinian security man and
the citizen, a high-ranking officer of the National Security Forces repeated the
oft-cited evaluation that Palestinian citizens have been raised in a state of rebellion. "Because of the history of Israeli occupation and oppression, the citizen
ties in his mind the security man to subjugation and oppression," one of his
handouts confirmed. Hence, the security service's problem was "how to teach
the citizen to be committed" to upholding the law, which required a "human relationship" between security and the citizen, who needed to better comprehend
"the complicated situation of the security man." "Citizens don't understand security," the NSF officer announced. An imposing but jovial gentleman dressed
in a military dress uniform with multiple shoulder stripes and bedecked with
medals, he paced in front of the audience as he spoke, having captured the

respectful and apparently interested attention of the officers. "We should co-operate and be a model for society," he preached. Among the characteristics required of security personnel that he listed were, "We have to be polite, know the law, know human rights, accept citizen complaints." From the audience he elicited further traits necessary in security personnel: bravery, respect, self-control, self-confidence, intelligence, strength, and being nondiscriminatory were some of the individual qualities they suggested. He acknowledged that the security services need reform. "There are deficiencies: clientelism, lack of institutions. There is injustice and occupation. There is discrimination inside and out." His final directive was, "Begin with yourself," and with that he strode out of the room, shaking the outstretched hands of the seated officers, who seemed eager for his recognition.

These human rights courses thus set a very particular tone of political discussion and constituted a field of political discourse in which the problems, characteristics, and goals of security were defined in specific ways. In lessons about how the "security man" should treat "the citizen," clear distinctions were drawn between the two social categories, their differences assumed. Such pedagogy illustrates the work that goes into producing a boundary between state and society, at least in the minds of security personnel. Timothy Mitchell (1991) has offered one explanation of how this mechanism of state-society separation generates and is a function of power. Mitchell describes how groups and institutions such as oil companies and banks are portrayed and believed to "lie outside the formal political system" (90), whereas in fact they are not simply in cahoots with, but a fundamental and driving part of, the political order. In the Palestinian case, however, we are confronted with a prior moment in this boundary-making mechanism, well before "the state comes to seem a subjective starting point, as an actor that intervenes in society" (Mitchell 1991:91). What the critiques of the PA show, however, is that many Palestinians have not been "misled into accepting the idea of the state as a coherent object clearly separate from society" (Mitchell 1991:90), nor do they accept what that not-yet-entity is being trained to be and do.

Rejuvenating Citizenship Through Human Rights Self-Esteem

Despite the presumed distinction between "the citizen" and "the security man," the meaning of citizenship, including who the category encompasses and what expectations and obligations it entails, remains unclear. Human rights workshops for security personnel that I attended partially illustrated Mudar Kassis's observation that state-building in Palestine is being undertaken in a way that focuses on "the power part of the state but not the state, building the regime not the citizens." In a properly functioning society, a workshop handout explained, "every citizen should be a security man, upholding the law even if he does not wear a uniform, caring for the nation and society and its individuals. So long as the citizen defaults on this security role, this means that there's a problem." Implicitly acknowledging the doubts that many Palestinians have about the nationalist loyalty of the security forces, the handout instructed the security man that it is up to him "to increase the Palestinian citizens' faith that the security man represents protection of the Palestinian national project in its entirety." In an oddly circular and vague formulation, however, the national project is to be guarded "by protecting the esteem for the authority of the PNA [Palestinian National Authority]." Even if forming better relations between the security agencies and citizens was a concern, it was filtered by a conception of the citizen-as-problem. Given the minimal levels of judicial and parliamentary oversight operating in Palestine, that these workshops reinforced the image of the citizen-as-problem was dangerous, potentially increasing a sense of antagonism that could foster abuse.

Among Palestinians outside the security forces, citizenship was understood rather differently. Influenced by the model of political participation inaugurated and fostered by the first intifada, the activists and academics I talked with associated citizenship with public engagement and active struggle. Citizenship meant doing "anything in the public sphere," whether struggling against the occupation at checkpoints, protesting the PA, staging demonstrations, participating in a political party, or demanding gender justice. The principles of gender and social equality and entitlement to political expression that undergird human rights standards were framed as the goals of active Palestinian citizenship. Palestinians who developed grassroots human rights workshops organized them as a way for young people to focus on social issues together and think about how to address them in their own communities, at the level of family, community center, and refugee camp.

Those who were engaged in human rights education at the two small HROs I focus on here were concerned about the fact that popular acts of citizenship had been on the decline since the early 1990s. In the assessment of these activists, and of many others who were no longer active, the generation of youth that was raised after Oslo "was demolished, made to feel that they had no influence," as Hani, a long time rights activist lamented. So too with those who had resisted the occupation during the first intifada, who also ended up feeling helpless. They were marginalized by the militarization of the second intifada, in which only a small percentage of the population was interested or equipped to participate in armed activities (Hammami and Tamari 2001).

Despite the general feeling of immobilization, during the second intifada NGOs were swamped with people, especially young people, wanting to volunteer. In an effort to rejuvenate earlier forms of popular political participation, Hani and other activists at a prisoner rights NGO sought to channel that spirit of volunteerism with a project designed to use human rights to teach students about leadership and civic engagement. Building from lectures on international humanitarian law (IHL) and human rights, "which were based on the perspective that rights are for all," students went on to learn how to campaign, how to mobilize the public, and how to do solidarity work. With the help of the program leaders, they implemented their own campaigns on topics they chose, from the nationalist to the local. Political prisoners, the Israeli boycott, and sexual harassment were some of their concerns. Hani said the goal was "to make human rights something relevant in the youths' own lives, to energize more activities." Citizenship required sparking a belief that people "could change things."

The legal clinic at Al-Quds University also taught human rights and IHL as "a tool of mobilization." Established in 2006 as the first clinical legal education program in Palestine, it promoted "an understanding of the precise legal nature of their situation in international law" in order to "decrease the feeling of powerlessness amongst the Palestinians." Sami, an extremely enthusiastic young coordinator in the program, believed that human rights "is a way to move society" and "a way to defend against violations in a legitimate way." He explained that most students did not think violent resistance was the right way to oppose occupation, and that the militarization of resistance had been a failure of the second intifada. Human rights offered an alternative framework. "The only other option is this discourse. Human rights are a way to defend against violations in a legitimate way," Sami said. Animated with the fervent passion of a new convert, he went on to describe human rights as "a new forum, something that people will listen to in the rest of the world. They will listen to me and believe."

Seemingly untouched by the cynicism toward human rights advocacy that I had come to expect from anyone working in the field, Sami believed that human rights work had a practical dimension. It "gives a sense of doing something, even if results come only in the future." A significant aspect of this program was its refusal of a dichotomy between collective and individual rights. Sami described how the human rights campaigns that the legal clinic students undertake "group Palestinians together." He illustrated by describing how the "Container" checkpoint (an infamous checkpoint on a major thoroughfare of the West Bank) affected "me as an individual" who has difficulty getting from one town to the next or getting to work or school, just as it affected "us as Palestinians, our right to education." Moreover, education in human rights as it pertains to rule of law and the PA brought a focus on abuses at home and "allows for self-criticism, which has been lacking here for a long time," he said.

Despite Sami's conviction that human rights are "a way to move" individuals and society, the successes of the program that he listed for me had to do more with its institutional strength, as it steadily attracted more students and began to influence other academic programs, rather than with instances in which rights were protected or abuses punished. In a context of increased surveillance at home, where Palestinians were becoming more wary of speaking up when PA security arrested a family member and more hesitant to report cases of torture out of fear that the PA might take revenge on them, the Al-Quds program staff considered the very knowledge that one has the right to speak out and the tools to speak out and mobilize collectively to be significant forms of empowerment.

Ann, an enthusiastic twenty-four-year-old law student, was the primary instructor for a human rights project for refugee youth. A cultural center in a West Bank refugee camp established the three-year-long program to "help combat the isolation imposed through travel restrictions that have contributed to the breakdown of the social fabric," which is what the NGO staff wrote in their successful grant application to the EU. Other goals included fostering an intellectual understanding and practical appreciation of democracy as a way of thinking and being in the world; helping to eliminate aggressive and irresponsible behavior among youth; eliminating negative social hierarchies, especially ageism and sexism, by promoting gender equality and anti-authoritarianism; and increasing women's leadership roles. The project began with workshops on human rights and democracy, which Ann taught and which were based on the human rights curriculum that Amnesty International developed, supplemented with local examples and case studies for discussion. The next phase of the project included workshops in journalism, "teaching principles of a free press and freedom of expression," all of which reached teenagers in six different refugee camps across the West Bank.

Ann was an active, outspoken, politicized woman driven by a range of principles that she described as "humanist" (*insani*) and that grew out of a long-held desire "to help the oppressed." As a refugee from a camp herself, she also believed that human rights work could help focus Palestinian society on refugee rights, an issue she saw repeatedly sidelined by the political leadership in the peace negotiations.

Her courses placed a heavy emphasis on freedom, nondiscrimination, minority rights (such as between Muslims and Christians in Palestine), and especially gender equality. This was a principle strongly encouraged and partially enacted by the NGO running the program, which insisted that all social activities must involve boys and girls together, despite the fact that this stance led some families in the socially conservative camp to object and withdraw their daughters from the programs. For those who stayed, the message was evidently getting through. During their group discussions, girls in the course often brought up examples of discrimination against them in their families and in the camp as illustrations of rights violations (and boys sometimes grumbled that their gender rights were being violated because they felt the instructor favored the female students over them). There was unanimous agreement that their rights to education and leisure, key rights in the UN Convention on the Rights of the Child, were regularly denied them, due to the obstacles that the occupation put in their way, and as a result of the authoritarian teaching styles they experienced in their UNRWA-run schools.

Ann's human rights sessions drew on a range of examples to promote discussion that reflected the program's emphasis on a balance between analysis of Palestinian society and of the occupation. As Ann noted, "These kids and Palestinians in general are used to thinking of violations as only coming from the occupation, but there are violations that have nothing to do with the occupation, like early marriage for girls and patriarchal male dominance. We focus on human rights not just because the funders want it. It's a way to build the society." Discussion of a recent event in which PA security forces had violently shut down Palestinian protests against Israeli attacks in Gaza illustrated how the right to freedom of assembly and political expression could be abused. "Human rights are also important to building a state," Ann said. "These kids have to know what form of a state that they want, the meaning of democracy and citizenship. They have to know the most important principles of citizenship are defense of nation and respect for laws. They have to know this so they know the right way to build a good state—a state that is going to be built by their hands."

Through the participatory, nonhierarchical pedagogical style of the workshops, participants were also encouraged to enact democratic and human rights principles. Rather than imitate the more authoritarian style that these students were used to at school, in which a teacher stands in front of crowded rows of desks, Ann initiated group discussion with students by arranging them in a circle. She reminded them of the importance of listening and understanding each other, encouraging even the quiet girls to express their opinions, and prompted discussion of how to resolve small conflicts between each other in ways that were fair. Group exercises emphasized leadership and voting skills, and she used newspapers to illustrate rights themes and provide discussion topics, thereby exposing participants to current events.

The very existence of the project, which the NGO organized in order to counteract the social dissolution caused by the Israeli occupation's cantonization of their country, was also an enactment of human rights.[15] Ann explained their thinking: "One right is the right to leisure and movement and travel. The occupation prevents us, but one can fight the occupation and go abroad and send one's message to the West. When they come from different camps and pass through checkpoints together to talk about Palestinian issues and their home villages, that is fighting the occupation itself."

Ann felt that she had developed an enhanced sense of self-esteem and empowerment as a result of her own human rights education. She believed that a similar transformation was happening among her students. Their growing comfort with interacting in mixed-gender settings and their aspirations for the future, such as one girl's assertion that she would become a "famous journalist and tell the world about our situation," were indications of success. Ann said that human rights education "will build a better generation. They will change themselves, their personalities, for the better, so they know what their rights and responsibilities are in this society, so they can face reality and our society thoughtfully, and create the change that Palestine needs." Like the high-ranking NSF official who commanded the security officers to "begin with themselves," the approach of human rights training for youth also focused on changing the consciousness, behavior, and aspirations of individuals. Only people who could demand their personal rights and be critical of systems that denied them would be able to demand the Palestinians' collective right to self-determination.

In contrast to Sami's understanding of HR discourse as an alternative to militancy, Ann thought that when her trainees "have a culture of human rights, they will want to choose a different form: not negotiations, but armed resistance—when they know their rights." Ann was not herself militant, nor did she advocate militancy in her courses. Given that she focused on non-violent ways of solving interpersonal conflict, her suggestion that knowing one's rights might lead people to take up arms may seem a somewhat odd conjecture. Despite this disjuncture between her speculations and her actual goals and actions, I was not surprised by her comment, because it is commonly believed and often declared that international law guarantees the right to resist occupation by any means (although it is a controversial issue).[16] This understanding of human rights awareness as a prompt for armed resistance also emerges from a nexus of beliefs and experiences common to many Palestinians, especially since the conclusion of the first intifada. There is broad recognition of the failure of negotiations at the highest levels of politics, of the inefficacy of the human rights system and the UN's inability to end the occupation and its abuses. These disappointments have combined with a rejuvenated notion of citizenship in which action and a concerted effort to change the status quo are central. For Ann, teaching human rights meant teaching people that they have the right to change their society. Because negotiations and other means have been unsuccessful, armed resistance should remain an option (even though it too has failed).

The significance of Ann's work of reminding Palestinians what their human rights are was brought home to me in a session dedicated to identifying rights violations in news items from the local press. Ann summarized a story about a woman who was in her ninth month of pregnancy trying to visit her family in a neighboring town. While being delayed by Israeli soldiers at a checkpoint, she went into labor, and because the soldiers refused to allow her passage, she could not reach a hospital and was forced to give birth at the military barrier—a common event during the second intifada (UNGA 2005). In response to Ann's call for commentary and analysis, the children offered their opinion that this woman's "husband should not have let her go, knowing she might get stuck at the checkpoint and have to give birth there." Not only did this response reveal the conservative gender attitudes among these teenagers, but it also showed the degree to which they had become accustomed to the occupation. They told me that getting used to (ta'aklam) the occupation should be a priority (see also Allen 2008). It was just this kind of implicit acquiescence to the occupation that one of the leaders of the NGO had been railing against throughout the second intifada, because this pragmatic adaptation was a harbinger of defeat (*hazimah*), an indication that the logic of the occupation had infiltrated people's consciousness. One of the goals of this human rights project, and of the work of the NGO as a whole, was to counteract such resignation. Ann offered a different perspective on the story, reminding the youth that everyone has "the right to move around." When she asked for suggestions on how to achieve that right, one student asserted clearly, "Get rid of the occupation." Another called out, "Freedom."

Conclusion

The central role that Palestinians and the international community accord to human rights as a badge of state legitimization means that the concept of human rights has come to mediate key aspects of sometimes opposing efforts at directing social change. On one side were the security officers, who received the message that they *were* the state in the making, or at least its most important reflection. They understood themselves to be the arm fundamentally responsible for the state's orderly progress and functioning. By regulating "the citizens" according to human rights standards (as embodied in the Palestinian Basic Law), they could acquire a better *image* in front of local and international audiences, and thus be better able to fulfill their role and deserve a state. Many citizens, however, had become afraid of the PA security apparatus. Civil and civilian society increasingly understood itself to be a distinct group, and "the citizen" was portrayed as a character inherently rebellious to security personnel. On the other side, NGOs mobilized human rights education to teach youth what their civil, as well as their national and nationalist, rights should be. Human rights workshops gave teenagers an opportunity to learn about the basics of democracy, and to acknowledge that they should not tolerate the abuses of the occupation. These sessions were also a forum in which to discuss what was wrong with the PA and its abuses. Human rights was a framework through which to articulate the egalitarian political, social, and family structure towards which they wanted to work.

One might object that human rights courses are an insignificant arena of struggle over power and meaning in Palestine. After all, they reach only a fraction of Palestinian security agents and the population as a whole. They are neither coordinated nor rigorously evaluated, and many bear signs of ineffectual pedagogy, which makes it easy for security trainees and observers to dismiss human rights training as farcical. It is precisely the superficiality of these train-ings and their utilitarian nature that contributes to a widely held perception that human rights are a tool for achieving power and status for the aspirational state and its functionaries, rather than a set of aspirational values or a means of instituting just relations between state and society.

For those running programs for youth and for the academics in the Birzeit master's program, however, human rights education offers a kind of "internal strength." Those who offered the programs I observed believed that the knowl-edge of one's rights and the understanding that human rights apply to one's own situation affect trainees' sense of self, their belief in their own agency. Unlike the courses for officers, the programs for youth were situated within a distinct political imagination in which the methods and discourse of human rights could underwrite and energize public activism in order to counteract the pacification wrought by Oslo. Across all levels of training—content, dis-course, performance—Palestinian organizations like those of Hani, Sami, and Ann mobilized human rights education to effect changes in the nature of social relations in Palestine. They understood, promoted, and enacted citizenship not primarily as a status moored to individuals with natural rights, but as a mode of social engagement.

Although EU states promote human rights training in order to support sta-bility and economic development and because it fosters markets and invest-ment, the Palestinian NGOs and institutions that focus on youth are not so interested in the economic value of human rights and, rather, develop rights training as a way to nurture nationalist consciousness. Palestinians' own tren-chant critiques of the human rights industry, which resonate with scholars' criticisms of human rights as "the leading edge of empire's vanguard" (Goodale 2005:556), have left open a space in which they produce their own meanings and political projects. These cannot be subsumed under the labels of "imperial-ism" or "liberalism," or be critiqued as a kind of false consciousness.

Human rights education has presented various models of citizenship and plans for Palestinian state-building: for individuals like Ra'id, who are making peace with a personal transition from nationalist rebel to child rights advo-cate; for a generation of college students trying to plan for their future in an unstable economy; and for security forces being told to "respect citizens" while following orders to quash the Islamist opposition but not get caught torturing. What remains to be seen is if the cultural processes of citizenship (cf. Ong 1996:737) activated by human rights training lead to, or reinforce, contrasting if not irreconcilable modes of subjectification that make not only state-building, but also nationalism, impossible. The next chapters describe the PA's and Hamas's efforts to perform and create a state in the West Bank and Gaza Strip, and the role that nationalism plays in the decidedly mixed results achieved among the many local audiences to whom those performances were directed.

Chapter 4

Making Up the Face of the State

Human Rights in the Creation of Political Authority

D URING A DISCUSSION I HAD IN 2009 with a Palestinian UN worker, Bashir, who is involved in human rights training for PA security personnel, recalled with amusement a telling exchange he once had with a civilian police director:

> One time the head of police in the West Bank and Gaza Strip said to me—this is the top security officer in the police—he said, "I don't send my cadre to your training because of you or because of human rights, but for my reports to the Europeans." He said, "As director of police I do respect human rights, but I want cars and arms. I want something out of this." He told me this straight out!

According to Bashir's analysis of the exchange, PA security personnel consider human rights to be something like makeup for a face that they present. It is a performance used "to send a message to the international community that we respect human rights and we deserve a state," not something related to their actual behavior or rules. Bashir, the police chief, and other trainers recognize the instrumental deployment of human rights discourse and activities. All these actors understand that they "do human rights" in order to get foreign goodies, and to demonstrate "stateness" through the illusion of complying with the codes of conduct expected of states. Much of the PA budget relies on donor funds, so if the donors are worried about PA rights violations, so is the PA.

The incorporation of human rights routines, rituals, and displays into a government's apparatus has become standard practice for most states (excepting those willing to suffer the label of "rogue"). The rights regime (including its professed values, institutions, actors, and practices), and law more generally, shapes subjectivities and political claim-making in Palestine (Allen 2009a; Fassin 2008; Feldman 2008; Kelly 2006), as elsewhere. From Colombia to Iran, the United Kingdom, and beyond (Kelly 2012; Merry 2011; Osanloo 2009; Tate 2007), the human rights system has become a central element of the conception of state legitimacy. It is necessary window dressing that is hung to prettify, and sometimes to block the view of what is really happening inside, where, in the Palestinian case, the pseudo-state is committing a range of abuses.[1]

A variety of actors take part in the performance of human rights and of the state in the West Bank, including PA security services and the Independent Commission for Human Rights (ICHR), the quasi-state human rights organization that monitors the PA. The United States and Israel make the loudest demands of the PA for "law and order" of a particular sort, one that tolerates and even encourages human rights violations in the West Bank PA's pursuit of political dominance,[2] but it also includes international donors who support the human rights system. The West Bank PA has hinged the production of its own stateness on distinguishing itself as a state and defining its relationship to society through two key performances directed toward these audiences: one is the use of force through its security sector, the other is a stated commitment to human rights law, in part enacted through its interactions with the ICHR. However, none of these performances is fully convincing to the Palestinian people. Affixing the banner of human rights or statehood to a nonsovereign entity like the PA, an assemblage that is not able to perform adequately many of the most basic exercises of governance, has paradoxical effects, at once building a facade of the state and drawing attention to its fragility.

Analysis of the interactions and performances of these actors and audiences reveals some key things about the discursive and ethical aspects of state-making in Palestine, and how the lines connecting performance and audience crisscross and convince, or not. Despite their antagonistic relations, the PA and the ICHR are important elements of each other's existence. Ironically, it is in their claims to autonomy from each other, and in their assertions of power over each other, that the PA and the ICHR constitute themselves to themselves. However, their squabbles for authority and influence occur in an echo chamber. Although human rights and security are the contradictory means by which the PA and the international community have tried to help build the PA as a state, what in fact shapes the actions, efficacy, and authority of the PA and the ICHR is a different political ethical complex. What determines their legitimacy in front of the Palestinian people are the values of nationalism and solidarity, populist principles, issues of class, and shared knowledge of political histories. The Westerners' money that buys the police cars and demands human rights performances is seen as having corrupted both Palestinian political values and the people who are bought and induced to act in insincere, non-nationalist ways. The PA's state-making efforts, with their focus on building up oppressive security forces and quelling the direct fight against occupation while performing support for human rights, are dissonant within a Palestinian nationalist idiom that speaks first and foremost of collective liberation. As the PA and the ICHR struggle to assert their authority over each other while seeking to please the United States, Israel, and donor countries, Palestinians' cynicism is incited. Their disdain grows in the cracks between the PA's pretensions to sovereignty, the ICHR's aspirations to protect human rights, and the overwhelming reality of military occupation and its abuses.

Max Weber, who defined the state as "'a compulsory association which organizes domination' through the means of physical force' also understood that 'in reality, obedience [to the legality of the state] is determined by highly robust motives of fear and hope—fear of the vengeance [. . . of] the power-holder, [and] hope for reward . . . '" (quoted in Aretxaga 2003:400; see also Weber 1978:54–56, 213–215). Missing from this definition is consideration of what happens when there is disdain and cynicism along with fear—not only of the state's vengeance, but also of its unchecked power—and for most people, not much hope, as is the case in Palestine. A state's powers are always subject to the observation, analysis, and more often criticism of the people, even when direct expression of this disdain is repressed (cf. Navaro-Yashin 2002:4). States, as Navaro-Yashin (2002) and Wedeen (1999, 2008) have demonstrated, can endure despite or even because of these critiques, because the discourses of deconstruction contribute to maintaining a fantasy of the state, which thereby remains "an object of psychic desire" (Navaro-Yashin 2002:4). In Palestine, however, because there is no fixed institutional arena of power that is accepted as "the state," because of the suspicion with which the human rights system is regarded, and because of the attachment that many Palestinians still have to a nationalist past, the critiques and cynicism have a special power to muddy the "state effect" (Mitchell 1999), blocking belief in the state as a separate authorized entity of power.

The Palestinian Independent Commission for Human Rights

An institutional site that has become common in processes of authorizing governments today is the national human rights institution (NHRI), sometimes called national human rights agency. Some five hundred such agencies exist today, the vast majority having been created during the 1990s (Cardenas 2003). Morocco, Saudi Arabia, and Jordan are among the Middle Eastern states that have set up NHRIs (Cardenas and Flibbert 2005). Like the ICHR, they are funded by international organizations, including the Ford Foundation, and in the case of the ICHR, by the state development agencies of Holland, Norway, and Sweden, among others. Most state human rights agencies, however, exist in states that are recognized as such. Palestine is something else, and it is this in-between condition of limbo, a condition that analysts and political actors only sometimes explicitly recognize as such, that makes it a particularly interesting place to observe how a state tries to prove itself, before people believe it, before it is reified.

The ICHR emerged in 1993 as the PA was being established. Based on a decree issued by the late president (then PLO chairman) Yasser Arafat at the urging of Hanan Ashrawi (a political negotiator, the ICHR's first director, and chair of the board of directors for the human rights NGO Miftah).[3] The ICHR, originally called the Palestinian Independent Commission for Citizens' Rights (PICCR), was set up as a Palestinian ombudsman and national human rights commission, with a mandate to ensure that all requirements to safeguard human rights are provided for in Palestinian legislation and in the work of the PA (ICHR 2009a). The PA has declared its commitment to international human rights covenants since its creation and has affirmed its adherence to these in Article 10 of the Amended Palestinian Basic Law of 2003.[4] The ICHR bases its analyses, interventions, and the curricula of its training sessions on the adoption of human rights standards in local law.[5] Also among its goals is the advancement of human rights in "propagating a culture of human rights through awareness raising and training" to make it part of "the value system of the Palestinian culture" (ICHR 2011a:5).

There are a variety of NHRI types, and the approach and structure of the ICHR is not unusual. Broadly speaking, the mission of most NHRIs includes "implementation of international human rights standards by acting as 'guardians,' 'experts' and 'teachers' of human rights" (Peacebuilding Initiative n.d.). The Principles Relating to the Status of National Institutions, known as the Paris Principles, were adopted by the UN in 1993 and outline what are considered to be the international minimum standards for national institutions.[6] The ICHR was certified in 2009 as an "A-status" NHRI, which indicates accreditation for its full compliance with the Paris Principles (ICHR 2009e).

Practitioners and scholars almost uniformly agree that NHRIs "have emerged as the most important mechanisms for domestic protection and promotion of international human rights standards," with one writer going so far as to refer to them as "almost revolutionary" (Pohjolainen 2006:8, 164). Numerous assessment reports and manuals have been written about how to increase their efficacy.[7] Critical studies of NHRIs may discuss the extent to which a given institution fails to live up to its mandate or serves as a legitimizing cover for a government that continues its noncompliance with human rights standards, but in most studies, human rights standards are left unquestioned and fixed as the benchmark of evaluation.[8] Less analyzed, however, are the clashes and concatenations of goals, memberships, techniques, and values involved in interactions between state, civil society,[9] citizens, and NHRI actors.[10]

The ICHR's work consists of, among other things, regularized forms of scrutiny of the PA, including scheduled visits to prisons; analysis of the PA's performance, judged according to Palestinian and international human rights law; and receipt of citizens' complaints against the PA for a range of abuses—from grievances over civil servants' delayed job promotion to torture.[11] They produce a variety of publications, including a quarterly magazine and annual report; they write reports for regional human rights publications; and they conduct awareness-raising sessions for the public on a variety of rights issues. Their reports circulate widely, and local, regional, and international news outlets convey their findings, from the Arabic language site of Agence France-Presse to the unofficial website of Hamas. They have become a trusted source of information for scholars and analysts interested in Palestine as well.

The ICHR has expanded noticeably in the decade and a half since its establishment. It has secured long-term institutional funding, especially from Scandinavian governments, which supports work in five regional offices in the West Bank and Gaza Strip and a large central headquarters in Ramallah.[12] Filling the well-appointed offices with an energetic bustle is a mostly young, educated staff of more than fifty employees. Many fieldworkers have undergraduate law degrees, as well as experience in NGOs, and senior members encourage newer employees to pursue advanced education. The head director and research director have master's degrees in human rights from universities in the United Kingdom and Geneva, and the most recent chief commissioner, Mamdouh Aker, is a practicing surgeon. There is a well-defined organizational structure, and a clearly organized website in both English and Arabic. As at other NGOs, employees at the ICHR vie for the perks of travel and training abroad, and squabbles over opportunities for career advancement attest to the professionalized nature of their work. Also similar to staff in other HROs, ICHR staff members come to work with a variety of motivations. Some described to me their dedication to their job in community service terms, as being fueled by a sincere desire to help their society. Others who were somewhat less enthusiastic recognized their work as having only very gradual and minimal effects. "We write letters to ministries. The security services are annoyed by our work, but not much beyond that."

Although the ICHR is self-defined as scrupulously nonpartisan (Azzam 1998:341), some of the individuals who work there come from political and activist backgrounds. Some are former communists, or leftists who previously channeled their activism into HRO work elsewhere, and others were part of Fateh's youth movement on college campuses or were active with that party during the first intifada. The ICHR is not a homogenous entity; it includes people—some with current or former party political ties—who together try to balance the organization along a fine line between outright opposition and collaboration with the PA.

Despite the PA being the ICHR's founder and the source of its legal mandate, there is mutual distrust between PA and ICHR actors, fueled by class divisions and sometimes oppositional political goals. Agents of the PA see the ICHR as part of "global civil society" and as too disconnected from the realities of the Palestinian political situation, a designation fraught with class resentments. Some in the ICHR see the PA as dangerous, in part because its members have not been suitably educated into "modernity," in which a state must be an honest, neutral broker. At the same time, the shared political histories of individuals in the PA and the ICHR can also facilitate the work of the ICHR.

The tensions were apparent during ICHR training workshops (see Chapter 3) where the members of the security forces expressed their sense that they were being "picked on" by the ICHR. One senior ICHR trainer recognized this tension explicitly in his presentation to a room of officers, insisting that the ICHR was there with them "as part of a partnership." "Maybe," he said, "you were used to thinking that the idea of human rights comes from the West, from the outside, that you are in one valley and we in human rights are in another; but now we must continue together." State and society, he urged, must work hand in hand through a partnership of security and civil society. In an attempt to forge an alliance, some ICHR staff highlighted shared political attitudes, but in these explicitly pedagogical spaces, the boundary between the PA and the ICHR was assumed.

Despite the senior ICHR trainer's cozy encouragement to the officers that they all "continue together," it was clear that many members of the ICHR did put themselves across a distinct dividing line that was marked by class assumptions as much as by human rights concerns. The class divide was expressed in a variety of forms, from dress to education. Whereas many of the ICHR staff I met were clothed in the hip fashions of the Ramallah elite (see Taraki 2008)—jeans, sports jackets, and pointy shoes for the men; form-fitting clothes for some of the women—the PA security trainees wore either uniforms or street clothes, with less of a studied chic casualness than their counterparts. The ICHR staff were well educated, many having a degree in law; some of the security personnel had not attended college at all. More than one ICHR trainer told me that the ICHR considered the ranks of the security forces to be filled with hardheaded "military types who won't change."[13] They made comments about the limited education of many of the officers and their overwhelming "ignorance" of human rights. A field researcher in one northern West Bank town said that he has better success with the more educated security personnel, who are "more open-minded," and he noted that a young, "baby-faced" ICHR lawyer was not faring well with his rougher security trainees.

On the other side, officers complained that human rights activists had idealistic expectations. Invoking the distinction between their circumstances and those of wealthy Europeans, more than one officer exclaimed that "Palestine is not Switzerland!" It was a frustrated response to what they saw as unreasonable demands being made on their limited resources, as individuals, as a security force, and as a poor nonstate. In a somewhat veiled acknowledgment of such tensions, a senior ICHR director confronted her employees during a staff meeting with the observation that there is a lack of "confidence and respect" between participants and trainers. The chilly and sometimes tense interactions between the ICHR and security personnel during training sessions, evident even in their segregation during breaks and lunches, reflected an entrenched and embodied divide between the two sectors.

In the context of ICHR trainings, sociological distinctions and popular resentment of "the NGO elite" contributed to the division between "state" and "society." The dynamic relationship between them is marked by a contest over who has the authority to oversee civil society. Since its establishment, the PA has been preoccupied with vying for authority over the NGO sector and its funds. In the years after the Hamas takeover of Gaza, officials and others sympathetic to the government's perspective explained to me that what motivated the PA's interactions with HROs was a matter of ensuring proper oversight: not just anyone should be allowed to open an NGO and get all that donor money. Farid, a young lawyer at the Ministry of Interior (MoI), was also concerned about the inappropriate or even nefarious agendas that HROs pursued, such as an NGO advocating on behalf of what he took to be skewed priorities, including the rights of gay women in Palestine. To be sure, NGOs in Palestine, as elsewhere, are largely unaccountable to anyone but their donors. However, in Farid's opinion, it was not the Palestinian people who should have a greater say in the organization of NGO aid. Rather, the PA should be responsible for centralizing the funds and messages on behalf of Palestinians, including these NGOs. Members of the PA consider themselves to be the legitimate, rightful authority charged with organizing everything from traffic and the armed forces to the structure of civil society. Through such wrangling, the role of each sector was being negotiated, while the dividing line between them was etched ever deeper.

The relationship between the PA and the ICHR is not straightforward or singular, however. In practice, the two institutions are deeply intertwined, ultimately buttressing each other's authority within a mix of hostilities and convergences. The mitotic process dividing state from (civil) society, or creating the image of a clean parturition, which some scholars contend is a necessary ingredient for modern statehood, can never be fully achieved in a context in which people know each other too well. State legitimation is a unique kind of problem in a place where people carry intimate knowledge of the political histories of individuals, and where the antipathies toward social groups and political positions are deepened by class distinctions.

Red Tuesday

Analysis of the ICHR's involvement in an incident involving the PA reveals more about the multiple kinds of performances, audiences, and moral groundings that are involved in efforts to assert authority. On June 24, 2007, scuffles broke out between student members of the two rival Palestinian parties, Hamas and Fateh, at an-Najah National University, a private university in the northern West Bank town of Nablus. The clashes escalated and, in the end, one student was dead of a gunshot wound. Several were injured (PICCR 2007).

Relevant background to this episode, dubbed "Red Tuesday," returns to the ongoing struggle for power between Fateh and Hamas that led to the Islamists' takeover of the Gaza Strip in June 2007. This struggle went back to the democratic general elections—albeit held under Israeli occupation—that gave Hamas a majority in the Palestinian Legislative Council (PLC) in January 2006. An international financial and political boycott of the new Hamas government followed, led by the United States and the European Union, while a thoroughly disgruntled Fateh, which had grown used to dominating the PA and controlling its resources, posed a challenge on the inside. Repeated clashes between the military wing of Hamas and security forces belonging to the PA over the following year intensified into generalized fighting in Gaza on June 7, 2007. That round of fighting alone took the lives of 161 Palestinians, including 41 civilians, and left some 700 wounded (PCHR 2007a).[14]

Immediately after the bloody events in Gaza and the takeover of power by Hamas there, the administration of an-Najah National University decided to ban all student political and media activities, except those organized through the university's student union. The administration said that this was to avoid creating opportunities for friction among the students. Despite their verbal commitment to the decision, the Islamic students bloc engaged in public political actions on the campus. They also issued a declaration condemning the arrest of a number of students by Israeli forces. Fateh students were angered by what they saw as a breach of the rules against public student activities, and violence broke out.

Armed men who were not students but subsequently understood to be from Fateh or the PA or both, entered the campus and started firing shots into the air, as did members of the university security. Toward the end of the melee, a group of armed men in civilian clothes dragged a bearded student to the ground, beat him, and shot him point-blank. According to one eyewitness testimony published by the ICHR (then called PICCR), a few students had taken photographs of the incident with their mobile phones, but the university security "either confiscated or totally smashed them on the spot." Despite the large number of eyewitnesses to the killing, by August 5 the public prosecutor's office had declared the case closed and the perpetrator unknown, less than two weeks after the incident.[15]

The ICHR had commenced a separate investigation. According to the ICHR, it postponed the release of its fact-finding report "in order to allow time for the public prosecutor's office to complete its investigation into" (PICCR 2007:2) the killing of this student member of Hamas. The standard procedure that the ICHR follows is first to write a letter to the relevant organization or security service. If that is insufficient, they then write to the MoI, and then to the prime minister, sharing their observations. "Sometimes this results in the dismissal of the culprit," the chief commissioner told me. In the case of Red Tuesday, "when the prosecutor failed to reach tangible conclusions," the ICHR went ahead and published its fact-finding report (PICCR 2007). In it, the ICHR assigned blame to all the parties involved, especially the university administration, the security forces, and the public prosecutor. According to the ICHR, restrictions on freedom of opinion and expression and other liberties inside the university created the conditions leading to the violence. The report advised the university "to take all the necessary [steps] that would guarantee . . . the right to exercise freedom of opinion and expression." What was also generally understood—but nowhere stated in print—was that the public prosecutor did not pursue the case because it was allegedly a member of Fateh who had killed the student.[16] It is widely known that al-Najah's board of trustees and administration have historically been affiliated with Fateh, which is also the dominating party in the PA. A businessman from Nablus told me he would not be surprised if there had been a great deal of party pressure from Fateh and a cover-up.

In response to the ICHR report, a local newspaper published a denunciation of the ICHR in the name of Fateh at an-Najah National University (PIC 2007a). This statement condemned the ICHR for being biased, unobjective, and not independent.[17] It asked why the ICHR did not write reports about things that Hamas had done, it decried the ICHR for criticizing the efforts of the PA security forces, and it reaffirmed the work of the public prosecutor. The statement raised questions about the foreign funding of the ICHR, called for an investigation into its finances, and ominously accused the director and members of the staff of having particular—but unnamed—political leanings that are "known among our people."

Public denunciation—in the form of leaflets or published statements—is a common form of political discourse in Palestine (Peteet 1996). Raising suspicions about the nationalist commitment of a group or person can be a dangerous form of attack. Collaboration with the Israeli occupation, or treason, for example, is against the law and has frequently led to extrajudicial execution-style killings. In this case, it is the ties to foreign funding that offered fodder for casting aspersions. Although the statement was basically an ad hominem attack, it trotted out bald nationalist appeals to underwrite the defensive censure.

A lawyer at the ICHR told me, "We did not respond [to the attack] in the papers. We communicated with the university, we met with the president, and he assured us that they respect the Commission and its right to work, and it won't be obstructed." When I asked the same lawyer if he was worried by these attacks, he responded by saying,

> We are legal, working in line with the responsibilities we were granted by the presidential decree. The Commission will not back down from its responsibilities. . . . We don't face real threats, just the occasional challenge from one side or another—the police, the Preventive Security—but this is normal, part of our work. The Commission is established. Its existence is not in danger. It has proven itself. For example, we've called the director of the Palestinian police and met with him, and we've called Legislative Council representatives for meetings, and the head of the secret police . . . and the cabinet secretary. Even PA employees come to us with complaints.

In these responses, the authority of the ICHR is underwritten by the mere interaction it has with PA officials. The fact that it can call meetings with officials and they respond is cited as evidence of the ICHR's authority. It is a strange inversion of Althusser's (1971) notion of interpellation. In his example, it is the policeman who whistles and the random pedestrian who knows himself to be "hailed" and thus responds as a subject of the "Ideological State Apparatus." Here it is the state that is hailed, and it is in responding to that whistle that subjection occurs. The response is evidence of the PA recognizing itself as being responsible for abuses. It is a recognition that is part of enacting an accountable state.

Although the work of the ICHR is ostensibly to ensure that human rights and Palestinian law are implemented, in practice it bolsters both the legitimacy of the law as a standard and the legitimacy of the PA as being at once the implementing mechanism of the law and beholden to it. An ICHR fieldworker explained that one of his tactics in trying to obtain compliance from security officials is to "remind them that they *are* the legitimate government. They are not like Hamas; they didn't instigate a coup." Reaffirmation of the power and legitimacy of the law as a reflection and arm of the state occurred continually in practice and discourse. As in the human rights trainings, invocation of the law is a means of teaching PA representatives what the acceptable, and preferred, sources for authoritative action should be.

These ICHR and PA practices, including the human rights trainings, the prison visits, the bureaucratic interactions, the organization of state offices, and the stated regulations that define them, have shaped the self-understanding of these officials from both the ICHR and the PA. For example, a prison director told me that he permits ICHR visits to his prison "because this is the law. The law says this organization should have access. I'm not afraid of him," he said, indicating the young, clean-cut ICHR staff member there on a monthly inspection. "I am required to let him in by the law." It is no excuse if the law is idealistic or we lack the supplies to fulfill legal requirements in the prison, he said. "The law is the law. The law is my situation." (Of course, what he left unsaid was the extent to which his prison—with its overcrowding, political prisoners, and torture—does not, in fact, always obey the law. They justify themselves to themselves by maintaining the facade of following the letter of the law, including human rights standards.)

So why do these officials come when called, so to speak? What *is* the source of the ICHR's authority? And what *kind* of authority is it?

The people I spoke with at the ICHR agreed with one simple response: everyone wants to *look like* they respect human rights. In the estimation of one fieldworker, individuals within the security apparatus may have different attitudes, approaches, and motivations. There are those in the security forces who are educated and who want to respect the law. Some were themselves tortured by the Israelis and, continuing the cycle of abuse, do as they were done to. There are others who dismiss the concept of human rights as a foreign import. The head of a security force baldly stated to a British member of an international "reform project" that all the bother about human rights was so much bunk. However, no one can afford to *appear* to contravene human rights standards. Such standards, in and of themselves, are a measure of international legitimacy. Security agents responsible for rounding up Hamas took great pains to assure me that their agency respects law and human rights (disregarding much evidence to the contrary, including the fact that the trial of civilians in military courts and their incarceration in military prisons is in absolute contravention of Palestinian law).

This all may seem obvious. Of course they want to appear to respect human rights, but that obviousness is just a testament to how central human rights performances have become to the conception of state legitimacy. Stateness is similarly performed in other "weak" states, such as Colombia (Tate 2007), and engagement with the human rights system justifies the exercise of power in many places, including the United States and Iran (Abu-Lughod 2002; Osanloo 2009). The PA, in order to be a state, has to respond to the ICHR as a record of its own responsibility. The ICHR functions partially to substantiate the state to itself as a manifestation of its own power.

In a system in which everyone understands that they have to *look like* they respect human rights, a space opens up for what Ilana Feldman (2008:273) calls bureaucratic "citational practice," in which the regularized human rights monitoring of the PA produces a kind of "self-referential reiterative authority." Human rights categories are being engraved into the work and public face of the PA as a state that recognizes its own responsibilities. They have become institutionalized in new bureaucratic structures, such as the Democracy and Human Rights Unit and the complaints department, which are part of the civilian police department. In stating, reproducing, and insisting on a catalog of the rights and responsibilities of state authorities and citizens, the ICHR carves the PA itself into a more fixed form.

The self-authorizing effect of repetitive human rights practices is evident in the ICHR's own self-perception. It believes that it has some kind of authority—and legitimacy—because state officials want to look like they respect human rights, because they "have to" listen to the ICHR, "have to" respect human rights—all because the ICHR was established by the PA. A research director told me, "We're not just another run-of-the-mill NGO," sniffing with offense at what he took to be my putdown of his authority when I asked him why the MoI would bother to take his calls. The ICHR was established by a presidential decree, he reminded me; thus its existence likewise substantiates the state, because being the product of a presidential decree is a manifestation of the state's power. "After fifteen years we have proved that we are professional and respectable. They listen," the chief commissioner told me.

It seems as though the lines tracing the paths of authority and legitimacy have begun to look like the art of M.C. Escher, in which the drawing hand and that which is being drawn are so intertwined one cannot determine figure from background, picture from frame. To spell out the circular logic of legitimacy: The president of the PA establishes a state human rights organization, funded by international donors. The PA also mobilizes massive resources to bolster the "security sector," also funded by international donors. The security sector commits human rights violations against the state's own citizens. The state human rights agency, the ICHR, condemns these violations. The PA responds to these condemnations—because the PA established the ICHR. The ICHR gains authority because the PA responds to it. The PA gains legitimacy because it responds to the ICHR, to look good in front of its citizens and its donors. However, who the PA and the ICHR are really performing for, at least in this human rights guise, is each other.

The battles between the ICHR and the security services, sharing human rights and nationalism as their common discursive and performative idioms, are in and of themselves performances of state authority. They "announce and enact" (Wedeen 2003:74) political power by acting like a state and a state monitor, thus sustaining each other's existence. Lisa Wedeen (1999, 2003) has addressed a similar set of questions about how states struggle to produce authority in circumstances of incomplete sovereignty. In her work on Syria and Yemen she has attended to the power of performances and spectacles, especially when the performances seem "bogus." As she argues, state power is further embedded every time a fake election is held or a spectacle of patriotism is well-attended by an unenthusiastic crowd, because the state's ability to induce actions or prevent revolt is performed for all to see.

Wedeen's analysis focuses especially on state-citizen dynamics, but the case of Red Tuesday draws attention to a tighter circle of state performativity. The frameworks of accountability for the PA and the ICHR are focused inward; as noted earlier, they are performing human rights for each other—and their international observers. For example, ICHR staff point to the growing number of complaints received and pursued as evidence of the Commission's success, as did the national officer of a foreign state funder that supports the ICHR (see also ICHR 2008:7). Although this actuarial logic obscures the minimal substantive results that come out of the ICHR's work, the ICHR is contributing to the "routines and rituals of state" (Corrigan and Sayer 1985:5). These loops of call and response illustrate Abercrombie and Turner's (1978:153) insight that the dominant ideology—in this case, that of state authority—"has far more significance for the integration and control of the dominant class itself" than for the rest of the citizenry. Palestinians' general recognition of the PA as a conglomeration of interests squabbling in an echo chamber, devoid of sincere nationalist concern, is part of what undermines the credibility of those trying to create a state.

At play as well, however, are prosaic features of the organization's authority—an authority that simply contributes to staff members' ability to carry out their tasks. Despite the fact that the Palestinian national human rights institution has been compared favorably to other Arab NHRIs for having "attained a degree of autonomy in confronting governments"—unlike those in Saudi Arabia or Egypt, which "have been unable to establish legitimacy in society because they are seen as government organizations" (El Fegiery 2008)—networks of personal ties, subtle forms of persuasion, and the character and reputation of individuals shape the dynamic in Palestine as well. Although the ICHR grounds itself in a "modern" logic of bureaucratic rule—in which the source of authority is supposed to come not from the person but from his or her structural position in an institution (Osborne 1994)—what happens on the ground is more fluid.

The informal aspect of ICHR's functioning is encouraged by the nature of the judicial system in Palestine, which is not fully functioning. Rumors of political partisanship sully the reputations of district attorneys. Judges are afraid to work, lest rulings unfavorable to powerful people or extended families ricochet back against themselves.[18] Many people do not even bother to pursue a case in the courts, believing them not to be fair or even functioning. This is what a working group at Birzeit University's Institute of Law labeled "alienation from the judiciary," which they attributed in part to the Israeli occupation for entrenching a general "disrespect for the law and thwart[ing] the development of a rule of law culture in Palestine" (Birzeit University Institute of Law 2009:8, 41; see also Brown 2003:24).[19] Instead, more local methods of dispute resolution are favored, in which face-to-face conversation mediated by respected members of the community tends to—or is at least intended to—lead to mutually accepted solutions (Birzeit University Institute of Law 2006:39, 2009:8; Welchman 2008). Criteria that depend on more intimate knowledge, such as individual personality, a reputation for fairness and level-headedness, and the social prestige of a particular extended family, constitute more meaningful sources of authority.

Nationalist motivations, solidarities, histories, and values are still fundamental to how many things get done—or are blocked—in Palestine. An ICHR fieldworker said his successes negotiating with security personnel were largely based on his personal relationships with members of the security agencies. He himself had been a member of Fateh, active during the first intifada and imprisoned for seven years for his efforts. That experience gives him some credibility and authority in the society. Many of the members of PA security are men of his generation, people who were part of the same nationalist struggle, people he knew well from their time in prison together. He is not happy that his work depends on these social factors, he told me, but he recognizes their utility. Others in the ICHR are quite close to the state as well. The commissioner himself has the easy ear of Prime Minister Fayyad and President Abbas, as he had the ear of Arafat before them. Even if blueprints for the state-building of institutions like those of the World Bank advocate for an impersonal bureaucratized state, the work of institutions involves actual personal relations, with their own nationalist histories and moral logics that are quite separate from "human rights," bureaucratic rules, and national and international law.

Yet such personal ties can hinder the work of the ICHR as well, and once again it is the political, national context that informs how and why this happens. Yasser, an ICHR fieldworker in the north described the difficulties he faced when he started working with the ICHR. One of his cousins, with whom he shares a last name, was a regional Hamas commander. The PA officials with whom Yasser had to interact took an immediate dislike to him, associating him with Hamas, their bitter enemy. When he went to visit Hamas political prisoners as one of his ICHR duties, he was escorted by security guards who announced him to the Hamas prisoners scornfully as "the cousin of your leader." Family ties and their intertwined political associations still often determine how people regard one another.

Moreover, some ICHR staff members' work histories with other human rights organizations play into the ways in which state officials try to discredit ICHR. Unsurprisingly, many people with experience working at HROs have been employed at the ICHR. The director was once a director of Al-Haq. Other field researchers from Al-Haq did the same work at the ICHR. A lawyer from the MoI described these people as being leftist opponents of the PA and of the Oslo Accords. He referred to these human rights genealogies and the personal and political histories of ICHR staff in his assertions that the ICHR is not independent. The same logic partially dictated the nature of the attack against ICHR after Red Tuesday. As one lawyer familiar with the case explained to me, "It is likely that Fateh was more concerned to smear the general commissioner [Mamdouh Aker], not the organization itself, because the director had publicly denounced the actions of both Hamas and Fateh for causing the bloody turmoil in Gaza."

After this incident, the MoI in Ramallah launched a more bureaucratic and formal attack, undertaking an investigation into the legality of the ICHR itself. This approach may be one more step in the PA's nascent attempts to lay the legal framework for its authoritarian practices, following patterns established elsewhere in the Arab world (Brown 2003:20). The MoI has called into question the legitimacy of the presidential decree that established the ICHR, as well as the ownership of the land on which its headquarters is built. A lawyer for the MoI presented the MoI's case to me, insisting that the presidential decree actually carried no official authority. "It was written on the back of a napkin," he said. "It was just something Arafat said, a decree, not a law—and this was in 1993, before the Palestinian Authority was officially established."[20] The PA and the ICHR both perform their legitimacy through legal and human rights discourse. Even as they contest the others' application of that discourse, they reproduce it, and hence their own authority as representatives of it.

The question of how the performers perceive their audiences is crucial. As Prime Minister Fayyad understood the dynamic, Israelis are trying to cast "doubt on our trustworthiness, responsibility, and worse." The result, he said, was that "the international community put us virtually on trial, putting our capability and competence to the test." He had received the message that "the more immune from criticism our people were, the more we would be able to protect our political rights" (Farraj et al. 2009). It is generally understood that within the PA it is especially Prime Minister Fayyad who has been good with the international community in matters of finance and his finesse with PA presentation; this is "good" insofar as the EU and US governments seem to like him and his ways. As a Palestinian employee of an international funder told me, "He knows the jargon. Fayyad is claiming to build a state institution. He is a good manager and would never reject a donor report critical of PA abuses. His two-year state plan goes on about the importance of human rights and the role of civilian police. All of this looks good on paper, but in reality? It's something else." This contradiction between ideals and reality, between human rights and security, is lost on no one.

Law and Order in West Bank Cities

Any state-building process is more than a discursive exercise of self-definition or proclamation, and it constitutes itself only partially through pomp and human rights talk. The PA's engagement with the human rights regime highlights the performative aspect of state-making, but also reminds us how significant are the elements of what Blom Hansen and Steppurat (2006:296) have referred to as "de facto sovereignty . . . the ability to kill, punish, and discipline with impunity," and its often uneasy interaction with "sovereignty grounded in formal ideologies of rule and legality." The PA's ability to kill and punish has been heavily bolstered by the international community, which has been pouring millions of dollars into PA security forces, training them in "counterterrorism" measures and providing equipment. In the view of these donors, security sector reform is "essential to state building" (Y. Sayigh 2009:1).[21] A Palestinian security director I spoke with in Nablus had taken this sentiment on board. "We have to get our internal house in order first. Negotiations need calm. We have committed to a peaceful approach. In order to take control, first we have to prove ourselves. We have all this funding because we uphold our side of the bargain."

When the second intifada started to wind down around 2004 to 2005, English language news on Palestine began to focus on the successful efforts of the PA to impose "law and order in West Bank cities." One particularly glowing assessment published by the U.S. Department of State applauded the addition of "some 300 members of a special Palestinian Authority National Security Force equipped with new Kalashnikov assault rifles and wearing immaculate olive-green uniforms" as they "now cruise the streets of Nablus in soft-top jeeps, setting up checkpoints and arresting common criminals" (Bradley 2007). By 2007, the general chorus of praise for Prime Minister Fayyad and President Abbas and their crackdown on chaos in the West Bank had become persistent and widespread (see, for example, Harel and Issacharoff 2010).

As far as many in Palestine are concerned, however, the security agencies have been establishing something very different from law and order. In the midst of all the redeployed Palestinian police, along with their colleagues in the Presidential Guard, the secret police, the Preventive Security Agency, and the National Security Forces, many see on the near horizon an oppressive police state, an authoritarian regime along the lines of the Egyptian dictatorship under the now deposed Hosni Mubarak.

In 2007, human rights activists I spoke with insisted that Palestinian democratic traditions and an active civil society with long years of experience fighting the tyranny of military occupation would provide an adequate block to the PA's authoritarian tendencies.[22] Two years later, however, those same observers were not so sanguine. The HRO workers I talked to in 2009 expressed more worry about the renewed efforts of the PA to intimidate them. An activist from a prisoner support organization told me how the PA's repressive activities were expanding:

> Even a demonstration organized by an NGO was not allowed! They even tear-gassed PLC members. They set up checkpoints between Ramallah, Bethlehem, and Nablus so that nobody could get into Ramallah for a *Hizb al-Tahrir* [a non-violent Salafi group] march [see ICG 2011]. Anyone who looked Islamist, anyone who had a beard, was pulled over. Hizb al-Tahrir doesn't do anything! It's just because the PA doesn't want anyone organizing anything.

The PA's ongoing refusal to allow public demonstrations has been praised by Israeli security analysts, but has incurred the disdain of the public.[23] Street demonstrations were a nationalist ritual throughout the first and second intifadas and have long been a central form of political expression in the occupied Palestinian territory. To Palestinians, it was anathema that their own government was preventing the performance of this nationalist practice, regardless of which political party was marching or which ideology was being expressed. The fact that those demonstrators who did dare to come out were violently beaten back—some fatally—was another cause of Palestinians' concern (Haaretz 2007).[24] The ICHR continues to publish reports documenting and condemning these and other violations committed by the governments in the West Bank and Gaza (see, for example, ICHR 2011b), but given the repetitive and ongoing nature of the abuses, it is difficult to see that those publications have enhanced human rights protections. Although there were a variety of opinions about how far the PA would go in trying to stymie HROs, or about how successful they might be, everyone outside the PA with whom I spoke agreed that the quasi-state's repressive apparatus was becoming more powerful. Further developments had cast a chill on their attitudes, and on their work. The increasingly active MoI in Ramallah had started questioning the legality of long-established NGOs, digging around for excuses to revoke their licenses and shut them down. Despite their concerns about possible recriminations, local NGOs continued to report on the PA's violations alongside Israel's, of which there were many. Censorship and the obvious ways in which media outlets affiliated with the PA present news biased in favor of that government were criticized (*Guardian* 2009; Electronic Intifada 2008; CPJ 2000), as was the PA's continued trying of civilians in military courts (Rabie' 2008). The death in PA detention of numerous political prisoners, including a mosque imam and others with suspected Hamas links, throughout the West Bank was another sobering trend.[25] The ICHR's general commissioner himself confronted Prime Minister Fayyad with evidence of ferocious forms of PA violations against Hamas, asking him if he was trying to turn Palestine into a police state. Ongoing incidents of oppression have fostered this pessimistic expectation among Palestinians in general. In addition to these concerns about personal safety and civil rights, what citizens have objected to most is the absence of a nationalist ethic in public displays of force by PA security agencies. That the PA is so beholden to its international audience, so anxious to try to prove its "responsibility" and protect itself from criticism in front of that audience, is an affront to other conceptions of the right relationship between state and society, a relationship in which nationalism and populism underwrite notions of legitimate authority.

Javier Solana, EU High Representative for the Common Foreign and Security Policy, said he was "very happy that everybody recognises the efforts
by the Palestinian Security Forces to guarantee security in the territories that
the Palestinians control" (EUPOL COPPS 2009). What that notion of security refers to is a matter of debate. In these Western discussions of Palestinian
"law and order," invasions by Israeli occupation forces get relegated to some
other analytical category—that of Israeli security—if they are considered at all.
Israeli incursions into areas supposedly under Palestinian control are not considered to be part of the dynamic that defines the "social order" demanded of
the PA. The fact that Israeli raids and arrests were a daily occurrence throughout the West Bank, that assassinations in the Gaza Strip were ongoing, and
that the pace of home demolitions in East Jerusalem was picking up was not
within the ambit of the Palestinian forces' security guarantees.[26] Never mentioned was the effect of the Oslo accords that established the PA in 1994, entailing Israeli withdrawals from occupied land that were only "partial, phased,
conditional and reversible."[27] Nor was the fact that Israel stipulates how the
security services can operate, and that the PA could do little to protect its citizens from such Israeli attacks anywhere in the occupied territory.[28] None of
this figured into the international evaluations of Palestinian law and order as a
precondition for state-building.

Solana's happy estimation that "everybody" positively recognizes the PA security efforts was, then, based on an exaggeration. Although some Palestinians
praised the increased levels of law and order in their neighborhoods (Lynch
2009), people grumbled to me privately about the ostentatious displays of the
security services' armed power on the streets. Many Palestinians I spoke with
had become afraid to speak at all, in fact, because they worried that the increasingly active secret police would overhear critical words not to their liking.[29]

The State's Compulsory Association

Such protestations are most evident whenever the PA-as-state presents itself as
a threat of violence and gives proof of its powers of coercion while performing
for the international community, such as when an important official comes to
town. What happened on Christmas Eve in 2007 during the Palestinian president's annual attendance at Christmas Mass is an apt illustration of how domination is organized, even when *dis*organized, and the disdain it provokes.

Following a tradition started by his predecessor, Yasir Arafat, PA President
Mahmoud Abbas (commonly known as Abu Mazen), was set to attend mid-

night Mass at the Church of the Nativity on December 24. Midmorning, Palestinian police and Presidential Guards spread out through the city and lined the main street of Bethlehem. Every few meters a young man stood, dressed in black uniform, pant legs tucked into high boots, black stocking caps on close-shaved scalps, carrying rifles and walkie-talkies, some importantly sporting wired earpieces. Both sides of the streets were covered with these sentinels. Police car horns blared as officers ordered drivers off the road in garbled voices amplified through loudspeakers. Their presence could be seen, and heard, everywhere.

The Guards were stern but very young. When I remarked on this to a friend he replied, caricaturing the logic of security, "They take them young. The test for being in the Presidential Guard is bringing the candidate a jar of sand and telling him to count the grains. Those who accept the task are hired." Others pointed out to me that high school diplomas are not a requirement for employment in the security services, and some claimed that candidates for the Presidential Guard must specifically promise not to pursue their studies (or get married). Using a fairly harsh local put-down, one critic concluded that "they only want donkeys"—stupid, stubborn animals; it was a sentiment echoed by many.

Abu Mazen came in shortly before midnight with a cavalcade of big SUVs ferrying important personalities. The streets had been a mess all day as civilian cars had been trying to get through intersections blocked off by security vehicles that were not sure where to go themselves. Everyone I came across that day complained about the chaos they caused. People were disgusted.

In Manger Square, Palestinian security had set up metal barricades to guide the line of visitors waiting to get into the church. By that evening, a large portion of the square was filled with SUVs with darkened windows, the favored vehicles of the *mukhabarat*—the not so secret police. Many were quite nattily dressed, all slicked up in long leather coats and gelled hair. Shepherding the waiting pilgrims were more young members of the Presidential Guard. There were two soldiers patrolling, rifles in hand, atop every building. One friend said it reminded him of the days when the Israeli occupation was still in town and there were *Israeli* soldiers everywhere. Likening the security services to Israeli occupation forces, the enemy of Palestinian nationalism, indicated just how suspicious people had become of the PA.

Such uncomplimentary views of the president and his enormous security retinue resounded whenever Abu Mazen moved anywhere within Ramallah, the seat of the PA in the West Bank, because it was always such a production.

Before he approached, the main streets of the city leading to his compound (the *muqata'ah*) were blocked off by security vehicles, and armed guards would stand all along the president's path. Cars were held at intersections for several minutes, some honking impatiently, no one exactly sure what was going on. Pedestrians would sometimes be directed to alternate routes, or they might stand around waiting to see the show. A procession of six or seven large SUVs and luxury cars with blackened windows would then speed through, a police motorcycle at the front and back of the line. Once they were through, traffic would resume and pedestrians would continue on their way.

After one such exhibition a friend remarked to me with contempt that such displays were in fact an indication of how little respect the president really commanded. "This shows you how unpopular he really is. He has to be so protected. He is so afraid." She initially thought, mistakenly it turns out, that the Palestinian security services were holding the rows of young men stopped along the sidewalks against their will, indicating just how likely people were to expect the worst of the security forces. (The youth were in fact just hanging out, watching the show.) Referring to the previous, departed president by his nickname, she went on: "Abu 'Ammar never had to stop traffic that way. He was never so afraid." A shopkeeper who had just watched the brief parade added, "This is how Arab leaders are. They're not for the people. Not with them." "Even the Pope, such an important person, drives around in an open car!" my friend pointed out.

Palpable in this and other, similar displays of PA force is a very self-conscious tension between the West Bank PA, trying so hard to assert and perform its authority, and the people's absolute unwillingness to go along with the show—or at least be convinced of it.[30] The PA is a state in the making that is being given many of the tools and trappings of a state—especially by the United States, which has been donating to the PA much of the technology and training so self-consciously displayed on the streets during these events (Stern 2007). It is, however, precisely such ostentatious performances—and the deep US pockets that fund them—that cloud the PA's authority in the eyes of the people. It was not only the chaos and inconvenience that caused disgruntled drivers to joke and sneer. Neither was it merely the inefficiency and apparent disorganization that was at the root of their disdain. It was the *excess*—the gratuitousness of these efforts. In their eyes, the PA did not have the right to block traffic, because it had not earned the respect of the people; it had no populist credentials. The PA was all show and little substance, and its shows were farcical.

Although these practices—blocking roads and disrupting daily life, incarceration and torture—may exemplify the excessive acts of brutality that some theories identify as the basis of sovereignty (Blom Hansen 2005:171), such practices can also delegitimize that sovereignty, contributing to its instability. It is the obvious efforts to create the dividing line between "state" and "society," physically enacted in such orchestrations of traffic separating the "official" from the people, that much of Palestinian society rejects.

The control or use of violence is not the only barometer according to which the PA is judged. Services, including education, water provision, and infrastructural upkeep, are other obligations that Palestinians in the West Bank expect the PA to fulfill. However, it is the misadventures of the security services that prompt much of Palestinians' talk about the PA. Decades of Israel's brutal occupation practices undertaken "for reasons of security" have made Palestinians acutely sensitive to the insecurities that security forces can inflict. An elderly man in a refugee camp provided another angle of insight into local conceptions of the PA and its failings. He told me with some indignation about a census that the UN had been conducting in the camps, to determine "who is in need and who isn't." He said that the UN, which has provided education, health, and other basic services to Palestinian refugee camps for decades, "now wants to reduce its services and limit what they provide to health and let the PA take over—but the PA is not taking over. Fifteen years of the PA and what have we got? Just more police, repressing the people; the PA taking money for themselves, not for the people." Pragmatic concerns regarding unfulfilled service provision, attention to the moral failings of self-serving politicians, and the risible overblown shows of force combined to discredit the PA.

What happened to Daoud, a recent college graduate and short-term PA security detainee, illuminates the extent to which the idea of the state, "as a claim to legitimacy, a means by which politically organized subjection is simultaneously accomplished and concealed" (Corrigan and Sayer 1985:7), has yet to convince or conceal in Palestine. During the Israeli attacks on Gaza in the winter of 2008 to 2009, Palestinian demonstrators marched in protest, some in support of Hamas, others simply in solidarity with the Gazan people. Daoud, a graphic artist with no official political affiliation and not sympathetic to Hamas, went out to observe a pro-Hamas rally that was passing through the center of Ramallah. He was watching the event from the margins, hundreds of meters from the center of the action. Suddenly, four men in civilian clothes grabbed him roughly when he raised his cell phone to take a picture. "Apparently there was a directive: no pictures. He didn't know it," his father, 'Abed, explained. Daoud was first arrested by the Preventive Security, then transferred to the civilian police, who then handed him over to the *mukhabarat*. All of his interrogations centered on his political party affiliation. "They thought he was Hamas," 'Abed said. He added that he and his son—who are politically independent but of leftist inclinations—are still being asked around town if they are Hamas.

I asked if they had complained to anyone about this treatment by the security services. I provoked them somewhat by asking how they could expect their rights to be respected if they did not demand them. Daoud's parents both shook their heads in frustration at my naivete. "No, no. To whom would we complain?" I suggested that the ICHR might be an option. "What would be the point? If you have no backing [*dhahr*], no political organization [*tanthim*] to protect you, you have nothing. You have no voice." Daoud was released after several frantic hours of his family calling around to friends and hospitals. In the end, a relative of Daoud's mother who is a member of the *mukhabarat* in a neighboring town tracked down where Daoud was being held and secured the young man's release through his personal-professional connections. Daoud got out, his father said, "because we know people who know people. Others aren't so lucky."

Discussion then turned to other forms of bias in the government. 'Abed, his wife, and her sister spoke about the growing repression of Hamas. Abed was appalled that "to be religious or pray is now an accusation." Zeena and Nadia, one a grade school principal, the other a teacher, talked about how politicized the Ministry of Education had become, noting that each change of government has meant a change in ministers and directors, without consideration for professional qualifications. "And now anyone working in the Ministry of Education who looks a certain way, bearded, or in *hijab*, or seems to be Hamas, is dismissed from the job," Zeena said, confirming reports by ICHR and what I had heard from many others.[31]

I asked why there was not more public outcry against this inequity. "What if Nadia decided to wear a hijab and was dismissed from her job for suspected Hamas sympathies? Would no one stand up for her?"

"How can we?" Nadia said. "These dismissals are an administrative matter, or at least passed off as such. No one officially comes out and says publicly that they're firing someone because they are Hamas."

"And who would we complain to?" Zeena added ruefully.

"Even if someone did raise a court case," 'Abed noted, "it would be years and years before the case is heard. You might forget what your job even was by the time you got to court." 'Abed, himself trained in law, regretted the unfairness inherent in this situation and exemplified in his son's case, but he could not see that there was any alternative. Of course there are those who make much more direct challenges to the authority of the PA, such as the family in the natal refugee camp of Abed's wife who threw a policeman out of a window when he came to deliver a court order informing them that one of the men in the family had to pay alimony to his divorced wife. The majority of Palestinians refuse to make complaints to the ICHR or take cases to regular courts, but some make their dissatisfaction known in simpler ways. As Tobias Kelly has shown in great ethnographic detail, in the occupied territory "local understandings of legal rights are rooted in particular relationships . . . [and] legal claims constantly shift between the moral and the instrumental" (2006:24). In refusing to try to take advantage of the institutional or official means by which to call the state to account and instead relying on personal connections, Daoud and his family in effect helped delegitimize the PA and the ICHR. Their cynicism and distrust have led them to deny the state a vote of confidence that recognition of its official bodies would entail. The actions of 'Abed and his family are both moral and instrumental.

To add insult to injury, 'Abed went on, he and his son were forced to apply for a "certificate of good conduct" from the Preventive Security, a requirement to be fulfilled when applying for visas for foreign travel.[32] It is also the case that Palestinians in the West Bank are required to get a certificate from security officials in order to apply for PA jobs and sometimes for other local jobs (although the Hamas MoI says it no longer requires such procedures). 'Abed's first grievance was with the inefficiency of the system. "It took more than two weeks to get the certificate, whereas the Belgians gave him the visa in one day!" More objectionable, however, was the fact that they were forced to get these certificates from morally questionable authorities. "It's even worse that the guy who gives this OK is himself a bad person—morally. Who is he to determine a stamp of approval for 'good behavior'?" 'Abed asked in quiet outrage.

Intertwined throughout these incidents and stories—institutional performances of authority and critiques of them—are a swirl of moral judgments. They occurred in a context that is crosscut by supranational, international, and national agents and goals. Fundamentally shaping the contours of statebuilding in such a context are contradictions in how morality and moral behavior are performed and evaluated by citizens, state officials, those trying to become "official," and international actors. Because many of the PA's members and their material interests are well-known and much discussed by the Palestinian public, the ideological masking that theories of the state might predict is not working in Palestine. Nor is it even very evident. Instead, the PA flaunts a garish face of the state—the state as spectacle and font of physical force. However, because a still robust, albeit declining, popular nationalism, with its elemental system of political ethics, is a fundamental part of Palestinian society, that mask is unconvincing. The Palestinians I encountered recognized that mask as such, and rejected it.

Conclusion

The PA has failed to entrench its particular state image, not because stateness is performed, or performed badly, or is illegitimate in some objective sense. It is, rather, a combination of structural and cultural factors that prevent the crystallization of its legitimacy in the eyes of the people. Structural conditions imposed primarily by the Israeli occupation, donor states, and state mediators of political negotiations make it impossible for the PA to achieve that illusion of permanence and territorial sovereignty that other states manage. The most intransigent element of this snarl of impediments is the unfettered Israeli settlement project and military occupation.[33] This, in and of itself, means that the PA is not sovereign and has little local legitimacy as a state in anyone's eyes. As a municipal council member in a northern district told me, "Legitimacy of the government is décor. It's a joke." Class distinctions, political party rivalries, and moral evaluations of the use of force are other factors, as are values related to noble versus individualistic motives, courage and pride, transparency and honesty, and other prosaic concerns about the provision of services. Palestinians are tired and fed up, as they have been telling me since the beginning of the second intifada (see Allen 2008). Such antipolitics discourse is key to understanding the waves of popularity of Hamas, one organization in Palestine that has been seen, by at least some of the physically and politically stifled people living in the occupied Palestinian territory, as a source of moral guidance, ideological inspiration, and political horizon.

Chapter 5

Nationalizing Human Rights
The Political Ethics of Hamas

A SHARP CONTRAST to the ways in which the West Bank PA plays at human rights, betraying and even emphasizing the falsity of its performances, is the politics of sincerity that mark the human rights engagements of the Hamas-led PA in the Gaza Strip. As part of its own state-making efforts, Hamas has become entwined within the human rights system, by engaging with HROs, providing human rights training, and submitting reports to UN bodies. However, it does so in ways that are announced as ethical and effective, placed in an explicitly nationalist context, and opposed to what are portrayed as the perfidious ways of Fateh. In its insistence on Palestinians' right to be nationalist, on their right to demand rights that will be guaranteed by a political rather than a technocratic solution, Hamas presents an alternative to the cynical human rights system and to the limbo status quo in politics. Despite the fact that Hamas's declarations of sincerity and ethical behavior are recognized by some as more of a claim than a description of actual actions, their political-ethical approach resonates with a nostalgic nationalism in which many Palestinians take comfort. It also fuels their critique that has enabled their unique engagement with the human rights system, which is both critical and bureaucratic. Hamas has continuously named many of the human rights system's faults, calling attention to the hypocrisies that so many Palestinians recognize as being inherent within that system. They publicly condemn what others see and stew over. Even though their bureaucratic interactions with the human rights regime bespeak an organization trying to instantiate themselves as regularized state actors in a system of global governance, Hamas members still present themselves as noncynical nationalists acting on behalf of the people. Their alternative take on human rights, engendered within this nationalist framework, goes some way toward explaining why the movement has been a preferred political alternative for some Palestinians.

Hamas's understandings and uses of human rights are continuous with the Palestinian history of forms of claim-making and a system of shared values, reflecting a "moral polity" (Roberts 2002) that encompasses particular political and social ideals of sincerity and national solidarity. Ajantha Subramanian's (2009) discussion of the "dialogical relationship between claims and rights in which the practice of claim making is generative of new understandings and subjects of rights" (19) is relevant here. In contrast to anthropological figurations of rights either as "flowing from the West outward" where they are "vernacularized," or as a "form of governmentality through which subjects are incorporated into a normative legal framework" (18), Subramanian's approach should prompt observers to see in Islamists' engagement of human rights something other than an opportunistic appropriation of a Western discourse (albeit one that claims universality) for the purposes of pursuing local and political goals. Instead, it should encourage us to note the continuities among present-day human rights practices, principles, and idioms that reveal temporal ties with the past and links across different realms of practice and thought, thus obviating the oft-repeated question of whether or not Hamas is "really" democratic or "really believes" in human rights principles.

Seeing the mobilization of human rights in the context of this ethical world helps us understand what human rights "really mean" to Hamas, and to Palestinian society, in a unique way. It also sheds light on the kind of government Hamas has attempted to produce. It is one that is trying to engage the international community in a self-confident, self-consciously agentive, nondefensive manner, one that asserts its own principles but also tries to find points of political intersection and bases of mutual recognition. Also evident in Hamas's interactions with human rights and UN organizations is a concern with bureaucratic form that is nevertheless still firmly rooted in nationalist substance. In Hamas's negotiations with the human rights system, we see another way in which the human rights system shapes state practice.

Islam, Hamas, and Human Rights: How They Fit Together

Human rights fits distinctly within the framework of Hamas's discourse and governmental activities because Hamas is an Islamist movement, and because of its place in the history of the Palestinian-Israeli conflict and intra-Palestinian contests, as well as in the international context that crystallized after 9/11 and the "war on terror." The case of Hamas in Gaza demands an analysis that is situated within a broader debate about the ways in which predominantly Muslim societies engage with questions about "liberal human rights," democracy, ethics, and social justice, in part because these are the themes that Hamas representatives themselves insert into the conversation.[1] The stakes of the debate about Islam and human rights became sharper after the electoral victory of Hamas's Change and Reform Party during the municipal and legislative elections in late 2004 to early 2005 and in 2006 in what were universally acclaimed to be free and fair elections (to the extent that they could be, occurring as they did under occupation, which restricted the free campaigning of candidates and the movement of voters). Indeed, among the ways in which Hamas has strived to enact "stateness," its participation and victory in democratic elections, as well as its interactions with the human rights regime, are perhaps most recognizable to an audience that takes Western, liberal values as the norm.

By virtue of the universalism of human rights—that is, their universal availability and hegemonic presence—Hamas's interactions with the human rights system make it, as a political movement with religious motivations, part of a shared intellectual debate that extends across the globe (see also Dubois 2006:7).[2] It is not an extremely cohesive or harmonious space of deliberation. It takes place in multiple venues, among politicians and scholars, pundits and policy advisors, Palestinians and others, and many countervailing voices seek to mute Hamas. Thus, my access to many of the central Palestinian actors in these debates has been as a somewhat distant observer. Due to the ongoing repression of Hamas by Israel and the PA in the West Bank, it was difficult to find people who would speak freely to me, an outsider, on behalf of or from the perspective of Hamas. Also, Israel's refusal to let most people in or out of the Gaza Strip meant that I could not talk to people there.[3] However, interviews with official spokespeople and legislators from Hamas in the West Bank, and conversations with some affiliated young men, in addition to publications— books by prominent members, written pronouncements, news media, and the Internet—provide a clear sense of Hamas viewpoints. Although I could not follow the "social life" of any particular Hamas document, speech, or item of cultural production in order to interrogate the intent of its author or the reactions of its audience, I was able to situate these various genres of expression within a broader sociopolitical scene. These jigsaw puzzle pieces, taken in tandem with reports on what Hamas is actually doing, along with Fateh and nonfactional perspectives, show that all sides are involved in confirming the general "universal" human rights framework while also using it to buttress their own claims to legitimacy. They also reveal a consistent set of ethical principles at play in Palestinian national politics in general. This parallel nationalist ethical discourse is one to which both Fateh and Hamas refer. Even if they do not adhere to it fully, it is the frame of reference that has the most overarching significance within their society.

Hamas in particular is clear in its pronouncements that human rights practice must be subsumed within a broad set of cultural, political ethics, one that places a high value on sincerity, honesty, and substance over show. Hamas has put the principles of sincerity and honesty into action by, in their own words, "serving the people and identifying with their hopes and pains" (Amayreh 2010:15; see also S. Roy 2011:5). Drawing on Webb Keane (2007), I refer to this notion as "the moral load of sincerity" in order to draw attention to the "value and authority of the relations between speakers, their speech, and other persons" (212).[4] Ethical dimensions can be, and for anthropologists probably should be, recognized in most spheres of action (Lambek 2010), and they are particularly critical in Palestine.[5] The political strife that has been so acutely extant in the occupied Palestinian territory for so long has produced a context in which justifications for political behavior are demanded. Having lived for decades under military occupation, Palestinians are not willing to hold in abeyance questions of political legitimacy and credibility (cf. Feldman 2008:135), and political accounts and excuses (or lack thereof) are a specific object of continual reflexivity (see also Keane 2010:69). The realm of Palestinian public discourse is a lively space of critique and criticism, where every change that is promised, service rendered or neglected, and speech uttered is noted and appraised. In a context in which everything and everyone is suspected of being politicized (*musayyas*), it is the evidence contained in actions, not words, that can gain political credit for an individual or organization—and it is more often its absence that reduces it.

Although the antagonistic views expressed by the people I talked with were sharp, the consistency in the discourse across political divides suggests that an ongoing, even if underlying, coherence of Palestinian political and social values persists. As previous chapters have shown, a tug of war between different visions of the state is occurring across that transforming moral economy. There are those who advocate for and see themselves as working toward a "modern state," with "transparency" and "rule of law" as the professed principles guiding that process. Abiding by, or appearing to abide by, international agreements and standards, including human rights standards, is part of that state. So too is a notion of impersonal citizen-state relations and of a neoliberal market-driven political economy.

In the populist-nationalist version of the state, by contrast, material resources should rightfully be shared among the people. Those who subscribe to this perspective see a bureaucratic, less nationalist, or even anti-nationalist state being built by global patrons with corrupting influence, patrons who feed the power-hungry people motivated more by private concerns than by the popular good. The value of sincerity, and specifically the lack of it within the human rights system, is a basis on which it has lost credibility and inspired cynicism in Palestine. It is within this framework that we can understand the ways in which Hamas draws on the moral load of sincerity to translate notions of human rights in a distinct way on the ground—in both language and practical action.

Changing political, economic, and social conditions within the occupied territory are also important factors shaping Hamas's engagement with questions of human rights. Hamas has moved from a focus during its early years in the 1980s on inculcating greater religious observance and working through social welfare activities to a greater emphasis on militant resistance to occupation during the first intifada. In response to its acknowledged defeat by Israel and the PA (S. Roy 2011:38) by the end of the first intifada in 1993, the movement shifted away from political violence and moved toward social sector charity and educational initiatives during the Oslo period. After Hamas's victory in the 2006 elections, state-building came to the fore as well (10). The concentration on "civism"—a commitment to strengthening society through "community life, order and stability . . . individual and collective rights, [and] the public good" (9)—reflects Hamas's self-identification as "a reformist movement that believes in working from inside society and convincing its members of the justness of [the movement's] thoughts" (ICG 2011:22).

One way they do this is through the education and activation of the women cadre, who were credited with bringing out a large number of female voters in support of Hamas. A number of leading women activists from the movement were elected members of the Palestinian Legislative Council (PLC), among whom was Mona Mansour. It was through meeting Mansour and reading her late husband's text on human rights in Islam (Mansour 2000) that I began to explore Hamas's particular take on human rights.[6] In my conversation with Mansour and other members of the movement, it became clear that they understand human rights principles to generally fit with Islam. Ultimately, what emerges out of Hamas's critiques of the human rights system, of how its members deployed human rights discourse, as well as Palestinians' critiques of Hamas, is a picture of Palestinian nationalism as a fundamentally moral discourse in which sincerity of word and action remain key principles.

"Brothers in Humanity": An Islamist Perspective on Democracy and Human Rights

During the winter of 2007, I visited Mona Mansour in her home in Nablus. She welcomed my assistant and me into her formal living room, where her college-age daughter, a student of journalism, sat quietly taking notes in one corner. Hanging on one wall was a large portrait of Mansour's late husband, Jamal. Once a spokesperson for Hamas in the West Bank, he was killed in an Israeli airstrike on July 31, 2001, in Nablus.[7] After I introduced myself and explained my research to her, and before I had a chance to ask a question, Mansour launched into an analysis of the international hypocrisies that have fueled what she called the tragic nature of the Palestinians' situation:

> The whole world calls for democracy, and the result of this democracy is the punishment of the Palestinian people for their choosing Hamas in the elections. This is despite the fact that the elections here were clean and credible. There's never been anywhere in the world an election process as clean as the elections here. The world requests democracy, but not for Palestine if it means the formation of a Hamas government.

The international siege placed on the Gaza Strip since June 2007 has left the 1.5 million Palestinian residents with substandard health and sanitation facilities and a lack of basic goods and services, including inadequate electricity supplies.[8] There has also been a political blockade against Hamas. Mansour went on to describe the many ways that the PA and Fateh have harassed and oppressed her party in Nablus, including by closing more than one hundred Hamas charitable institutions, dismissing 1,880 employees from government jobs (a purge that is ongoing), and carrying out an arrest campaign against Hamas members there and elsewhere.[9]

Mansour's analysis reflects an understanding of the various (even arbitrary) deployments of the category of "democracy" in East-West relations, one expression of which is the special relationship of Israel to the United States, which is justified on the basis of the former's self-proclaimed unique status as the "only democracy in the Middle East." The banner of human rights and democracy has been flown at the head of US incursions throughout the Middle East and deployed to justify military involvement in Afghanistan and Iraq. Hamas waves that flag in return as a semaphore of civilization. They raise it in discourse about the successes of the Hamas government in Gaza, in arguments about the failures and abuses of Fateh and the West Bank PA, in their meetings with representatives of international human rights and humanitarian organizations, in human rights and international humanitarian law trainings, and in their responses to the UN. In so doing, they try to show that they share the same standards of truth and value that they presume outsiders use to evaluate them. Human rights and democracy are a central idiom in those efforts.

As my assistant and I stood to leave, Mansour offered me a copy of a publication written by her late husband. It was a lengthy study elaborating an Islamist perspective on democracy and human rights. It is interesting that in this text Jamal Mansour, like foreign funders and West Bank NGOs, also conceptualized "democracy-and-human-rights" as a unit. Despite the fact that the meaning, practice, philosophical foundations, and historical developments of democracy and human rights are, in many places and for many theorists and scholars, distinct from each other, democracy and human rights come together in the work and talk of many civil society actors in Palestine. Both terms have accrued an ideological load that makes them, together or separately, indices of a certain civilizational status for all political contestants. Jamal Mansour was taking part in a symbolic battle within a discursive terrain that is common throughout occupied Palestine, asserting with his scholarship an Islamist presence within it.

His analysis draws heavily on the position of the Muslim Brotherhood and places the notion of human rights within a framework of global human evolution and yearning "for justice, equality, and respect." For Sayyid Qutb, a leading Egyptian ideologue in the Muslim Brotherhood in the 1950s and 1960s, social justice was the essential goal of an Islamic polity, which he believed should be based on unity and mutual responsibility between individual and society (Moussalli 1992:173–174).[10] Qutb's thought is relevant because the Islamist movement in Palestine emerged out of the Muslim Brotherhood Society, which was established in Egypt in 1928. The Palestinian branch was set up in 1946, and Hamas announced itself on December 14, 1987, soon after the outbreak of the first intifada. Defining itself as a "Palestinian national liberation movement" that "struggles for liberation of Palestinian occupied territories and for the recognition of the legitimate rights of Palestinians," Hamas declared Islam to be a "frame of reference," but establishment of an Islamic state was not the goal of the organization.[11] Guiding principles evident in Hamas practice and discourse reflect the Muslim Brotherhood's focus on social justice. Mansour (2000:15) quotes the Muslim Brotherhood in his discussion of human rights, to confirm that "any attack on these rights and freedoms under any name, be it even the use of Islam itself, represents the degradation of humans. These rights transform talents and abilities into development and prosperity."[12] According to Mansour, "equality, freedom, and just distribution" are inextricable features of the moral outlook and political culture of Hamas (44).

What counts as justice is a relative concept, as all moral notions are, and the concept has developed throughout the history of Islam (Khadduri 2001). How people should determine standards of justice and how they are to achieve it in society are always matters of ongoing debate for any community. Their articulation at any given moment draws on multiple traditions, contexts, personalities, and historical events. Jamal Mansour recognized the influence of this mélange, writing that human rights have

> become a partner of international political development demanded and valued by the authority of the people, who call for the rights of equality, respect, and participation in their totalities. . . . I believe that Islamists will generally accept the rights and freedoms listed in the international charters, will guarantee them in their constitutions, and will work towards incorporating [them] within religious requirements. This course of action has been accepted and is on the rise around the world. [2000:15]

There is little that is remarkable about the rest of Mansour's overall account of human rights, and it accords closely with principles set out in international conventions. The prohibition against torture, freedom of expression and assembly, and the rights of religious, cultural, ethnic, and racial minorities are presented favorably and in familiar terms. Mansour's elaboration of a Hamas outlook on democracy and human rights even resonates with that of Western development agencies. His understanding of human rights as the necessary grounding for "development and prosperity" echoes the view of the UN that an understanding of human rights is the necessary grounding for security and development (UN 2005). In all of these quarters, human rights are being positioned as a foundation for social progress in general.

To the extent that Mansour's account suggests that the Islamist formulation may diverge from secular human rights, it is to assert that although there is overall acceptance of human rights standards and of the position that people are the same, with equal rights and duties, these standards must be worked out in practical detail "so that we do not fall victim to accepting in theory what may cause religious contradictions in practice" (15).

Even before the human rights system was established with the Universal Declaration of Human Rights (UDHR) in 1948, one of the ongoing debates surrounding human rights was about their relative or universal nature. Concern over the cross-cultural applicability of human rights standards, or their possibly exclusively Western origins, plagued the formulation of the UDHR (Waltz 2004; Goodale 2009; An-Na'im 1999) and has remained a central issue ever since. One of the most sensitive topics has been the question of Islam's accordance with universal human rights standards, especially Muslim women's human rights (Abu-Lughod 2010:31–32; Afary 2004; An-Na'im 1987a; Moosa 2001–2002). In public debates and scholarly analyses, the problem is sometimes presented as primarily an ideological one: a conflict between a local tradition, Islam, and global demands for human rights. One position in these debates holds that Islam, through reinterpretation, can be made to support human rights as articulated in international declarations (Moosa 2000; Al-Hibri 1997). Some Islamists claim that human rights are inherent in the *shari'a* (Islamic law) (Mawdudi 1980), with the 1990 annual session of the Organization of the Islamic Conference affirming this (to a degree) in the Cairo Declaration of Human Rights in Islam.[13]

In contrast, some view the clash between secular Western and Islamist approaches as inherent and irreconcilable. Of course any critical scholar would have to acknowledge that there is no single Western or Islamic conception of human rights (Bielefeldt 2000:114; Dalacoura 1998; An-Na'im 1987a, Khadduri 2001), but there are those who frame their arguments in such generalizing terms, producing pronouncements on "how contemporary Muslims think about the rights of women under Islamic law" (Mayer 2007:113). Mayer has insisted that Islam, and the canny politicians ruling Muslim states (118), attempt to disguise their discrimination and "avoid acknowledging that they want women to be subjugated. . . . [T]hey deploy formulations that minimize or hide their discriminatory impact" (117) and "deliberately [obscure] crucial issues" (123). Other scholars, in contrast, recognize Islam as part of a moving history, with changing ideas about rights understood as a product of that history (Moosa 2001–2002). They work toward developing a reformed vision of Islamic law that accords with international standards of human rights (An-Na'im 1987b). This latter approach typified that of my Hamas interlocutors and the organizations' official statements.

Sheikh Radwan, a municipal council member with Hamas affiliations and former mosque preacher (before the PA fired him after the 2007 split with Gaza)[14] explained to me the basis of Islam's concordance with human rights in terms of the esteem that is placed on the human being as the most favored creation of God. The sheikh quoted 'Umar Ibn Al-Khattab, the second caliph of Islam, who asked, "Why have you enslaved people who were born free to their mothers?" a rhetorical question that is frequently cited by those making the case for the applicability of human rights in the Palestinian context. The sheikh offered more Qur'anic verses to back up his explanation of human rights in Islam, and he expressed his belief in a universal humanity and the universal values that are common to it. He said, "We are brothers in humanity anywhere, no matter where, Europe, America, Australia, or otherwise. From my reading of history, I find that morals and values are the same the world over, no matter whether for the Muslims or Europeans. In the past, honor was honor and honesty was honesty and lying was lying."

Although the intricacies of the scholarly discussions about Islam, democracy, and human rights extend beyond the scope of this book, their terms of reference are revealing. Whether Islam can or should accord with international human rights standards, the perceived necessity of elaborating how they might harmonize, the extent to which Islam or Muslim-led governments protect women's rights, and whether or not any assertion by Islamists regarding human rights can be taken as sincere are all issues that attract similar levels of intense attention in the Palestinian context. Such questions swirl amid battles over who is best suited for governing Palestinians, along with questions about what kind of polity can ensure the full flourishing of moral subjects, citizens who are enfranchised and committed to pursuing the nationalist struggle and achieving liberation from occupation.

Empty Politics, Empty Words

If numerous scholars have observed the lack of "faith in anything that comes under the label of 'politics'" (Lybarger 2007:102; see also Brown 2011) in the occupied territory, so too have politicians. Sensitive to this pervasive distrust, Gaza Prime Minister Isma'il Haniyyah justified Hamas's military action against the then Fateh-ruled PA in the Gaza Strip as a "necessary security step to abort a vicious plan concocted by enemies of the Palestinian people with the aim to ignite a civil war, and that it *had nothing to do with politics*," affirming his government's concern with preserving unity of the Palestinian land (Haniyyah 2007, italics added). As opposed to actions taken sincerely for the benefit of the people, politics is a vulgar, despicable game that entails deception and betrayal, backstabbing, unprincipled pragmatism, and hypocritical empty slogans (see also Lybarger 2007:102). "People need work, not words," the governor of Jenin, Qadoura Musa, told me. "We want there to be closeness between speech and implementation," a former PLC member from the same town opined. Most people, however, saw the gap to be wide indeed.

This intense suspicion is roused by almost everything that is said and written in official discourse or formal genres. As one young man from a West Bank refugee camp summed up the situation for me, "These days, people don't judge politicians' words; these days, people attack politicians *because* of their words. The simple people judge politicians' words by saying, 'They're all thieves and collaborators with Israel.'" Newspapers and political magazines were written off entirely as jargon and slogans, even by members of the political factions that published them. Zaid, from a family of prominent Fateh activists, noted that it was especially educated and politically active Palestinians who used to read political magazines such as *al-Hadaf* or *Fateh Al-Thawrah*. There was a time, he added wistfully, "when the political leaders and writers used to write." Now, however, his politically active siblings do not trust such magazines anymore, he told me. So much of the printed word is not relevant for people in Palestine these days because the politics from which it emanates is also irrelevant.

Likewise, political speeches during ceremonies and rituals are typically ignored. Even when they are bellowed through bullhorns, audiences usually continue their private conversations and pay little heed to the prepared rhetoric. During a ceremony in commemoration of political prisoners, for example, I asked the person who had accompanied me what the speaker was saying, but she had not been listening and could not relay it. After having walked in numerous martyrs' funerals and finding myself never able to understand the fuzzy words being yelled through the microphone, I finally asked a friend what they were saying during a funeral for a number of members of Hamas who had been killed by Israeli occupation forces. I could understand that the speech included numerous nationalist and religious references, but the distortion was too great for my non-native ears to sort out each word. My friend also had no idea what was being said. Moreover, he did not really care and was ignoring the official-ese, as most do, considering it to be so much *haki fadi* ("hot air," literally, "empty words").

There are, of course, other genres of discourse that are attended to with great interest. The Friday *khutbah* (sermon) seems to keep the attention of many worshipers. Breaking news on stations like Al-Jazeera or, more locally, Al-Watan TV was attended to with rapt attention, especially during the first few years of the second intifada, when dramatic and too often deadly events were common. The speeches of Hizbullah leader Hasan Nasrallah during the Israeli war in Lebanon in the summer of 2006 were listened to, discussed, and appreciated by most of the people I knew in the refugee camp where I spent much of my time. The immediacy of live news coverage and the reputations of certain religious authorities as being plain-speaking and sincere gave value to their words. However, these were the exceptions, and even the news flashes eventually incited only ennui (Allen 2008).

In the context of political cynicism that holds the occupied territory in a tightly knotted fist, it is Hamas that has released that grip for some. The movement was embraced by some Palestinians because of the new kind of politics and the newly sincere kind of personhood that Hamas sought to cultivate. Hamas presents itself as offering an alternative way of doing politics that is about action and leading by example, not proclamation: "We must plant the seeds for an Islamic future in the next generation" through an Islamic value system, a prominent political official in Hamas said. "We do this through example and education . . . spreading Islamic values without violence through good example, namely through the provision of social and community services" (S. Roy 2000:25).[15] Palestinians who turned to Islam had judged secular nationalists to be lacking in the kind of inner commitment that was necessary to liberate Palestine, and they were frustrated with those who had made grand statements about continuing the fight but did not act accordingly (Lybarger 2007:98, 201). They were profoundly disillusioned with secular-nationalist moral and political corruption and desired greater authenticity in religious and political life.

Islamic revivalists throughout the Middle East have posed similar questions about how to achieve social justice through greater national and religious authenticity (Donohue 1983). Hassan al-Banna (1906–1949), founder of the Muslim Brotherhood, preached about the importance of inner transformation, of reforming "the heart, soul and spirit of the individual" in order to return people to their authentic Muslim identity (Lybarger 2007:212). Islamism was a response to a widespread sense that there was a need for renewed dignity and self-respect among Muslims and Arabs in the face of Western political domination and secular encroachments (Haddad 1983, 1992; R. Mitchell 1993).[16] Some in Palestine saw in Hamas a more satisfactory means to achieving that aspiration. It was especially before their electoral victories in 2006, when they had less power among Palestinians, that Hamas concentrated on "collective empowerment within a civic framework."[17]

As Jeroen Gunning (2008:16, 59) has shown, Hamas is an organization that has "sought to create a vanguard of activists who exemplify 'genuine' or 'authentic' Islamic behaviour," with politicians who are expected to adhere to a moral code that accords with Islam. During the Oslo period especially, there was a focus on the "social, cultural and moral renewal of the Muslim community in Palestine" (S. Roy 2011:15); but religious beliefs and goals have not been core to the professed raison d'être of the movement. As noted, Hamas describes Islam as its "frame of reference" while nationalist and political party goals are the overarching concerns (Tamimi 2007a:247; S. Roy 2011:165).[18] It defines itself as a "mainstream Islamic movement that is committed to the principles of democracy and legitimate and peaceful political participation on an equal footing for all Palestinian groups" (Yousef 2007). Hamas names as goals the establishment of social justice, including liberation from tyranny, care for the poor, and the maintenance of Muslim dignity by way of Islam's prescribed path.[19]

Through their disciplined networks of religious and social service provision and their networks of volunteers—including women (Cobban 2006; Jad 2005; Amayreh 2010)—Hamas produced new conditions through which people could be mobilized, not only in direct anti-occupation activities, but also in projects for the development and survival of the society. Their practices resonate with Islamist and nationally based principles that enjoy deep credence in Palestinian society: the value of self-sacrifice for the community, and the general precedence of community over the individual. The foreign minister of the Hamas government in Gaza, Mahmoud Al-Zahar, asserted the populist nature of the movement, describing their goal as being the reconstruction "of the poorer classes—raising their living standards and improving their quality of life," in contrast to the PA, which "created a new rich class, that's all" (S. Roy 2011:143). Many Palestinians perceived that, unlike other politicians or NGOs, Hamas consistently fulfilled its promises, because it did serve the neediest sectors of Palestinian society—orphans, the disabled, and the unemployed—when neither the PA nor any other organization had been able to ensure the social security of the population. This is a form of sincerity that gave Hamas credibility in the society (Milton-Edwards 2008:1588; S. Roy 2011:186–189).

As important as its provision of social services has been, Hamas's role as an active participant in the military resistance to the occupation has also been a defining characteristic of the organization and it frames those activities in similar terms of sincerity of action. A sympathetic analyst compared Hamas to the PLO, the leadership of which was "caught off guard" during the first intifada because "Yasir Arafat and his advisers were engaged in promoting their image to the world as peace-makers" (Tamimi 2007a:53). Hamas, on the other hand, came out as a full-fledged, proactive resistance group that was engaged in the struggle against the occupation. When Hamas was in the opposition, it decried the Madrid peace process (which began in 1991 and ended with the separately negotiated Oslo Accords of 1993). Since its public emergence, it regularly rejected negotiations in dichotomous terms, opposing "action versus talk." Action was the way to gain national rights, not negotiations and the international community. Article 13 of its 1988 Charter stated, "There is no solution to the Palestinian problem except by jihad. The initiatives, options and international conferences are a waste of time." In a subsequent article, Hamas wrote, "Only metal breaks metal, and nothing defeats corrupt belief except the true belief in Islam" (quoted in Milton-Edwards 1996:201).

In 1992, clashes broke out between Hamas and Fateh over the balance of power between the two factions. A series of articles published in *Filastin al-Muslimah*, a Hamas mouthpiece, discussed the reasons for and effects of the factional battles. In addition to the repeated calls for unity and the assertions that Hamas is "against fighting our brothers" (*Filastin al-Muslimah* 1992a, 1992b:14–15, 1992c:20–21) that appear in these pages, it is specifically the sincerity of Hamas's practices that is highlighted against the disingenuous nature of Fateh. In a discussion of a document called the "Honor Charter," which was supposed to spell out the nature of factional coordination, one article explains that Fateh was pressuring Hamas to sign it. Giving into such demands would not have been an honest acceptance of the agreement on the part of Hamas, the article asserted. Instead, it was "working on developing a charter that actually fulfills the wishes of the Palestinian street, not just something that can be exploited for public relations" (1992b:14–15). Hamas's refusal to join the PLO is explained as being, in fact, a refusal to back down on its principles. The faith expressed in the members of Fateh, who "are still part of this people and can distinguish between a nationalist and a collaborator, between someone loyal and a betrayer," thus reiterates Hamas's key principles of sincerity, clarity, and honesty of intent and behavior. Although it may be the empirical case "that every known society values honesty and expects people to honor their promises" (Lambek 2010:17), sincerity is especially highlighted in the Palestinian nationalist context.

More than a decade of Hamas competition with the ruling Fateh party finally led to the election of Hamas to national leadership in 2006. The standard narrative of Hamas's surprising victory holds that this landslide vote was really a vote for change, and a vote against the corruption of the reigning PA, dominated by Fateh (Milton-Edwards 2008). Hamas described itself in a *Washington Post* article as a "reformed government that embraces the empowerment of the people, facilitates freedoms and protects civil rights" (Tamimi 2007a:269). A key element of Hamas's own account of its popularity is the "honesty" of the party (*Filastin al-Muslimah* 1992a, 1992b). The conclusion of its Change and Reform platform during the 2006 election campaign stated, for example, that the party's "methodology depends on decent and professional representatives who carry the slogan of honesty to God and loyalty to him, to the people and to the cause" (Barghouti 2007:27).

Many non-Islamist voters supported the party because they believed this statement. Hamas was seen as producing a rupture with the corrupt traditions of politics that had held sway in Palestine in the era of Yasir Arafat. In a 2007 poll by AMAN—the Palestinian branch of Transparency International (TI) (an organization focused on fighting corruption)—a significant 84 percent of respondents said they think there is corruption in civil organizations (AMAN 2007), and Hamas has been decrying the corruption of Fateh for decades (Ramadan 1992:20–22). As Akhil Gupta (1995:389) has observed of the Indian context, the discourse of corruption marks actions that constitute an infringement of rights. Discourses of corruption thereby represent the rights of citizens to themselves. Discussions of corruption in Palestine, and reports about it by organizations such as TI, are part of how Palestinian citizenship is defined. One of TI's studies reported that the poor hold corrupt individuals and institutions responsible for their conditions of deprivation; whether due to Hamas, Fateh, or the PA, this corruption causes their poverty.

In this "corruption talk," a paradigm of rights and obligations between citizens and the state, or statelike structures, are increasingly crystallized. The populist critique of corruption within this ethical discourse reveals a Palestinian "moral economy" (to recall E. P. Thompson [1971]) animated by a "legitimizing notion" that bespeaks a belief in agreed-upon rights, customs, and social standards, and in so saying, confirms those rights and values.[20] The norms are partly economic, insofar as corruption talk is a reaction against incorrect disposal of public wealth. More broadly, however, it is a commentary on political ethics (Roberts 2002:9). Hamas responded to Palestinians' disgust at the crony politics, patronage, and patrimonialism that had been the political status quo for so long. Since the 1990s, Hamas had been promising that through transparency and accountability they would put all of this to an end (see, for example, Abu Marzook 2006). In an op-ed piece in the *Guardian*, Hamas political bureau chief Khaled Mish'al (2006) explained that Hamas was elected because it "is immune to bribery, intimidation and blackmail." The article, "We Will Not Sell Our People or Principles for Foreign Aid," went on to assert that Hamas is "keen on having friendly relations with all nations," but they will "not seek friendships at the expense of [their] legitimate rights" (see also Hamad 2006).

The principled nature and anticorruption stance of Hamas, central to its self-professed identity, have been their unswerving focus across differing realms of interests and activity, from politics to religious behavior. As Mahmoud al-Zahar, Hamas spokesman at the time, affirmed in 1995, "You can't compare the institutions of the PLO and Islam. In the former there is corruption, bad management, violation of human rights . . . and a failure to meet promises" (quoted in Milton-Edwards and Farrell 2010:75; cf. Khadduri 2001). The established leadership does not keep promises, as al-Zahar said, meaning that their words do not match their actions. Regional representatives of Hamas point to the fact that the party did not need to spend enormous amounts of money on campaign advertising, as its rivals did, because it had sincerely motivated volunteers, who worked for free. Hamas could forego such wasteful, expensive posters and commercials because its "advertising" did not have to be so superficial; the movement was long ago rooted in the hearts and minds of the voters through the good works of the movement (PIC n.d.). A similar distinction is drawn in discussions of proper religious behavior. Those who confuse being a good Muslim with always making it to the front row to pray or with always being somber and frowning are chastised for missing the point of Islam, for mistaking show for substance.

Notions about prayer, politics, and honesty that Hamas has articulated can be usefully compared to debates about correct ways of praying and speaking in the encounter between Christian missionaries and Sumbanese people that Webb Keane (2007) has studied. Keane analyzed the regnant language ideology about sincere talk for what it reveals about the nexus of "speaking (and reading and writing) practices, moral values, political institutions, and concepts of the person" (16). In the Protestant context that he considered, ideas about sincerity contribute to "commonsense notions about the agency and freedom that often are supposed to define persons" within Protestant and secular traditions (5). The concept of sincerity is tied to "the idea that language could be transparent, that it could be a clear and direct vehicle for the communication of thoughts from one person to another" (15).

In Palestine, this ideology of sincerity functions within a nationalist value system that idealizes social ties and social welfare over individualistic motives. The land and "the people" (*al-sha'b*) are to be valued and their safety and independence fought for, even if it means personal sacrifice. Upholding these values and sustaining the collective depends on honest, cooperative interaction geared toward shared goals. Hamas exhorted in an online article, "Our society must cooperate to avoid selfishness and be governed by altruism, exactly like the Ansar [supporters of the prophet] and the immigrants" (those who migrated with him from Mecca to Medina) (PIC 2007c). The moral ramifications of sincerity are linked not only to ideas about inner thoughts, but also to intentions about future plans. The concern is with what one says one will do, and how that accords with what that person truly intends to do (or is already doing). *Filastin al-Muslimah* (1992c) proclaimed that "Hamas will continue with its promise, carrying the banner of unity of arms and pulling together in the fight against the enemy," in comparison to Fateh, which is accused of giving in, submitting to the plan of autonomous rule, and thereby deepening the occupation. The broken promises and the agreements to which Fateh did not adhere only underscore by contrast Hamas's sincerity of action (*Filastin al-Muslimah* 1992d:17).

The place of the "moral load of sincerity" (Keane 2007:212) in ethical debates between Fateh and Hamas is the result of a longer history in Palestine. Rochelle Davis's (2010) study of village memorial books shows how central the values of honesty and cooperation have been in the nationalist discourse throughout Palestine's history of dispersal. Palestinian refugees produced these texts about their villages that were destroyed in 1948 with both historical and instructive intent. These pedagogical histories show that among the shared values that dominated village life of decades ago were honesty, "cooperation [*al-ta'awun*]," and "assistance [*al-'aun*]." One of these texts describes how the people of a particular village "would fly to help each other in building, harvesting, and agriculture," sharing resources, maintaining their commitment to collectively held values, and placing collective needs before individual interests during times of crisis (72). The author of a book about another village, Ijzim, portrayed a community of Palestinians cooperating with each other against colonial forces (77). Stories from Gaza also recount the primacy that refugees placed on communal assistance and on the "ethic of care" that sustained them (Feldman 2008:131), principles that my interlocutors stressed were important during the first intifada and too scarce during the second.

Similar to the village books, biographies of Hamas leaders have been published not only as appreciative eulogies of martyrs, but also as didactic accounts emphasizing their moral code. Presenting their subjects as laudable characters, such biographies are available on the Web and in print.[21] While browsing in a bookstore in the West Bank town of Ramallah, I came across one such text, the memoirs of 'Abd al-'Aziz al-Rantisi, a Hamas leader assassinated by Israel in April 2004. The introduction tells readers that they will find in al-Rantisi's life story only jihad, *da'wah* (proselytizing), troubles, and suffering. He was arrested by Israel and faced constant pressures and inhuman practices. However, the editor, 'Amr Shammakh (2004), avers that throughout it all al-Rantisi held on to religion and what is right. Much of the text that follows elaborates on the superior moral character of the Hamas leader. He was mild-tempered and calm, modest yet self-confident; he stood up to the intimidation of Israeli forces and did not let his dignity become tarnished by the ignoble treatment of Israeli prison guards. The publication offers his personal anecdotes and the testimony of others, recounting both the hardships of al-Rantisi's life and the firmly principled stances he held in the face of grave challenges.

Al-Rantisi's story metonymically represents the character and approach of Hamas, which he characterized as being in full concordance with Islam and the principles of Palestinian rights: "There is absolute correspondence between what we say and what we do. As a result, we enjoy high credibility and the people trust us." It is this joint principle of sincerity of action and honesty of speech that runs throughout Hamas discourse, from the Friday sermons and other public speeches of its representatives to its op-ed pieces published in English-language dailies. Similar values are highlighted in the memoirs and hagiographies of prominent political figures across the political spectrum. In his autobiography, Na'eem Khadar (n.d.), a PLO ambassador in Belgium who was assassinated in 1981 (probably by the Mossad), declared in almost mystical tones that earnestness is fundamental to Palestinian identity: "It's something spontaneous . . . that a Palestinian can identify another Palestinian. When we discuss with a Palestinian . . . from the first sentence we can identify that he is Palestinian, from his political conviction, his determination, and the way he presents his thoughts. . . . There is a tone of honesty and conviction . . . that stays in the basis, the depths, of the Palestinian" (31). These principles are also a key to understanding the ethical dimensions of contemporary internal Palestinian politics. They are the same standards—valuing action over talk—against which the Palestinian public has judged both the politicians of Fateh and Hamas, as well as the human rights system.

Hamas into Human Rights

As Hamas increased its strength and popularity in Palestine and developed ties with regional players, it announced its commitment to engaging with a broader political realm. In so doing, Hamas incorporated references to human rights in its efforts to reach out to the international community. This extension is part of its political program, but according to a Hamas spokesperson, it is also behavior appropriate to the ideal believer who integrates "his past with the present . . . and with his view of the future, and the culture of Islam with the other human cultures around him" (cited in Klein 2009). Hamas's attitudes copy some of Al-Haq's early notions regarding the importance of human rights as a language that could mediate political convictions and express mutually recognized, or at least universally claimed, values. According to its own pronouncements, Hamas saw the necessity of persuading "governments and international organizations . . . to condemn the repressive measures adopted by the occupation in contravention of the principles of international law and the values of human rights" (Tamimi 2007a:264–265).

Whether or not members of either organization would agree to the comparison, and without implying any line of causation, similarities are clear between Al-Haq and Hamas in their emphasis on international dialogue through a human rights idiom as a means to secure Palestinians' rights, just as there is a shared conviction of the universalism of human rights as rights for all. A leading PLC member, Musa Ramadan, confirmed this principle to me, saying that "human rights don't have religion. It is for everyone. It is without nationality." Ramadan cited an agreement that Mohammad signed before he became the prophet of Islam—"an honor agreement about human rights, robbery, and so on," the legislator said. After becoming a prophet, Mohammad asserted that if the tribe invited him to sign that agreement again, he would, even if they were not Muslims. For the legislator, this meant that "everyone should support human rights." Another Hamas representative I interviewed in the West Bank asserted that it is "a big mistake to prevent human rights. For example, if we as Muslims decided to force the *hijab* on women, then we will be making a mistake. This is a personal freedom for women." The representatives of Hamas are fully aware of common perceptions that are held, internationally and at home, about their conservative social values, especially as they pertain to the status and rights of women (see, for example, Amayreh 2010; Yousef 2010). Explicitly tying human rights to civilizational status and arguing for their accordance with Islam, Fathi Hammad, minister of interior in the Gaza Strip, made a public statement that his ministry trains its personnel in "piety towards God and respect for human rights." He went on, saying, "We attempt to implement the loftiest laws in practice. We have observers in the PLC and an inspector-general and inspectors in all governorates. We allow wide space to rights organizations and open the prisons to everyone, and fear no one. We know that civilizational progress is tied to Islamic teachings and see no contradiction between civilization and progress versus Islam" (Cabinet Secretariat 2010, quoted in Y. Sayigh 2011:90–91). Because the person is God's favored creation, it is not permitted in Islam to violate his dignity or honor, or his possessions, or to take his life, Sheikh Radwan explained. "Because God created that person, anyone who attacks that person, it's as if he attacks God."

The extent to which the views of Ramadan or Hammad reflect how the Hamas-led PA in the Gaza Strip governs is a matter of debate. The fact that religious study has been beefed up in the PA school curriculum there (Milton-Edwards 2007:312), that memorization of the Qur'an is rewarded with automatic promotion for police officers in the Gaza Strip, and that classes for Qur'anic study are provided in prisons are just a few examples of the distinctly Islamist nature of the government. Since Hamas gained political power, the curbing of some personal freedoms in Gaza (what Hamas refers to as "moral enforcement") has been amply documented, including the banning of male hairdressers from women's salons, as well as other steps that narrow political pluralism (Y. Sayigh 2011:22; S. Roy 2011:223–224).[22] Capital punishment is also meted out against those whom the Hamas government deems traitors and other criminals. Although the universality of human rights was indeed a belief shared among my religious interlocutors, the extent to which the Islamist movement has prioritized that belief in its political practice has varied considerably.[23]

Nevertheless, there is a common thread running throughout these arguments about the fit between Islam and human rights principles, and a stress on the importance of bringing human rights into practical operation on the ground. Here, then, we return to the theme of sincere action over empty talk, values that members of Hamas brought to the fore in their critiques of the human rights system. Jamal Mansour (2000:15–16) asserted that "Islam has not been satisfied with merely the acknowledgment of human rights to life and individual integrity, rather it has made it a sacred obligation of the society, the individual, and the government to implement it, on the principle of the Caliphate and respect of humanity." He quoted the Muslim Brotherhood's belief "that the path to freedom is through an organized, legal, and ethical framework" (15).

Sheikh Radwan expressed a similar concern over the political context in which rights are realized. After mentioning the many authoritarian Arab states in which citizens do not live securely, he cast his critical eye upon the West, calling attention to the lack of human rights implementation there as well: "As for European countries, and America, they get some human rights, but there is nothing about changing the political system. So there is freedom of religion, worship, and morals, but they are not able to change the political situation." He correctly noted that many in the United States criticized President Bush, and that Europeans opposed the war in Iraq, but nevertheless the war was pursued. "Even though they can speak as they wish," he said, "in some things they have lost their freedom and cannot determine the policy of their countries."

By refusing to leave human rights in the realm of mere aspiration or idealistic pretense, these and other Hamas representatives repeatedly interjected into human rights discourse a variation on the principle of sincerity that runs throughout Palestinian debates on human rights and on politics in general. As Musa Ramadan observed, the universality of human rights, so widely professed, is often hypocritically ignored when convenient. "The problem in the West with the idea of freedoms is that they choose what they want from them and leave the rest."

The Repoliticization of Human Rights

Hamas calls on human rights standards in a variety of contexts for multiple reasons. For the Gaza government, human rights are undoubtedly one element of a PR system, as they are for any state.[24] With insistent repetition, Hamas officials underscore the increased security that occurred following their eradication of armed lawlessness in the streets of Gaza, which they say allows citizens to enjoy their rights. Human rights require a social system that provides the structures that not only protect but also enable the enjoyment of human rights, not merely the shielding of citizens from violation. During his Friday sermons, Prime Minister Isma'il Haniyyah regularly reminds his listeners of the greater calm that has let citizens feel more at ease since Hamas's election (see, for example, Haniyyah 2007) and affirms the "keenness of his government on preserving and protecting human rights in Palestine," sentiments echoed in speeches and articles published on the unofficial Hamas website, the Palestinian Information Center (Al-Jazeera 2007).

Human rights standards are held up especially as a measure of the movement's moral and practical superiority over their rival, Fateh, or the West Bank PA (PIC 2007b, 2007c). Hamas's engagement with human rights does more than simply shoot another arrow from the political rhetoric quiver, however. It also repoliticizes human rights internationally by inserting the problem of rights violations and the impunity of the perpetrators into the political context of occupation and international siege.[25]

A case in point is the Hamas government's responses to the international attention given to Operation Cast Lead, the Israeli incursions in Gaza from 2008 to 2009 (often referred to as a war; see Allen 2012).[26] In a Friday sermon marking the one-year anniversary of the war, Prime Minister Haniyyah chastised UN Secretary-General Ban Ki-moon, saying that "words of condemnation and denunciation are not enough." He called out to "remind the free world of its legal and moral responsibilities toward besieged Gaza" and exhorted the international community "to raise the siege on the people of Gaza and plant hope in the spirits of the oppressed," warning that the "faith of our people in the UN and international community is corroded year after year as it neglects the realization of justice for our people" (Haniyyah 2009).

A little more than four months after the Goldstone Commission presented its report of the UN Fact Finding Mission on the Gaza Conflict to the UN Human Rights Council on September 29, 2009, the Hamas Minister of Justice, Mohammad Faraj Al-Ghoul, issued the Hamas response to the questions and advice posed to the Palestinian government in the Goldstone Commission report (Palestinian Government, Gaza 2010). The Ministry welcomed the Commission's report and expressed hope in seeing results from the investigation and its recommendations on the ground. What is notable is that the fifty-one pages of the Ministry's response (not including eight annexes) were mainly dedicated to recounting the many ways in which *Israel* continues to resist implementing the Goldstone Commission's recommendations (by not opening borders, by using internationally banned weapons, and so on). The response was replete with charts and statistical tables describing the effects of Israel's actions on the Gazan economy, including specific information on agriculture and fishing, details about levels of home destruction during the war, and a review of Palestinian legislators detained as political prisoners by Israel.[27]

Although Amnesty International judged Hamas's response to be insufficient, especially for failing "to address adequately the firing of indiscriminate rockets into southern Israel by Palestinian armed groups during the 22–day conflict," the Ministry's report asserted that the PA had implemented all of the Commission's recommendations (AI 2010:5; see also HRW 2010).[28] Thus, the Hamas government did not opt out of the human rights conversation or wholly refute its terms of reference. Its response did, however, reframe the discourse by redirecting the focus onto the occupier's noncompliance.[29] In reply to the Goldstone report's recommendation that the Gaza PA ensure that international funds and support reach their intended recipients, the Hamas response detailed steps taken, including the formation of a coordination council for the rebuilding of Gaza (Palestinian Government, Gaza 2010:40–43). It stated that despite the government's efforts, the international community has itself fallen short in fulfilling their obligations necessary for rebuilding Gaza (see also S. Roy 2010). It also argued that Israel has maintained the closure of borders, preventing passage of goods needed for rebuilding with its tightening of the siege, which the report characterizes as "an international crime and collective punishment on the residents of Gaza" (Palestinian Government, Gaza 2010:44).[30]

In addition to highlighting Israel's violations, the Hamas response also discussed broader human rights issues, including the status of political prisoners held in Israeli jails, and the conditions of Palestinians held in Gaza prisons (who Hamas insists are not detained for political reasons). The report notes the Hamas government's cooperation with HROs—including shared programs between the Gaza-based HROs and the Ministry of Interior (MoI)—which is amply documented with copies of official letters exchanged between them. The text frames the government's efforts as being generally in accordance with the Palestinian Basic Law, and human rights and international law. The form, tone, and intent of Hamas's response was not dictated by that of the UN report. Instead, it tidily laid out the extent of the damage from Israeli attacks, pointed out Israel's unfulfilled obligations, and detailed Hamas's efforts to protect human rights. One could dismiss this response as an obvious dodging of Goldstone's core criticisms of Hamas (AI 2010; HRW 2010), or as the shoddy job of a naive and inexperienced government, but it would be a mistake to overlook the multiple kinds of work this document does.

The very existence of the report propels the Hamas government into a routinized international human rights round robin in which the UN produces reports and demands further reports and responses from states on a regular basis. (For example, state signatories to the Convention Against Torture are required to submit reports to the monitoring committee every four years.) Hamas's participation in this chorus of call and response normalizes the government as both the proper address of UN requests, and as the responsible respondent that fulfills its obligations to the international community. The "official" nature of the report is repeatedly announced in documents, which are correlates to the performances of the state in pageants and parades. Its stamps and letterhead prove its production by the Ministry of Justice; its approval by the Minister is affirmed by his illegible but stylized signature on the cover letter.

Self-referencing elements of the report help build Hamas's "field of bureaucratic authority" (Feldman 2008:91). Just as the West Bank PA confirms itself in its dealings with ICHR (see Chapter 4), the circular process of "auto-authorization" that Feldman has identified as a key feature of governance in structurally ambiguous conditions (2008:15) is at work even within the confines of this individual report's covers. Included in the report is the copy of the government's official notice from November 5, 2009 (Annex 4), inviting any citizen to come forward to the general prosecutor with complaints about any "internal violations" between June 1, 2008, and August 1, 2009 (a period of intense fighting that left the Fateh-ruled PA routed out of Gaza). The notice articulates itself in a broad legal framework, declaring the announcement as part of the government's observance of international and local directives. It calls for submission of complaints in "respect of the international laws and agreements, following from previous decisions, following the national and legal responsibilities, respecting the recommendations of the UN Human Rights Council, respecting the decision of the UN General Assembly with regard to the 'Goldstone Report.'"

The correspondence with HROs also demonstrates that the Hamas government is responsibly partaking in a circle of human rights–government relations. In so doing, the government presents itself as responsive but also benevolent. Supplicant organizations like the International Committee of the Red Cross, which requested permission for a photographer to accompany delegates to a prison in Gaza (Annex 5), praise and thank the government for its cooperation before making requests. The Ministry letter granting permission for the photographer was also included in the annexes, performing further documentary evidence of this government's sovereignty. In these displays of bureaucratic consciousness, the report's form and content assert the government's right to grant and deny access. It thereby produces another dimension of the "state effect" (T. Mitchell 1999), defining some people as those authorized to control, forbid, or allow particular kinds of movements and interactions, and defining others as those who must seek authorization.

In many ways the report submitted in response to the Goldstone Commission's report parallels Hamas's governmental websites, another arena of self-representation. The Hamas-linked websites of the MoI, the Palestinian Information Center, the Palestinian Police, and *Al-Resalah* newspaper discuss their official meetings with international human rights delegations and HROs, highlighting the confirmation by those organizations of the humane treatment of prisoners in Gaza prisons, or decrying biased human rights reporting.[31] In 2009, moreover, the Ministry of Interior and National Security (MoINS) incorporated units dedicated to human rights issues, and in 2010 the Civil Police set up a complaints bureau to receive submissions from human rights organizations and citizens' complaints (Y. Sayigh 2011:29). The MoINS also "devoted considerable resources" to a public awareness campaign to convince the public of the security forces' commitment to human rights (ICG 2010; Y. Sayigh 2011:30). With every meeting, every public announcement of those meetings, and the establishment of every office and campaign, the Hamas government places itself in an international dialogue. Its contributions to the loops of human rights–related meetings, reports, and replies simultaneously proffers recognition of the legitimacy, or at least the necessity, of that conversation, and situates its claims to statehood in a normalized world of nation-states. That Hamas is willing to jump through the human rights hoops, complete with standardized forms of "bureaucratic inscription" (Hull 2008), makes the Hamas state legible (Scott 1998) to "the international community."[32] In turn, the human rights system, in the guise of a UN commission addressing itself to Hamas in Gaza, a Red Cross representative seeking permission to visit prisons, or human rights training sessions, validates the state effect of those ministers and ministries.

At the same time as they draw attention to their active involvement in the international human rights system in these ways, Hamas representatives express doubts about the work of HROs in Palestine and abroad, doubts that echo Palestinians' general criticisms recounted throughout this book. PLC representative Ramadan summed up the problems as being those of funding, bias, and efficacy. "Our local human rights organizations are politicized through the funding that they get. Their reports are not based on what is happening, but based on what the country who gave them money wants to hear." Despite these critiques, the Hamas-led government in the Gaza Strip continues to respond to human rights NGOs, including the ICHR. In fact, the Ministry of Information in the Gaza Strip responded in great detail with critical comments and corrections to an ICHR report on the media and freedom of information, calling their nomenclature into question. Not only was the author of this critical response offended by the term *deposed government*, which is how ICHR refers to the Hamas government in Gaza, but he also wondered why the report called the security services in the West Bank by their proper names but did not do so in the case of those in Gaza, referring to them instead as "security services belonging to [*al-tabi'ah li*] the Interior Ministry of the deposed government" (PIC 2009). This commentary repeatedly drew attention to what the author considered to be "political terminology" that was not in accord with "legal correctness and legislative customs." Articles defending the government in Gaza that are posted on the unofficial Hamas website, Palestine Info, and on other news outlets have regularly condemned ICHR for being biased and the actions of the Commission as being "unprofessional." The Hamas government thus reiterates the ideal relationship between the ICHR and the state, and insists on its own legitimacy as an elected government that should be held to account in a nonpartisan way (cf. Winegar 2006:137–174).[33]

If Hamas legislators generally trust the work of the ICHR, as some of them told me they do, it was in contrast to a number of other organizations that were not viewed as credible. They "don't follow all the details," Ramadan said, citing specifically Al-Haq's coverage of a clash between PA police and Hamas members in the West Bank town of Qalqilya (Elshobaki et al. 2008:6–12).[34] The legislator complained that the NGO had adopted the PA's narrative of the events without proper investigation. He went on to criticize the small circle of NGO debate and NGOs' poor outreach and efficacy:

> What do they do on the ground? People are convinced that these centers are just working to collect more money. If a place published a book, people will say, I wonder how much money Switzerland gave them to publish it. Unfortunately, the NGOs' goal these days is money. It is very strange: they hold conferences

in hotels and rent rooms for us, and food and drinks that may cost fifty to sixty thousand dollars. They spend all of this money on a conference, and no one will read the research or report that might come out of it. So, the people don't trust the NGOs.

Honesty and Sincerity of Action: The Social Values Guiding Hamas

Contrasting the Islamists' efforts to those of the (secular) NGOs, the parliamentarian Musa Ramadan repeated the theme that is at the core of Hamas's principle of sincere action versus empty show. He observed that the "only organizations left on the ground are the Islamic ones. They have charity centers, hospitals, and schools. They give charity to people." Indeed, Islamic charitable institutions affiliated with Hamas are widely considered to be honest, professional, efficient, and impartial. Most agree that they deliver aid regardless of the beneficiaries' party or religion (ICG 2003:ii; S. Roy 2011:173), but there are accounts of service provision having been biased toward Hamas sympathizers in Gaza. Even people who do not support Hamas recognize the efficiency and efficacy of its work (ICG 2003:ii), because its actions yield tangible, and much needed, services. During a visit to the Al-Bireh public library, a secular leftist grudgingly pointed out to me the high quality and efficiency of services provided in the Hamas-led institutions. He compared the polite demeanor of Hamas civil servants and the well-organized services that developed when Hamas gained control over numerous West Bank municipalities in 2005 to the disorganized nature of their Fateh-run counterparts. From extensive financial donations to the needy, to establishing neighborhood libraries, sports clubs, and schools, the focus of Hamas institutions is social welfare for the society as a whole. They do not, as Ramadan's critiques imply, simply collect information about rights violations; they attend to the people's problems and treat them.

Ramadan's disapproval of the wasteful, money-driven nature of NGOs was not just centered on the inadequacy of the secular groups' services; it also echoed a common conviction that the NGOs were led by materialistic motives. The stated missions of those NGOs include rights awareness and protection, but their efforts did not appear to be truly geared toward those ends. The effective service provision of Islamic groups, in contrast, is evidence of the sincerity of their efforts.

Although Hamas won some supporters as a result of its substance-over-show approach, not all Palestinians are convinced; and it is against the same criteria embedded within the moral load of sincerity, a concern for the closeness between words and actions taken on behalf of the nation, that some seek to discredit Hamas too. Those who were not inclined toward Hamas's position, especially staunch members of Fateh, worked hard to convince me of the two-faced nature of the Islamists. Any nod toward human rights or claims to liberal democracy, they believed, were mere discursive manipulations. They were full of "tactics and PR," as a sheikh who had left the party told me. According to this perspective, beneath the "beautiful words" of Hamas, in the actual inten-tions and actions lurking beneath the ritual language of democracy and human rights, is a movement readying itself for an Islamist takeover in the West Bank. It is true that Hamas's behavior is not always ethical, even by its own stan-dards, and many of its policies and actions in the Gaza Strip do not accord with human rights standards.[35] However, whether or not Hamas is plotting some-thing is a question the answer to which is, in addition to being unverifiable, less relevant to my point here about the shared baseline values according to which Palestinians evaluate political behavior.

Although scholars have warned against replaying in our analyses the di-vorce between the material and discursive dimensions of states that is crucial to "the state effect" (T. Mitchell 1999:76–77), Palestinians are already thoroughly wary of that distinction. They are quick to detect and dismiss pretenses to power and authority by the undeserving, always ready to name a base scrabble for the seat of power for what it is. They clearly recognize and are suspicious of the discursive work that can go into a performance of state that has no material foundations. The reputation that Hamas has sought to build, through its self-representations in deed and word, is built out of that collective national sus-picion. Since being elected to the government and taking over the Gaza Strip (while still existing under occupation), Hamas has negotiated between, on the one hand, nationalist commitments to act sincerely (against occupation, for the people) and, on the other hand, international demands to engage the human rights system. To negotiate those apparently conflicting requirements, it shuns both the West Bank PA and HROs for offering words and no reality, insisting that rights can be realized only within a suitable political system. In so doing, Hamas has opened itself up to the same kind of critique from its foes. However, all Hamas supporters agree that without the appropriate actions to build the political reality, human rights are empty words in the air.

I N SEPTEMBER 2011, the PA made a bid for full membership in the United Nations. Although it gained the support of numerous foreign countries and many hailed it as a way for the PA to break into the international fellowship of states, it also prompted vocal opposition among Palestinians. Some pointed out the senselessness of announcing a state that had no sovereignty or economic viability (AIC 2011; Samaha 2011). The PA's rival, Hamas, characterized the UN bid as "tactical" and refused to support it because it was not based on "national principles" (DPA 2011). A human rights worker from Ramallah expressed his disdain for the PA's efforts in a message to me over Facebook with some well-placed scare quotes: "What do we need from a 'State' as we have a 'president' and 'security forces' and 'cabinet(s).' So, we have everything." A smiley face, and then a frowney face, followed, in case I did not grasp his full meaning. His sarcastic remarks stemmed from a number of things: the fact that the legal mandate of the president, Mahmoud Abbas, ran out in January 2009 (or January 2010, by some accounts); that the cabinets of the West Bank and Gaza Strip are led by rival parties and do not coordinate or exercise real oversight; and that the security forces' discretionary power to violate citizens' rights with impunity—spying, imprisoning, torturing—has made many, like this rights worker, worried about what kind of authoritarian state the PA is trying to make.

The UN bid and debates about it illuminate the always incomplete ways in which the authority and legitimacy of states are produced, attempted, refuted, or refused. It highlights the significance of international recognition to the authorization of state powers, and underlines the importance of the observations, analyses, and, more often, criticisms of the people that a state is claiming to represent. Although the continuing inability of the PA to be granted sovereignty and be recognized as a state makes the processual nature of statehood more obvious, the inherently incomplete and transnational element of nation-state projects (Cowan 2008:342) pertains not only to Palestine. It is true that the critiques of state-making efforts in the occupied territory are particularly loud and marked by moral evaluations, and aspects of this are specific to the Palestinian experience and related to the particular place of the "question of Palestine" in the international system (which is in turn tied to Israel's own symbolic and geostrategic significance). However, the tangled problem of consent, authority, and legitimacy in the constitution of "stateness" is a general one. The ongoing interplay of the international human rights system with nationalist ideologies, the centrality of populist ethics, and the repeated failures that mark the struggle over statehood in Palestine all point to issues that are applicable to state-making and its analysis more generally: the state as everyday and institutional practice, as performance and ideal negotiated across international and local realms, as a process of moral argument.

Even if human rights are particularly significant in the occupied territory for the historically and politically specific reasons spelled out in this book, they are also an important feature of state performances elsewhere. In the United Kingdom, Colombia, Iran, and beyond (Kelly 2012; Merry 2011; Osanloo 2009; Tate 2007), the human rights system has become a central element of the conception of state legitimacy, a core mediating grid through which states are debated and constructed, a specific form of supranational governmentality (Cowan 2007:546) that imposes criteria of legibility on supplicant states (Chatterjee 2011).[1] In addition, although this system has specific effects in each context, it has had similarly paradoxical effects everywhere. Whereas human rights projects are touted as a way to promote tolerance, democracy, and international harmony—to advance, as the U.S. State Department contends, "timeless values, which empower people to speak, think, worship, and assemble freely, to lead their work and family lives with dignity, and to know that their dreams of a brighter future are within reach" (U.S. Department of State 2009)—in many places engagement with the human rights system raises the suspicion that what it is advancing is quite the opposite.

For Palestinians, speaking the language of human rights can actually index a discredited and immoral subject, what a good person should not be: insincere and selfish, or "political" in the utilitarian, scheming, all talk, self-serving sense.

Activists and analysts have observed similar attitudes across the globe, wherein a resignification of notions of "human rights," NGOs, and politics more generally has occurred from post-perestroika Russia (Hemment 2007) to Southeast Asia (A. Roy 2004) and the United States (Berlant 1998; Brown 1995). Human rights—once a concept encompassing notions of sincere and selfless collective activism—evokes images of selfish, power-hungry, money-grubbing scoundrels. Julie Hemment (2007), for one, has noted that the predicament of feminist activists in Russia—familiar to NGO professionals everywhere (including Palestine)—is "one in which they find themselves preoccupied less with local issues than with pleasing donors and securing their own organizational sustainability" (6); and in East Africa, observers and practitioners have criticized the lack of "moral authority" among NGOs, which often do not practice the human rights that they preach (Nassali 2011:28). Donor-driven projects and international donor monies have produced a fat-cat mentality among NGO workers, who have become a new elite ever more out of touch with the communities they are meant to serve. Human rights discourse has been delegitimized because it is seen to be merely the tool of those who want to turn local problems into money for projects (Mutua 2009:31).

This view would seem to support the arguments of those who have described human rights as a hegemonic ideology that cripples collective action (Brown 2004:461) and "masks and legitimizes a concrete politics of Western imperialism, military interventions and neo-colonialism" (Zizek n.d.). However, Palestinians' varied engagements with human rights challenge simple condemnations of the human rights system as the thin end of an imperial wedge. Although the human rights regime shapes the context, it is not hegemonic and all-determining of Palestinian social relations and politics. If scholars have thoroughly critiqued the false universalisms of the human rights regime, what we know less about are the forms and effects of local critiques of the human rights system, in particular the generative power of the suspicion and cynicism directed at human rights at a time when "the whole idea [has] lost some of its romantic appeal and moral purity" (Moyn 2012).

In the occupied territory, members of Hamas have expressed one kind of critique, insisting on recognition of the disjunctures between human rights ideals and practices that plague the human rights regime. Their constant attention to these hypocrisies comes out of an ethical world with different and wider roots than that of the human rights system, and thereby challenges that regime. These other nationalist and, for many, religious systems of value have more meaning, more credibility, than purported universal norms and internationally guided state-building efforts.

Although similar neoliberal dynamics have shaped the work and effects of human rights and other kinds of NGOs throughout the global South, in Palestine a code of entrenched nationalist values creates particular kinds of friction between the transforming parts of this political ethical system. How politics and human rights are enacted and judged is a function of Palestinians' own understandings of rights and dignity, of authority to rule and sources of moral authority. I have shown the travails of people who continue to speak and try to act within a nationalist idiom, the counter positions of those who pursue state-building, and those who have withdrawn from both arenas, foregoing formal politics all together, and how cynicism is woven through all these positions.

This book has emphasized the cynicism that has grown up around human rights in occupied Palestine, but it does not necessarily lead to the argument, hypothetical and fantastical as it would be, that the human rights system should be abolished. *Cynicism*, as an analytical concept, indicates something other than apathy; it is not simply a normative judgment on the stance of people who use the human rights system for their own purposes. Cynicism is also part of how people continue to critique and search, or at least hope, for something better, and the human rights system is one way that Palestinians engage in that search. Many Palestinians continue to work with human rights principles and the human rights system in creative ways. They may be cynical, insofar as they do not have huge hopes for the future or in the efficacy of HROs. Yet they persist within the human rights system because they think it is a channel for being politically engaged, for doing something useful, for making a living, for articulating ideals of proper social relations and state forms.

Extracting the term *cynicism* from its normative and scholarly baggage in order to use it as a concept useful for broader social analysis has been tricky. What is its analytical purchase, I have been asked by fellow anthropologists, when it clearly relates only to intellectual critique but not to emotion? Or to the extent that it indexes emotion, isn't *irony* a better term than the amoralism implied by cynicism? Some have questioned its applicability to other places, such as India, where cynicism does not counter politics and instead the expectation of corruption and a robust subaltern politics persist side by side; or Turkey, where cynicism sustains the state (Navaro-Yashin 2002). My response is that cynicism, as I use it in this book, is a conceptual term meant to encompass dimensions of emotion (the culturally mediated expression of feelings) and conscious thought, which can only be captured ethnographically.[2] It has a specific texture and set of effects that is particular to the Palestinian situation, where cynicism comes out of asynchronous moral systems in transition and bears within it the seeds of its opposite. Because cynicism is also a result of how global structures function on the ground, it seems to be relevant in other contexts where political failures and personal disappointments have been funneled into NGOs and human rights work too, even if the specific experiences and outcomes of political cynicism may be distinct. It is not only what my interlocutors have to say about the human rights system that I read as cynicism, but also the fact that they say it, and my interpretation of what kinds of alternative political horizons or more hopeful stances such moments of articulation might index. My use of cynicism derives from the substance and fact of the analytical self-reflexivity among my specific interlocutors, but shades of its existence appear at the edges of ethnographic observations in other contexts.

Not all of the people I talked with are similarly pessimistic or view human rights in the same way, but they all have a diagnosis of their own personal position and of the general situation of Palestine. Cynicism is a critical stance by which those who are displeased with choices available in the present hold on to the belief that such limited options are not all that there should be. For many Palestinians, a horizon, however vague, of alternative possibilities and hopes endures because a history of more satisfying political bonds and of contributions motivated by more sincerely held political values is remembered, or at least nostalgically imagined. Their national imaginings persist through ethical debate despite the absence of a nation-state. That critical stance is part of what is sustaining Palestinian nationalism, allowing a variety of uses of the human rights system and blocking the entrenchment of an authoritarian state apparatus. How cynicism looks and feels and its effects elsewhere are questions that others must answer. What I suggest here is that it is a phenomenon ripe for wider investigation.

The Dark Side of the Moon

A prison director who welcomed the ICRC and ICHR to inspect his facilities (see Chapter 4) took me on a tour of the jail where I interviewed him—or at least a section of it. Abu Showky spent some two hours assuring me of the pristine rights standards of his prison, including by taking me into the wing where Hamas political prisoners were being held. It was somewhat ironic, given the illegality of political imprisonment in both the Palestinian Basic Law and international human rights law. He ended his pitch by saying, "Security and law is like this. It's like the moon. You know how the moon shines: it's beautiful, people use it to say nice things, they flirt through metaphors about it; but the moon—its reality is in the dark." A couple of floors underground, beneath the very room in which we were talking, were interrogation cells of the Palestinian Preventive Security and General Security where just the week before a prisoner had died under unclear circumstances. All that the director had shown me was the bright side of human rights, but it does not mean that the dark side is not still there.

When we left I asked Yasir, the ICHR staff member who had gained me entrance to the prison, what he thought this director was saying. Was he really admitting to an outsider the abuses that actually took place underground? Why would he? The human rights worker laughed and said it was because Abu Showky is stupid. But the security officer had not struck me as in any way dumb or unsavvy. Although he had performed his congenial concern for the well-being of his imprisoned charges in a somewhat unconvincing way, shaking the hands of the bearded men crammed into overcrowded cells, clearly Abu Showky saw the need to impress his foreign visitor in a particular way. He had to perform care and respect and his obeisance to human rights, and it was clear to us all that he was doing so. Yasir thought that, with his parting comment about the moon, the prison director was being careless in drawing too much attention to the curtain on the stage, and to the fact of the backstage realities. I am still puzzling over why he told me to remember the dark side of the moon.

I think he was making particular choices (to let me into the prison, for example, to see what he hoped I would see) out of a range of dictated options. He had described himself to me as a pragmatic man. As Abu Showky had said to me earlier in our meeting, "the law is the law," and the law is his situation. So he opens his doors to human rights and governmental monitors because the law demands it. If those monitors are keeping track, he said, he has proof that he's doing what he's supposed to be doing. "It would be even better if they were here twenty-four hours a day." He also told me he had a family to support and he needed to do well in his job and please his supervisors. He asked me about how he might get funding for higher education; having only managed to finish some high school, he thought a degree might help him progress in his career. He was caught trying to navigate a path between various pressures, including the need to fulfill familial obligations and his own personal ambitions, the need to satisfy perceived external demands, and the need to respond to internal requirements in order to maintain "order" of a certain kind that did not allow Hamas's political opposition to get out of control (the boundaries of which were, of course, always shifting). He could have resigned his position, or blown the whistle on the torture happening in the dungeons beneath his feet. Instead, he seemed to be performing the script laid out for him by his various audiences, trying to get along by playing his part.

Abu Showky expressed and enacted one form of cynicism, a type that I came across less often during my research, possibly because my contacts with members of the PA were briefer. The way he chose to act was cynical in a way that is captured more closely in the standard English language meaning of the word. The double character of critique and hope that I found in others' cynicism was less obvious in Abu Showky. His actions seem more clearly to have helped perpetuate corrupt and inhumane structures of power, and the malevolence of his cynicism is starker because of the nature of the abuses going on in the gaols beneath his feet. Obeisance to the human rights system "as if" human rights principles are really the motive and goal when, as in the case of Abu Showky, they are not, at once reaffirms human rights and the international community as sources of authority and arbiters of justice, and at the same time reduces the credibility of the human rights system and of civil society itself. In line with the arguments of Wedeen (1999) and Navaro-Yashin (2002), we could judge Abu Showky to be like those in Syria and Turkey who, if they are not part of the solution, are part of the problem. However, by calling attention to the dark side of the moon, this person, so deeply dependent on the PA and so directly implicated in its abuses, indirectly told me that he was acting in human rights performances that are staged to cover them up. In so doing, he pulled the curtain back a little, perhaps revealing his cynicism as well as his desire for something different.

My focus in this book on the internal processes of local power and authority formation is by no means intended to make Palestinians appear as the sole source of their own oppression, but rather to show something of the way power, authority, and influence are negotiated under conditions of domination. Palestinians are trying to produce a state out of the residue of an anticolonial nationalist movement during an efflorescence of global governance structures while still existing under occupation. Part of this process involves the dialectical interaction between, on the one hand, the role of human rights in political claims and their framings for international interlocutors and, on the other hand, the role of human rights in Palestinian state creation and the formation of local governance and political subjectivity. Although he was not representative of most people I knew in Palestine, Abu Showky's situation, if not his specific choices, is one indicative result of that set of interlocking structures.

International donors might act as if they can produce a state through their demands for human rights performances, bureaucratic "professionalism," and security agencies. However, as long as Palestinians do not recognize themselves in that state, the internal struggles will go on. As long as the state and its agencies are unaccountable to the law and unsupervised by a democratic structure, the state will remain nonexistent or fragile, with only a tenuous hold on the people it is meant to govern. Palestinians' responses to the PA's human rights and security performances reveal radical inconsistencies in the criteria of legitimacy that exist among the PA, other Palestinians in the occupied territory, and those acting in the name of the international community. Notions of rights (not just *human* rights) remain drastically disjointed, a key feature blocking convergence of visions of the state among the many actors involved in trying to produce it.

This perpetual tug of war is not only a paradox of the supranational support for state-making; well-intentioned efforts to produce stable, rights-respecting states will backfire and promote instability because the snarl of interlocking structural conditions, nationalist histories, and a past of disappointed political goals and sedimented cynicism shaping Palestinians' experience of the state-building process cannot be taken account of by the logic of the supranational. Demands by agents of global governance render nationalist politics illegible and illegitimate within the supranational framework. The requirements that specific governments and international institutions have placed on Palestinians to prove their "worthiness" and "readiness" for statehood and independence are read by many Palestinians as anti-nationalist, as serving the particular interests of others, not "the Palestinian people," as a populist conception would figure it. The liberal idea that matters of global concern can be managed and regulated on a global scale by international bodies and funders through the promotion of democracy and other values perceived to be universal and desirable has been proven, once again, not only inadequate to reality, not only productive of "side effects" that can expand state power (Ferguson 1994), but also productive of oppositional forms of consciousness. The seeds of failure are inherent within projects of global governmentality; cynicism is the form of immanent critique (cf. Postone 1996:87–88) that can water those seeds.

. . .

The theoretical question of what sovereign authority is and where it resides and the normative question of who should have it and what its social effects should be are the subjects of ongoing and newly reinvigorated debate in Palestine and many other places. In these times of revolution across the Middle East and economic upheaval throughout Europe, analysts need to consider anew the issues of consciousness, critique, and consent that the Palestinian case highlights. How to take account of the growing consensus that the human rights system and the UN cannot provide meaningful change? How to account for the new level of popular awareness and growing public critique of the masks of state? These masks are falling down to reveal, broadly and starkly to all, the corruption, cronyism, elitism, and internationalism of state institutions and the interests they serve. These struggles against authoritarianism and austerity in the Middle East and Europe are mostly not driven by antistate, pro-anarchy motivations. However, they do articulate ideals of moral authority and legitimate sovereignty, and desires for a renewed social contract. How do we analyze the state in these conditions of collective awareness when alternatives are in demand and the powers that be are scrambling to persuade cynical publics that the emperor still has clothes? We must first learn how to appreciate the multiple powers of cynicism in politics and the possibilities of solidarity and, yes, the resistance to oppressive forces that are contained therein. I intended with this account of political transformations in the occupied Palestinian territory to provide one model for what form that appreciation might take. I hope t offers some reason for healthy cynicism—and hope too.

Notes

Introduction

1. For the text of this convention, see http://www.hrweb.org/legal/cat.html.

2. Although sometimes referred to as the occupied Palestinian territories, the UN Office for the Coordination of Humanitarian Affairs uses the singular, which is the convention I follow here. See http://www.ochaopt.org.

3. See, for example, EUPOL COPPS (n.d.).

4. See Glendon (2001), Lauren (2003), and the UN's history of the drafting of the UDHR (UN n.d.).

5. William Sewell has usefully defined structures as "sets of cultural schemas, distributions of resources, and modes of power" that "combine in an interlocking and mutually sustaining fashion to reproduce consistent streams of social practice" (Sewell 1996:842).

6. All names have been changed.

7. For important early analyses of NGOs in the occupied Palestinian territory, see Hammami (1995).

8. For United Nations General Assembly Resolution 2443, which established this committee on December 19, 1968, see http://unispal.un.org/UNISPAL.NSF/0/1FE2116 573C8CFBE852560DF004ED05D.

9. See especially Tanabe (2007).

10. Paul Chamberlin (2011) interprets Fateh's open letter to the UN General Assembly in October 1968 (in which it claimed the status of a legitimate national resistance movement fighting for self-determination as set out in the UN Charter and the Universal Declaration of Human Rights) as an indication that Fateh posed the Palestinian issue as being at its core a problem of human rights.

11. Yael Navaro-Yashin's (2002) influential work on Turkish politics uses this notion of the "faces of the state" in a distinct manner to draw attention to politics as "unstable," because it exists in a range of domains, from the public square and national monuments to the police and media images. See also Obeid (2010). The PA also creates state performances through various groups, conducted across a range of venues, from courts and security services (Brown 2003) to the news media (Bishara 2008, 2012) and interactions with international aid agencies (Hilal 2003).

12. The Universal Periodic Reviews conducted by the UN's Human Rights Council, for example, are one way that states are publicly and internationally audited (Cowan 2012).

13. For a brief history of NGO-PA relations, see Jarrar (2005).

14. Here I am not calling on theories of performativity, such as those developed by Butler (1990) and Morris (1995) to discuss the embodiment of gender, or by Taylor (1997) to analyze "nation-ness." Rather, the notion of human rights performance that I am trying to get across resonates more closely with Sartre's concept of "bad faith," or performance as a kind of self-deception (Coombes 2001).

15. See for comparison Diane Nelson (2010) on the "ethnographic fact" of duplicity or being duped and reckoning as modes of understanding in Guatemala.

16. A key text on Palestinian national identity is Khalidi (1998).

17. Such critiques of the human rights system echo Hannah Arendt's understanding of the national basis of "the right to have rights" (Arendt 1994; see also Isaac 1996). For exploration of these ideas in the context of Israel, see Blecher (2005).

18. Abrams' theoretical contributions have been useful specifically to many anthropologists who are rethinking the state (e.g., Blom Hansen 2001; Blom Hansen and Stepputat 2006; Kelly 2006; Ong 2000).

19. For discussions of the state in global or transnational context, see Chalfin (2010), Cowan (2012), Gupta (1995), and Sharma and Gupta (2006).

20. The Fourth Geneva Convention prohibits an occupying power from transferring citizens from its own territory to the occupied territory (Article 49). The Hague Regulations prohibit an occupying power from undertaking permanent changes in the occupied area unless these are due to military needs in the narrow sense of the term, or unless they are undertaken for the benefit of the local population.

21. See, for example, Al-Haq (2006) and DCI-Palestine (2001).

22. Even after this change in the placement of the wall, 85 percent of the amended route runs through the West Bank (B'Tselem 2011b).

23. Administrative home demolitions are carried out by Israel purportedly because the houses were built without the required license. For statistics through 2012, see ICAHD (2012).

24. The controversy over Dayton's involvement in Palestinian security sector reform exploded in 2009 after the US security coordinator made a speech to the Washington Institute for Near East Policy implying that the Palestinian security forces were helping—or in the eyes of many Palestinians, collaborating—with the Israel Defense Forces. See Washington Institute for Near East Policy (2009) and ICG (2010:11–12).

25. See, for example, Carapico (forthcoming) on donor dynamics and NGO professionals' critiques of it throughout the Arab region, and Goldstein (2007) on Bolivia.

26. For a novel theoretical and ethnographic exploration of the role of "everyday" cynicism and agency in Syria, see Anderson (forthcoming).

27. Raymond Williams (1977:132) describes "structures of feeling" as "thought as felt and feeling as thought: practical consciousness of a present kind, in a living and inter-relating continuity . . . a social experience still in process, often indeed not yet recognized as social but taken to be private, idiosyncratic, and even isolating, but which in analysis (though rarely otherwise) has its emergent, connecting, and dominant characteristics."

28. For details on Israeli use of weaponry against Palestinians, see B'Tselem (2011c).

29. These NGOs included, among others, Addameer Prisoner Support and Human Rights Association, Al Mezan Center for Human Rights, the Democracy and Workers' Rights Center, the Mandela Center for Prisoners' Rights, the Palestinian Working Woman Society for Development, the Treatment and Rehabilitation Centre for Victims of Torture, and the Palestinian Center for Human Rights, as well as the international human rights NGO Amnesty International, and semi-official organizations such as the Palestinian Prisoners' Club (*Nadi al-Asir*).

30. The UN Office for the Coordination of Humanitarian Affairs, commonly known as OCHA, provides updated information on economic and humanitarian conditions in the occupied territory. See http://www.unocha.org.

31. For one report on PA repression in the West Bank, see Freed (2008).

Chapter 1

1. Additional details about the nature of Israeli violations can be found in the annual reports of the United Nations Special Committee to Investigate Israeli Practices Affecting the Human Rights of the Palestinian People and Other Arabs of the Occupied Territories, established in 1968 by United Nations General Assembly Resolution 2443 (XXIII).

2. The *Sunday Times* of London published a long exposé on the use of torture in 1977.

3. For information on settler violence and how the Israeli judicial system deals with it, see B'Tselem (2011d).

4. For information on house demolitions during the early years of the first intifada, see B'Tselem (1989a); and for information on the later years, see Israeli Committee Against Home Demolitions (ICAHD 2010). For information on torture and detention from 1990 to the present, see reports by the Public Committee Against Torture in Israel (n.d.); and for details on the human rights situation in the occupied Palestinian territory in general, see Amnesty International (n.d.).

5. Bishara (1979) recounts how a US Consulate official in East Jerusalem was punished for reporting information about Israel's torture of Palestinians in the West Bank. E. Said (2000) and Mearsheimer and Walt (2007) have demonstrated how Israel and the Zionist lobby have dominated and defined the terms of the debate on the Arab-Israeli conflict across public discourse in the West, especially in the United States.

6. Chomsky's (1999) indictment of the United States' support of Israel's repressive measures toward the Palestinians includes extensive citation of how positively Israel has been portrayed in the mainstream US media.

7. Originally called Law in the Service of Man, which became the West Bank affiliate of the Geneva-based International Commission of Jurists, the organization later changed its name to Al-Haq. In Arabic, the term *al-haqq* connotes something that is right, correct, true, and just, as well as the just thing or action that someone deserves in order to put things right. (Its plural, *huquq*, also refers to "law" and is the term used in the phrase translated as "human rights," *huquq al-insan*.)

8. Unless otherwise noted, quotations are from interviews with current and former Al-Haq members conducted by the author between 2007 and 2009.

9. Israeli officials and sympathizers have invested great effort in portraying the occupation as benign (Morris 1999:341), and in trying to justify Israel's military occupation (e.g., Dershowitz 2003).

10. This Israeli use of law is quite distinct from that of other colonial regimes. Israeli colonial law did not aim to impose new ideologies of personhood and social contract (Comaroff and Comaroff 1997:269) as colonial law did in Africa, but rather facilitated the dispossession of Palestinian land and quashed political mobilization against occupation (Shehadeh 1988:vii; Playfair 1992:266–267; Arsanjani 1982:426, 442).

11. For more references to Palestinian political engagement with the UN, including the statement of political leaders from the occupied territory addressed to the president of the UN Security Council and the UN secretary-general calling for the implementation of Palestinians' right to self-determination and sovereignty, see Chamberlin (2011) and Rangwala (2001:144, 153n79, 164).

12. For discussions of how objectivity came to be understood as knowledge that is distinct from the particularities of the knower, see Daston (1992), Daston and Galison (2007), and Dear (1992).

13. On "the irrational native" in colonialism's justifications, see Asad (1974), Fabian (1983), Luhrman (1994), and Mehta (1990). See Edward Said (1979) on orientalism in the Jewish colonial project in Palestine.

14. See E. Said (1979). For discussion of the role of orientalism in Zionism and American relations with the Middle East, see Shohat (2003), McAlister (2001), and Shaheen (2001).

15. In 1967, Israel annexed East Jerusalem and additional territory in the West Bank. Those Palestinians who were present when an Israeli census of the area was conducted were identified as "permanent residents" but did not have full citizenship rights. On the status of East Jerusalem and its residents, see B'Tselem (2011a).

16. For an early legal examination of Israel's administration of the occupied Palestinian territory in light of international law, see Playfair (1992).

17. Among the bases for this claim in international law is Article 49 of the Fourth Geneva Convention of 1949, which states, "The Occupying Power shall not deport or transfer parts of its own civilian population into the territory it occupies." *The West Bank and the Rule of Law* detailed the Israeli system of military orders that governed the West Bank. It was translated into five languages by national sections of the International Commission of Jurists, and the UN and foreign missions made bulk purchases, which contributed to increasing the legitimacy and exposure of Al-Haq abroad (Tolley 1994:150).

18. The Israeli government contends that it is not an occupier of what the international community considers to be the occupied Palestinian territories. Instead, they consider themselves "administrators," on the basis that Jordan and Egypt were not sovereign in the West Bank and Gaza Strip, respectively, and therefore the Geneva Conventions governing occupation of enemy territory do not apply (Kuttab and Shehadeh 1980:10–11). The international community has rejected these arguments (Gorenberg 2006:101–102).

19. As Kuttab (1992) wrote, for example, among the more than one thousand military orders that Israel used to govern the occupied territory, Military Order 101 of 1967, "Order Regarding Prohibition of Incitement and Hostile Propaganda Actions," prohibits meetings of ten or more people where political speech can be heard, or marches of ten or more people, or trying "verbally or in any other manner to influence public opinion in a manner which might endanger public security or order" (492). Among those who have restated the principle that an occupying power cannot change local laws except for security reasons, David Kretzmer (2002), an Israeli legal scholar, confirms that "the occupying power has the duty to take over the first and most basic task of every government: Maintaining law and order and facilitating everyday life. . . . the occupying power may not use the occupation as a means of changing the political status of the occupied territory" (57). Although Israel maintains that the Geneva Conventions do not apply to them, they say they are willing to abide by international conventions that apply to occupied territory. For an account of Israel's position on the applicability of the Geneva Conventions, see Anderson (n.d.).

20. These experts included Antonio Cassese and John Dugard. Cassese, an Italian jurist, was the first president of the International Criminal Tribunal for the Former Yugoslavia, serving in this capacity from 1993 to 1997. In October 2004, Cassese was appointed by UN Secretary-General Kofi Annan to be chairman of the UN International Commission of Enquiry into Violations of Human Rights and Humanitarian Law in Darfur. John Dugard is a South African professor of international law. He has served as judge ad hoc on the International Court of Justice and as a special rapporteur for both the former UN Commission on Human Rights and the International Law Commission.

21. Early fieldworkers, along with the lawyers and foreign volunteers, had completed their college education, many obtaining social work degrees, which contributed to the eventual professionalization of the human rights field. Some staff members had volunteered with Amnesty International in other countries, but many employees' initial involvement at Al-Haq was mere happenstance and their first exposure to human rights work.

22. The sparse funding acquired in the beginning came from Oxfam and ICCO (a large Netherlands development cooperation NGO affiliated with the Protestant Church in the Netherlands; see http://www.icco-international.com/int/about-us) and later from the Ford Foundation, which has been a key funder of international and local NGOs across the globe since the mid-1970s (specifically supporting work on political and civil rights and not on economic and social rights; Carmichael 2001:257).

23. The goal of the Palestinian nationalist movement until the mid-1970s was to establish a nonsectarian, democratic Arab state in all of Palestine through a people's war. After that came a period when Palestinian representatives called for a two-state solution that would entail Israeli withdrawal from the occupied territory and the establishment of a Palestinian state (Rangwala 2001:151–153; Tamari 1988:26).

24. The Likud Party is the major conservative party in Israel.

25. The UN, United States, and Great Britain have declared these settlements and outposts illegal and an obstruction to peace in the Middle East. See, for example, UNGA (1977) and Haaretz (2009).

26. In 1968, Fateh addressed the UN's International Conference on Human Rights and called for the application of the concept of human rights in Palestine, thus portraying itself as a "movement struggling to achieve those same ideals that formed the basis of the UN Declaration on Human Rights," and portraying the Palestinian problem as fundamentally "a problem of human rights" (Chamberlin 2011:35).

27. Worth noting is the contrast with Amnesty International, which specifically says they do not adhere to such high levels of evidential requirements. Their standards "are lower than those which would lead to conviction in court. AI is prompted into action by 'credible evidence of torture,' irrespective of whether the individuals responsible have been, or can be, identified. It is for judicial inquiries and courts to establish the guilt of individuals 'beyond reasonable doubt'" (Welsh 2000:3).

28. It is worth noting that in his study of a science lab and of the Conseil d'État (the French Council of State), Bruno Latour (2004) has diagrammed vast distinctions between scientific objects and legal objects, despite the epistemological overlaps between the two domains.

29. This characterization of Australian and Canadian NGOs is from sociologist of human rights, Dominique Clément of the University of Alberta. E-mail communication, January 8, 2010.

30. Howard Tolley's (1994:200, 206) history of the ICJ mentions MacDermot's defense of Al-Haq publications in the face of Israeli denunciations and denials, and his advocacy for Palestinians in general, including his pressing a "reluctant" ICJ Executive Committee to recognize Palestinian rights (196). The ICJ provides legal expertise at both the international and national levels to ensure that developments in international law adhere to human rights principles and that international standards are implemented at the national level. The organization emphasizes "its impartial, objective and authoritative legal approach to the protection and promotion of human rights through the rule of law." See ICJ (n.d.).

31. Affidavits did sometimes include subjective comments about detention conditions from the detainee's perspective, including descriptions of how cold the holding cells were, the fact that the food was "awful," or that the guards used "extremely unpleasant techniques of interrogation," such as kicking the detainee in the shins and threatening to assault a sister (Al-Haq 1983:29), or dragging a detainee "off like a dog" (LSM 1985:25).

32. For more information on Israeli policies of tree uprooting and home demolitions, see B'Tselem (2002).

33. For more information on the Israeli military courts, see B'Tselem (1989b).

34. During the first year of the intifada, "the army imposed a minimum of 1,600 curfews in the West Bank and Gaza, at least 400 of which were prolonged," lasting more than three days (Hiltermann 1989b:128–129). For a more recent account of how the permit system functions, see B'Tselem (2004).

35. For more summaries of the first year of the intifada, see Hiltermann (1989b) and al-Haq ([1988] 1990).

36. For critical discussions of the role of donors in Palestine, see Keating, Le More, and Lowe (2005) and Hanafi and Tabar (2005).

37. For reports on this case, see Cohen and Golan (1991). For one account of how human rights activists responded to the growing number of Palestinian deaths in detention, see Hiltermann (1990).

38. Shehadeh's (1997) legal analysis of the Israeli-PLO accords includes two proposals that he developed as part of the negotiations team.

39. For a summary and generally positive take on the Oslo peace process, see Shlaim (1994).

40. For an explanation of how different areas of the occupied Palestinian territory were designated by the Israeli-Palestinian Interim Agreement of 1995, see Al-Jazeera (n.d.)

41. For one, the more ambiguous legal status of the occupied Palestinian territory after Oslo muddled the legal framework in which HROs would operate (Hajjar 2003:49–78). See Bowen (1997) for legal analysis of the relevance of international law and human rights to the Palestinian territories after Oslo.

42. Levels of foreign aid to NGOs plummeted from US$170–240 million in the early 1990s to barely US$100–120 million after Oslo (Sullivan 1996).

Chapter 2

1. For another ethnographic account of the notion of solidarity in Palestinian social relations and moral evaluations, see Kelly (2006:31–42).

2. On the importance of family in Palestine, see Hasso (2011), Kanaaneh (2002), Kelly (2006), Peteet (1991, 1994, 1997), R. Sayigh (1998), and Taraki (2006).

3. On the meaning of martyrs and their social and political value, see Allen (2002, 2009b).

4. More than 80 percent of survey respondents believed that NGOs are corrupt and afflicted by nepotism or *wasta* (personal connections), and that they misuse public property (AMAN 2007; Nazaha 2006). The meetings at which the Code of Conduct was drafted were funded by the Konrad-Adenauer-Stiftung (a German political foundation related to the Christian Democrats) as part of the European Union's Initiative for Democracy and Human Rights, and organized in conjunction with the Coalition for Accountability and Integrity (AMAN), a Palestinian organization headed by Hanan Ashrawi (Konrad-Adenauer-Stiftung 2007a, 2007b). Ashrawi has been a Palestinian spokesperson and negotiator to the peace talks, director of the ICHR, and head of Miftah.

5. Donors working in Palestine include state aid agencies such as the UK Department for International Development (DFID), the Norwegian Agency for Development Cooperation (Norad), and the US Agency for International Development (USAID); religion-based organizations such as Christian Aid, Caritas, and Trócaire; and party-affiliated groups such as the Heinrich Böll Foundation, which is part of the Green political movement.

6. One rights NGO produced sixty-nine separate reports for different donors in one year and spent more than $70,000 on "servicing donors" in order to cover their administrative demands (Guest 2007:57; see also Carapico forthcoming, chap. 4).

7. For more on this struggle between the PA and Palestinian NGOs, see Jamal (2007:66–74). A UK House of Commons Report (House of Commons 2004:52–53) recounts concerns of PA ministers and officials "about the shift on the part of donors to fund what they termed NGOs' 'academic' activities, such as democracy-building and governance, rather than the provision of essential services," which the report suggests is "defensiveness on the part of the PA."

8. For a critique of how US aid has been used to support the Oslo process, see Lasensky (2004).

9. Peter Bauck of Norad stated explicitly that development policy from European countries is part of those countries' foreign policy, and NGO funding is increasingly recognized and wielded as a tool of foreign policy work (Hanafi and Tabar 2002). For a discussion of development aid as part of Cold War foreign policy, see Rieff (2002:103) and Pitner (2000).

10. By building infrastructure and trying to improve people's living standards in conjunction with the Oslo process, foreign donors tried to ensure support for the political project of Palestinian autonomy. They believed it was "important for the people to see very early that their situation will improve under peace" (Bouhabib 1994:66). It gave people an illusion of progress and potential prosperity, because the faltering Palestinian economy was being artificially propped up by aid, although it did not spark economic growth or ensure good governance as it was purportedly designed to do (Jamal 2007; Lasensky 2004:212; see also Nakhleh 2004). Meanwhile, the occupation continued in another form, one now protected by the PA. In the estimation of one Palestinian analyst, Western donors and foreign NGOs "primarily conceived of the role of NGOs in Palestinian territories as 'the promotion of confidence in building for peace and stability' rather than promoting democratic change," despite their pro-democracy statements (Hilal 2003:167; see also Jamal 2007).

11. Prior to the second intifada, the popularity of Islamic parties was also declining. "Those who said they do not support any political group or movement rose to 23% in Sept 2001 from 11.4% between Sept 1993 and Dec 1994, plus 12.3% who gave no answer" (Hilal 2003:167; see also Challand 2009:17).

12. In 2001, researchers put the tally of human rights and democracy organizations at thirty, with approximately one half dedicated specifically to human rights (Hammami, Hilal, and Tamari 2001:31).

13. Studies from the 1990s estimate the number of NGOs (including human rights and other organizations) in the West Bank and Gaza to be between 800 and 1,500 (Jarrar 2005; Hammami 2000; Sullivan 1996). Later figures indicate that the number of Palestinian NGOs across all sectors increased from approximately 930 to 1,500 between 2000 and 2007 (DeVoir and Tartir 2009:i). Palestinian NGOs also saw a dramatic increase in external funding between 2004 and 2005, much of it to fund governance, democracy, and human rights projects. Islamic NGOs, which comprise from 10–40 percent of social institutions in the occupied territory, have dedicated themselves to service provision (and not human rights) (S. Roy 2000).

14. In 1999, a report by the Office of the UN Special Coordinator gave an ac-

count of donor money showing that 16.7 percent of the funds were devoted to human rights and development projects, approximately $21 million going specifically to human rights. Other studies reported that "human rights and democracy" NGOs received 10.5 percent of total funding to PNGOs between 1995 and 1998 (Hanafi 1999), and that the international donor community has given approximately $1.5 to 2 billion in support of Palestinian civil society organizations in the decade spanning the mid-1990s to mid-2000s (Sidoti and Daibes-Murad 2004:37).

15. For more on the history of the link between politics and civil society organizations in Palestine, see Hammami (1995); Hammami, Hilal, and Tamari (2001); and Hiltermann (1991).

16. These social categories are ideal types (even if negative in tone), not representative of actual social dynamics. They are, however, social categories that resonate with many Palestinians who use these labels to discuss their attitudes toward others and to describe their own place in society. According to one study, more than three-fourths of Palestinians believe that international aid is creating in society an elite class guided by international agendas, while only 16 percent say that it is not (De Voir and Tartir 2009:83).

17. See Hanafi and Tabar (2004) for a discussion of the relationship between international donor assistance and the emergence of an NGO-based globalized elite in Palestine.

18. The investigation by Ernst and Young revealed that LAW misused or failed to report on 3.9 million of the 9.7 million it received in donations between 1997 and 2002 (Guest 2007).

19. It is also worth noting that Mustafa's approach is not much different from what goes on in many sectors in any country. In the United Kingdom, for example, there are many law firms that take on asylum cases and charge high fees of refugees who are unaware of the free legal assistance provided by legal aid offices, and private sector lawyers who charge the home office but deal with asylum cases hastily and shoddily.

20. For more on corruption and negative opinions about Palestinian NGOs, see Hanafi and Tabar (2004) and Challand (2009).

21. Nearly half of all Palestinians lived below the poverty line in 2004 (US$2.1 per day in 1998 prices, or NIS 1,800 per month for a family of six) (World Bank 2004). In 2010 the number of people living in poverty was 25.7 percent (18.3 percent in the West Bank and 38.1 percent in the Gaza Strip), of which 14.1 percent were suffering deep poverty (PCBS 2011).

22. See N. Rose (1996) for his theory linking the growth of psychology and related fields to an expanded emphasis on producing governable, self-disciplining individuals.

23. See Bibi (1995), Browers (2004), Chandler (2001), and Pitner (2000).

24. Y. Sayigh (1997), whose focus is on Palestinian politics outside historic Palestine, locates the defeat of the Left in the 1970s. Giacaman (1998), writing from within, places it in the 1980s. For more on the disarray of leftist factions after Oslo, see Y. Sayigh (1997:648–649), Giacaman (1998), Hammami (1995, 2000), Hanafi and Tabar (2002), Hilal (2003), and articles in *Majallat al-Dirasat al-Filastiniyyah* (2002). See http://www.palestine-studies.org/ar_journals.aspx?href=current&jid=3. It is important to note that

NGOs and other voluntary committees have long been the home of the Palestinian left and political independents, which reflects "Fatah's historical neglect towards developing community-based organizations inside the territories" (Usher 1995:46–47).

Chapter 3

1. By contrast, the Association for Civil Rights in Israel (ACRI) is the only Israeli NGO that provides structured, ongoing educational programs on international humanitarian law (IHL) and human rights law in Israel. B'Tselem has sporadically provided lectures on IHL for NGOs and social activists, as well as tours in the West Bank to show how people experience the violations of international law and human rights by the Israeli army and settlers. The International Committee of the Red Cross conducts occasional presentations and trainings for Israeli Defense Force (IDF) units operating in the West Bank and for the public at large. Repeated requests that my research assistant made to the IDF spokesperson's office for more specific information regarding human rights training in the IDF went unanswered or were actively rebuffed.

2. See Feldman (2008) on citizenship and governance during the British mandate and Egyptian rule in the Gaza Strip.

3. In the human rights courses I attended and in associated literature I obtained, the gendered term *al-rajul al-amni*, or "security man," was the term typically used to refer to security officers, despite the fact that there are also women in the security agencies. Some people involved in human rights training for officers tried to use more gender-neutral language by referring instead to "the personnel responsible for implementing the law," a designation that was rather awkward to enunciate.

4. That "human rights" and "good governance" have merged into one funding category indicates much about the philosophy and assumptions of international donors. "Good governance" is equated with principles of liberal democracy, among which are political and civil rights, such as the right to fair trial and equality before the law. Human rights work has become subsumed within a technical mindset that conceives of a "good governance and rule of law" framework in which things like more training for police and better prison facilities are presented as solutions to what are structural, political problems (Bahmad 2008:256).

5. Funders supporting the startup of the program included the Ford Foundation, the Heinrich Böll Foundation, and the European Community.

6. Boyer and Lomnitz's (2005:107) definition of "the intellectual" as "a social actor who has, by local, historical standards, a differentially specialized engagement with forms of knowledge and their social extensions" is appropriate here.

7. According to this study, 94 percent of respondents said that the program has improved their ability to tolerate the different opinions of others and that their interest in democracy and human rights has increased, as has their confidence in critical thinking rather than ideology. At the same time, they report increased pessimism about the possibility of realizing human rights and democracy in the absence of a just international system, and 96 percent said they are convinced that the individual plays an important role in social change (Kassis 2006:9, 12, 14).

8. I do not conceive the relationship between collective representations and personal fantasy and identity as a psychoanalytically inclined anthropologist might (Kracke and Herdt 1987). For a review of psychoanalytic anthropology, see Paul (1989). For examples of anthropologists who deploy psychoanalytic frameworks, see Allison (2000), Blom Hansen (2001), and Navaro-Yashin (2002).

9. Warnings that the PA is being pushed into becoming, or has been allowed to become, a police state have been voiced by everyone from European diplomats to the head of the Palestinian Independent Commission for Human Rights (Buck 2010; Hass 2011).

10. See, for example, Byrne (2009, 2011), Kassem (2009), and Eid (2009).

11. "In several cases, mass arrests and prolonged detention without trial of suspected Islamist activists followed pressure from external forces, particularly Israel" (B'Tselem 1996:17). See also Human Rights Watch (2011), Cobain (2009), and ICHR (2009c). Between 2007 and 2010, PA security services were responsible for the deaths in custody of at least eight detainees in the West Bank (HRW 2010).

12. HRW (2008) reported that the spike in internal Palestinian conflict came "after a year of politically motivated arrests, torture and ill-treatment by various Palestinian security services or military agencies on both sides. Security forces from both sides have targeted activists and organisations of the other party. Their abusive behaviour has victimised Palestinians from all walks of life and weakened the rule of law." See also Al-Haq (2008a, 2008b).

13. This has long been a complaint of PA officials, who decry efforts by Israel, NGOs, and foreign funders to discredit the PA on human rights grounds. See comments by former Palestinian Minister of State Zayyad Abu-Zayyad and PLC member Hassan Asfour (Abu-Zayyad et al. 1999).

14. The human rights education programs I attended were funded by the EU and the Future Foundation, as well as by the long-term funders of the ICHR, which includes several Scandinavian countries.

15. For information on restrictions on Palestinian movement, see B'Tselem (2011e).

16. See Diakonia (2009).

Chapter 4

1. Political imprisonment and torture are among the PA's most egregious violations against Palestinian citizens. See Al-Haq (2008a), AI (1996), and ICHR (2009a).

2. The Israeli government has been pressuring the PA to crack down on Hamas and other Islamic groups for years. As the Israeli human rights organization B'Tselem reported in 1996, "In several cases, mass arrests and prolonged detention without trial of suspected Islamist activists followed pressure from external forces, particularly Israel" (17).

3. For a brief account, see Azzam (1998:340). ICHR was originally called the Palestinian Independent Commission for Citizens' Rights (PICCR).

4. This article states, "The Palestinian National Authority shall work without delay to become a party to regional and international declarations and covenants that protect human rights."

5. A draft law submitted in 2005 gives ICHR a mandate based on national and international norms. It gives ICHR the authority to deal with citizen complaints, human rights violations, and the integration of human rights into Palestinian legislation and practices.

6. The Paris Principles were declared in a UN General Assembly Resolution (UNGA 1993).

7. See, for example, Mohamedou (2002). See also, on legalism, Okafor and Agbakwa (2002).

8. See, for example, Cardenas and Flibbert (2005). For one critical account that argues that "NHRIs are being created largely to satisfy international audiences," see Cardenas (2003).

9. *Civil society* has become a term that is both loaded and an "empty abstraction," as Jean and John Comaroff (1999) point out. The search for civil society in the Middle East is motivated, from a Western developmentalist perspective, by the democratizing project and concerns about "Middle Eastern authoritarianism" (see Carapico 1998:8). It is also motivated by a veiled desire to find out where political energies reside and how social change can come about.

10. For one partial exception, see Cardenas and Flibbert (2005), who posit that "states with NHRIs are legitimizing the idea of human rights and, perhaps unwittingly, contributing to the construction of new social demands" (414).

11. For a study of five different European NHRIs, see Mertus (2009). Along with the growing number of NHRIs is an expanding academic and policy literature about them. See, for example, the International Council on Human Rights Policy at http://www.ichrp.org and International Council on Human Rights Policy (2005).

12. Other donors include the Swedish International Development Cooperation Agency (SIDA), the Swiss Agency for Development and Cooperation (SDC), the Royal Danish Representative Office, and the Representative Office of Norway to the Palestinian Authority (ICHR n.d.a.). Since the beginning of 2008, ICHR has been receiving 5 percent of its budget from the PA, with plans for that contribution to increase in 2009.

13. For more on civil society views of security forces in Palestine, see, for example, reports of the Geneva Centre for the Democratic Control of Armed Forces (DCAF 2009).

14. For more on the Hamas-Fateh fighting, see Chu (2007), Rass (2009), D. Rose (2008), and HRW (2008, 2009).

15. The public prosecutor, or attorney general, is appointed by the president. Khalid al-Qidra, the first Palestinian attorney general, was known to be politically biased (Brown 2003:25).

16. The incident and the PICCR (later the ICHR) report were widely covered in the local press. Unsurprisingly, articles published on Hamas-affiliated sites focused on the blame that PICCR placed on Fateh.

17. It should be noted that the Hamas government in Gaza has issued similar sorts of denunciations in response to other ICHR criticisms (PCHR 2009a).

18. See EUPOL COPPS (2009).

19. For more on the challenges facing the judiciary, see Kelly (2006, 2010).

20. On the laws establishing the ICHR, see ICHR (n.d.b) and AMAN and Transparency International (2009:87).

21. Between 2002 and 2009, international donor conferences pledged $30 billion in aid and development assistance to the PA, Lebanon, and Yemen. In each case, the United States and the European Union focused on security sector reform "as essential to state building and reconstruction" (Y. Sayigh 2009:1). Foreign ministries and security agencies of donor countries "tended to be more concerned with 'political stability,'" which translates into "a focus on crack-downs on 'radical groups' [that would almost inevitably] involve a substantial number of excesses" (Brynen 2000:178; cf. Hilal 2003:165; Y. Sayigh 2011).

22. Also see Brown (2003:9) and Y. Sayigh (2011). For critical discussions of civil society in Palestine from a normative perspective, see Jamal (2007).

23. The PA prevented and beat back Palestinians who were demonstrating in the West Bank against the Israeli attacks on Gaza in late December 2008, protesting then-President Bush's visit to Bethlehem the year before that, and showing support for the Egyptian demonstrations in spring 2011. See also Issacharoff (2010).

24. It should be noted that security forces under the government of Prime Minister Isma'il Haniyyah in the Gaza Strip have also been accused of torturing and killing detainees (see PCHR 2011).

25. See the call by Human Rights Watch (2008) for punishment of those responsible for a detainee's death in custody. See also ICHR (2009a, 2009b) and Al-Haq (2008a, 2008b, 2009).

26. See, for example, *USA Today* (2007), Reuters (2007), B'Tselem (2009), and Macintyre (2007:20).

27. This is the point of a critical discussion by PLO representative Husam Zumlot of the "security-first route" instituted by Oslo. See Khan (2004) and Euro-Mediterranean Human Rights Network (2004).

28. Palestinian security forces operate within Area A, but Israel retains overall security control, as stipulated in Oslo accords I and II. As Azmi Bishara, former Palestinian member of the Israeli Knesset, put it, the "very survival [of the PA] depends on security cooperation with Israel and the entire industry of gestures, steps, and dialogues with Israel" (Rabbani 2009b:44).

29. For more commentary on the growing repression, see Byrne (2009).

30. Tobias Kelly (2006:143–168) presents a distinct reading of the ongoing popular criticism of the PA in his discussion of why Palestinians sometimes do in fact go along with the authoritarian displays of the government, seeing this complicity as an expression of people's fear of the disorganization that would result from an absolute lack of state control. The discrepancy between our interpretations may be accounted for by the fact that Kelly's analysis pertained to an earlier period, when the "sense of collective possibility" (165) was not yet as eroded as it was after the second intifada and the Gaza Strip–West Bank split.

31. See, for example, ICHR (2009f). This document is an ICHR monthly report

that discusses the dismissal of teachers who were appointed when the Hamas government took office in 2006. See also Omar (2008).

32. On the ICHR's legal challenge to this practice, see ICHR (2009d).

33. For reports on settlement expansion, see FMEP (n.d.). For reports on movement and border restrictions, see OCHA (2009).

Chapter 5

1. For a consideration of Hamas, Islam, and governance, see the article by the general secretary of the Palestinian Constitution Committee, Ali Khashan (2006).

2. On the distinction between universalism and universal, see Goodale (2009).

3. On Hamas and its clashes with Fateh between 2007 and 2009, see Al-Haq (2009) and Fisher (2007).

4. Although Keene's analysis is related to a culturally specific elaboration of Christianity, I find his terms more useful than some other scholarship on sincerity in "Islamic cultural universe[s]" (Gilsenan 1976:194). Hamas is an Islamist movement and the occupied Palestinian territory has a Muslim majority, but the notions of sincerity and credibility relevant in the context I analyze are not specifically tied to Islam or to a religious imagination.

5. Following most of the contributors to Lambek's (2010) volume, I use *ethics* and *morality* interchangeably, but I favor *ethics* for its connotations related to action and judgments of action.

6. Hamas does not represent everything and everyone related to Islam or Islamism in Palestine, where a variety of opinions are held regarding the proper role of Islam in politics and everyday life (see Høigilt 2010; ICG 2011; Muhsin 2005). Despite its emphasis on unity, Hamas itself is also not one thing; internal divisions occasionally come to the fore.

7. For a profile, see BBC (2001b). Israel claimed that Mansour was behind attacks in Israel; Hamas said he was part of the political wing of the movement, with no military connections.

8. For discussion of the effects of the blockade on Gaza, see International Committee of the Red Cross (2011), OCHA (n.d.), and Christian Aid (2009).

9. On curtailment of the freedom of association, see ICHR (n.d.d.) and Reuters (2007). The purge of Hamas by the PA included the firing of more than three hundred mosque preachers for their suspected affiliation with Hamas, as well as the dismissal of schoolteachers and university faculty (S. Roy 2011:235). Fayyad excused the dissolution of *zakat* committees (which collect and distribute income from tithes), saying that "the needs of the poor must never be used for political gains by any party." He insisted that the government should prohibit political party involvement in providing material support "because it is a way to buy people's consciences and [is] therefore contrary to basic human rights" (Farraj, Mansour, and Tamari 2009). It should be noted that Islamic social welfare organizations "provide emergency cash assistance, food and medical care as well as educational and psychological services, to perhaps one out of six" Palestinians (ICG 2003:ii).

10. Qutb is often regarded as the radical, intellectual father of jihadists, and for this reason the Muslim Brotherhood only "acknowledges" him in its intellectual pantheon but does not teach his work to its members. In fact, the Muslim Brotherhood teaches Hasan al-Hudaybi's response to Qutb (Y. Sayigh 2011:98). Al-Hudaybi was the second leader of the Muslim Brotherhood, after Hassan al-Banna.

11. For histories of Hamas and its political evolution, see Tamimi (2007b) and Hroub (2000).

12. From a declaration issued by the Muslim Brotherhood in Cairo, April 20, 1995.

13. The Organization of the Islamic Conference has been renamed the Organization of the Islamic Cooperation.

14. See the *Economist* (2010) for a report on the PA's efforts to control the mosques in the West Bank.

15. For a study that calls into question the extent of Hamas's influence on education and Islamism in the occupied territory, see Høigilt (2010).

16. Islam as a force in anticolonial politics has experienced a resurgence throughout the Middle East and beyond since the mid-nineteenth century. For a summary of these trends, see Esposito (1983).

17. Sara Roy, personal communication, April 30, 2010.

18. The modification (and moderation) of the language of the Hamas Charter began in the 1990s, and emphasis on the struggle against occupation displaced talk of a struggle between Islam and Judaism (Crooke 2008).

19. Mutual responsibility, charity, and struggle for the sake of equality and justice are important features of the political philosophy laid out by Sayyid Qutb (2000). For more on morality in Islam, see the discussions in Hovannisian (1985).

20. For a discussion of Thompson's concept of a moral economy as it illuminates social movements in Islamic societies, see Roberts (2002).

21. For example, the website of the Hamas military wing posts short eulogistic biographies of their "martyrs" and leaders. See http://www.qassam.ps/martyrs.html. The term *martyr* refers to anyone who is deemed to have died as a result of the occupation. Many of the martyrs featured on this site are described as having been assassinated or killed during the course of duty. For more on the significance of martyrdom in Palestinian society, see Allen 2008, 2009a, 2009b.

22. See also, ICHR (n.d.c, 2010a), Associated Press (2010), Milton-Edwards (2008:1595–96), and Frykberg (2010).

23. For discussions of the internal and external factors affecting the development of Islamist social institutions in the Gaza Strip, see S. Roy (2011:70–95).

24. See Y. Sayigh (2010) for a discussion of the ambiguous line separating the government in Gaza and Hamas the political movement.

25. On the functioning of the siege and sanctions, especially with regard to fiscal control, see Milton-Edwards (2007:310–312) and S. Roy (2010).

26. The Israeli Operation Cast Lead attacks on the Gaza Strip lasted twenty-two days. They began on December 27, 2008, with a week of continuous Israeli airstrikes, followed by ground and air incursions (ICG 2009:1). In three weeks, approximately

1,400 Palestinians were killed, including some 300 children, and 5,300 were injured, the majority civilians. The Israeli military claims that 1,666 people were killed, listing only 295 as noncombatants (Kershner 2009). Thirteen Israelis were killed, some by friendly fire, ten of whom were soldiers. Some 2,400 Palestinian houses were completely or largely destroyed, including 28 public civilian facilities, ministries, municipality buildings, the PLC building, and tens of schools, factories, mosques, and civilian police stations (PCHR 2009b; AI 2009).

27. For more on economic conditions in Gaza as a result of the siege, see Oxfam (2007, 2008).

28. Musa Abu Marzook, vice president of Hamas's political office, said in an interview that the Goldstone report found Hamas innocent of all accusations leveled against it by Israel (Abu Marzook 2009).

29. For a critical review of Israel's response to the Commission's report, see Falk (2009).

30. For more on the status of the blockade and the Gazan economy, see World Bank (2004b, 2009) and OCHA oPt (2009).

31. Their positive relations with ICHR and other HROs are recounted in Hamas-affiliated newspapers and on government websites. See Ministry of Interior (2010, 2011), Palestinian Police (2010), and Al-Resalah (n.d., 2010).

32. It must be acknowledged that "the international community" is itself a realm of effects as nebulous as any state, a conglomeration of people, powers, and organizations that attempt to legitimize themselves as the correct address of appeal for states in the making.

33. Despite this engagement, the Haniyyah government has also obstructed ICHR activities in the Gaza Strip (as has the PA in the West Bank). See ICHR (2010a, 2010b).

34. On June 6, 2009, three Hamas members and three policemen were killed.

35. For example, during the "coup" in the Gaza Strip in which Hamas routed the PA, tens of Fateh-associated members of the PA security services were killed or maimed by Hamas forces (ICG 2008; B'Tselem 2011f).

Conclusion

1. Of course the extent to which a state's human rights violations may prompt action against it by other states depends on the relative power of the violating regime within the international system.

2. For a discussion of affect and emotion and how they signal different dimensions of social life and its analysis, see Mazzarella (2008).

Abbreviations and Glossary

AI   Amnesty International

ACRI   Association for Civil Rights in Israel

Addameer   Prisoner Support and Human Rights Association, a Palestinian prisoners' rights organization

AI   Amnesty International

Al-Haq   Palestinian human rights organization

B'Tselem   Israeli Information Center for Human Rights in the Occupied Territories

dakakin   shops

DCAF   Geneva Centre for the Democratic Control of Armed Forces

DCI-Palestine   Defence for Children International-Palestine Section, a Palestinian human rights organization

DFID   Department for International Development, UK

DFLP   Democratic Front for the Liberation of Palestine, leftist faction

DoP   Declaration of Principles, Israel-PLO

EUPOL COPPS   European Union Co-ordinating Office for Palestinian Police Support

haki fadi   empty words

hijab   head cover

HRO   human rights organization

HRW   Human Rights Watch

ICAHD   Israeli Committee Against Home Demolitions

ICHR   Independent Commission for Human Rights

ICHRP   International Council on Human Rights Policy

ICJ   International Commission of Jurists

ICRC   International Committee of the Red Cross

IDF   Israel Defense Forces

iftar   fast-breaking meal

IHL   international humanitarian law

inhiyar   breakdown

intifada   uprising

khutbah   Friday sermon

Knesset   the Israeli Parliament

LAW   Land and Water Establishment for Studies and Legal Services, Palestinian human rights organization

MoI   Ministry of Interior

mukhabarat   intelligence service, secret police

NGO   nongovernmental organization

NHRI   national human rights institution

NSF   National Security Forces

OHCHR   UN Office of the High Commissioner for Human Rights

oPt   occupied Palestinian territory

PA   Palestinian Authority

PCHR   Palestinian Center for Human Rights

PFLP   Popular Front for the Liberation of Palestine, leftist faction

PIC   Palestinian Information Center

PICCR   Palestinian Independent Commission for Citizens' Rights

PLC   Palestinian Legislative Council

PLO   Palestinian Liberation Organization

PNGO   Palestinian NGO

Ramadan   Muslim holy month

shabeh   position abuse; torture method

shari'a   Islamic law

suffayt wa tuffayt   parked and turned off the ignition; a colloquialism describing disaffected former political activists

UDHR   Universal Declaration of Human Rights

UNESCO   United Nations Educational, Scientific and Cultural Organization

UNICEF   United Nations Children's Fund

UNRWA   United Nations Relief and Works Agency; UN agency charged with providing basic services to Palestinian refugees

USAID   US Agency for International Development

wasta   nepotistic connections

Bibliography

Abdel Shafi, Salah. 2004. "Civil Society and Political Elites in Palestine and the Role of International Donors: A Palestinian View." EuroMeSCopaper 33, accessed October 28, 2012, http://www.euromesco.net/euromesco/media/paper33_final.pdf.

Abdelnour, Samer. 2010. "A New Model for Palestinian Development." Al-Shabaka: The Palestinian Policy Network, accessed October 28, 2012, http://al-shabaka.org/policy -brief/economic-issues/new-model-palestinian-development.

Abdelrahman, Maha M. 2005. *Civil Society Exposed: The Politics of NGOs in Egypt.* London: I.B. Tauris.

———. 2007. "The Nationalisation of the Human Rights Debate in Egypt." *Nations and Nationalism* 13 (2): 285–300.

Abdul Hadi, Lubna. 2006. "Human Rights Education in Palestinian Universities." Research Summary. Document on file with author.

Abercrombie, Nicholas, and Bryan S. Turner. 1978. "The Dominant Ideology Thesis." *British Journal of Sociology* 29 (2): 149–170.

Abrams, Philip. (1977) 1988. "Notes on the Difficulty of Studying the State." *Journal of Historical Sociology* 1 (1): 58–89.

Abu-Lughod, Lila. 2002. "Do Muslim Women Really Need Saving? Anthropological Reflections on Cultural Relativism and Its Others." *American Anthropologist* 104: 783–790.

———. 2010. "The Active Social Life of 'Muslim Women's Rights': A Plea for Ethnography, Not Polemic, with Cases from Egypt and Palestine." *Journal of Middle East Women's Studies* 6 (1): 1–45.

Abu Marzook, Mousa. 2006. "What Hamas Is Seeking." *Washington Post.* January 31, accessed October 28, 2012, http://www.washingtonpost.com/wp-dyn/content/article /2006/01/30/AR2006013001209.html.

———. 2009. "Hamas Does Not Seek to Establish an Islamic Emirate nor a Complementary Political System [Hamas la tas'a li-iqamat imarah islamiyyah wa-la tas'a li-nizam siyasi mutakamil]." Al-Mushahid Al-Siyasi, accessed March 3, 2010, http://www.almu shahidassiyasi.com/ar/4/7704.

Abu-Zayyad, Ziad, Hassan Asfour, Edy Kaufman, Iyad Sarraj, and Anat Scolnicov. 1999. "Building a New Society: Issues of Human Rights and Human Dignity." *Palestine Israel Journal of Politics, Economics, and Culture* 6 (1), accessed October 28, 2012, http://www.pij.org/details.php?id=954.

Adams, Laura L. 2010. *The Spectacular State: Culture and National Identity in Uzbekistan.* Durham, NC: Duke University Press.

Addameer. 2011. "The Civil Network to Protect the Right to Freedom of Associations Holds Its Ninth Meeting and Assures on the Need to Cancel Decisions That Are Related with Latest Laws and Regulations on Amending Charitable Associations and Community Organizations Law." July 12, accessed October 29, 2012, http://english web.aldameer.org/?p=1295.

Afary, Janet. 2004. "The Human Rights of Middle Eastern & Muslim Women: A Project for the 21st Century." *Human Rights Quarterly* 26 (1): 106–125.

Al-Haq. n.d. "Fieldworkers Affidavits." Al-Haq, accessed October 28, 2012, http://www .alhaq.org/component/content/category/63—fieldworkers-affidavits.

———. 1982a. "Civilian Administration in the Occupied West Bank: Analysis of Israeli Military Government Order No. 947." Al-Haq, accessed October 28, 2012, http:// www.alhaq.org/publications/publications-index/item/civilian-administration-in -the-occupied-west-bank.

———. 1982b. "Report on Human Rights Practices in the Occupied Territories During 1981." Al-Haq, accessed October 28, 2012, http://www.alhaq.org/publications/ publications-index/item/report-on-human-rights-practices-in-the-occupied-terri tories-during-1981.

———. 1983. "In Their Own Words: Human Rights Violations in the West Bank." Al-Haq, accessed October 28, 2012, http://www.alhaq.org/publications/publications -index/item/in-their-own-words-human-rights-violations-in-the-west-bank.

———. (1988) 1990. "Punishing a Nation: Human Rights Violations During the Palestinian Uprising, December 1987–1988." Al-Haq, accessed October 28, 2012, http:// www.alhaq.org/publications/publications-index/item/punishing-a-nation-human -rights-violations-during-the-palestinian-uprising-december-1987-1988.

———. 1993. "Palestinian Victims of Torture Speak Out: Thirteen Accounts of Torture During Interrogation in Israeli Prisons." Al-Haq, accessed October 28, 2012, http://www.alhaq.org/publications/publications-index/item/palestinian-victims -of-torture-speak-out-thirteen-accounts-of-torture-during-interrogation-in-israeli -prisons.

———. 2006. "Israel's Deportations and Forcible Transfers of Palestinians Out of the West Bank During the Second Intifada," accessed October 28, 2012, http://www.al haq.org/publications/publications-index/item/israel-s-deportations-and-forcible -transfers-of-palestinians.

———. 2008a. "Al-Haq Calls on the Office of the Attorney-General to Fulfill Its Legal Responsibility to Effectively Monitor the Detention Centres Managed by the Palestinian General Intelligence Service and Preventive Security Forces." Al-Haq. February 28, accessed October 31, 2012, http://www.alhaq.org/advocacy/topics/palestinian -violations/163-al-haq-calls-on-the-office-of-the-attorney-general-to-fulfill-its-legal -responsibility-to-effectively-monitor-the-detention-centres-managed-by-the-pal estinian-general-intelligence-service-and-the-prev.

———. 2008b. "Torturing Each Other: The Widespread Practices of Arbitrary Detention and Torture in the Palestinian Territory." Al-Haq, accessed October 28, 2012, http://www.alhaq.org/advocacy/topics/palestinian-violations/188-al-haq-releases -new-report-on-arbitrary-detention-and-torture-in-palestinian-prisons.

———. 2009. "Overview of the Internal Human Rights Situation in the Occupied Palestinian Territory." Al-Haq, accessed on October 28, 2012, http://www.alhaq.org/advocacy/topics/palestinian-violations/240-overview-of-the-internal-human-rights -situation-in-the-occupied-palestinian-territory-june-2009.

———. 2012. "Veolia Not Awarded Public Transport Tender in The Hague." Al-Haq, accessed October 28, 2012, http://www.alhaq.org/advocacy/targets/accountability/72 -hermesveolia/577-veolia-not-awarded-public-transport-tender-in-the-hague.

Al-Hibri, Azizah. 1997. "Islam, Law and Custom: Redefining Muslim Women's Rights." *American University International Law Review* 12 (1): 1–44.

Al-Jazeera. n.d. "NSU Memo to Tony Blair Re: Areas A-B-C," accessed October 28, 2012, http://transparency.aljazeera.net/en/projects/thepalestinepapers/201218231 4062631.html.

———. 2007. "Government Program of Prime Minister Designate Isma'il Haniyyah [Barnamij hakumat Ra'is al-Wuzura' al-Mukallif Isma'il Haniyyah]." March 17, accessed October 28, 2012, http://www.aljazeera.net/news/archive/archive ?ArchiveId=1035901.

Allen, Lori. 2002. "Palestinians Debate 'Polite' Resistance to Occupation." *Middle East Report* 225: 38–43, accessed October 28, 2012, http://www .merip.org/mer/mer225/ palestinians-debate-polite-resistance-occupation.

———. 2008. "Getting by the Occupation: How Violence Became Normal During the Second Palestinian Intifada." *Cultural Anthropology* 23 (3): 453–487.

———. 2009a. "Mothers of Martyrs and Suicide Bombers: The Gender of Ethical Discourse in the Second Palestinian Intifada." *Arab Studies Journal* 17 (1): 32–61.

———. 2009b. "Martyr Bodies in the Media: Human Rights, Aesthetics, and the Politics of Immediation in the Palestinian Intifada." *American Ethnologist* 36 (1): 161–180.

———. 2012. "The Scales of Occupation: 'Operation Cast Lead' and the Targeting of the Gaza Strip." *Critique of Anthropology* (32) 3: 261–284.

Allison, Anne. 2000. *Permitted and Prohibited Desires: Mothers, Comics, and Censorship in Japan.* Berkeley: University of California Press.

Almbladh, Karin. n.d. "Scandinavian Human Rights Funding: Scandinavian Funding for Democracy and Human Rights in the Areas Under the Jurisdiction of the Palestinian Authority, 1994–2003," accessed October 28, 2012, http://www.phrmg.org/ Scandinavian%20Human%20Rights%20FundingScandinavian%20Funding%20 for%20Democracy%20and%20Human.htm.

Al-Resalah (al-Risala). n.d. "A Delegation from the Red Crescent Visits the Office of MP 'Amad Noufal [Wafd min al-Salib al-Ahmar yazur maktab al-Na'ib 'Amad Noufal]," accessed October 28, 2012, http://alresalah.ps/ar/index.php?act=post&id=3395.

———. 2010. "In a Visit to the ICHR Headquarters, MPs Discuss the Human Rights Situation in the Palestinian Territories [Khilal ziyarah li-maqarr al-Hay'ah al-Musta-qillah, al-nuwwab yunaqishun wad' huquq al-insan fi al-Aradi al-Falastiniyyah]," accessed February 27, 2010, http://www.alresalah.ps/ar/?action=showdetail&seid=7107.

Alternative Information Center (AIC). 2011. "Palestinian UN Bid and Refugee Rights: Questions and Scenarios," accessed October 28, 2012, http://www.alternativenews .org/english/index.php/news/news/3828-palestinian-un-bid-and-refugee-rights -questions-and-scenarios.html.

Althusser, Louis. 1971. "Ideology and Ideological State Apparatus." In *Lenin and Philosophy and Other Essays*. London: New Left Books.

Alvarez, Sonia E. 1999. "Advocating Feminism: The Latin American Feminist NGO 'Boom.'" *International Journal of Politics* 1 (2): 181–209.

AMAN (Coalition for Accountability and Integrity). n.d. *Code of Conduct on Transparency and Accountability for Palestinian NGOs*, accessed October 29, 2012, http:// aman-palestine.org/arabic/activities/nazahaweb/Publications/CoCeng.pdf.

————. 2007. "A Public Opinion Survey on the State of Palestinian NGOs," accessed October 29, 2012, http://www.aman-palestine.org/arabic/activities/nazahaweb/ html/ActivitiesEng/Act12307.htm.

AMAN and Transparency International. 2009. "Occupied Palestinian Territory: National Integrity System Study: Palestine 2009," accessed October 30, 2012, http://reliefweb .int/node/338113.

Amayreh, Khaled. 2010. "Islamist Women's Activism in Occupied Palestine: Interviews with Palestinian Islamist Women Leaders on Women's Activism in Hamas." *Conflicts Forum*, February, accessed October 29, 2012, http://conflictsforum.org/briefings/ IWAIOP.pdf.

Amnesty International (AI). n.d. "Israel and Occupied Palestinian Territories," accessed October 29, 2012, http://www.amnesty.org/en/region/israel-occupied-palestinian -territories.

————. 1996. A Synopsis of Palestinian Authority: Prolonged Political Detention, Torture and Unfair Trials, accessed October 29, 2012, http://www.amnesty.org/ ar/library/asset/MDE15/070/1996/en/999974af-ead4-11dd-b6f5-3be39665bc30/ mde150701996en.pdf.

————. 1998. "Israel/Palestinian Authority: Security Must Not Be Used as a Pretext for Human Rights Abuses," accessed October 29, 2012, http://www.amnesty.org/ en/library/asset/MDE02/006/1998/en/b271a529-d9ab-11dd-af2b-b1f6023af0c5/ mde020061998en.html.

————. 2009. "Israel/Gaza—Operation 'Cast Lead': 22 Days of Death and Destruction," accessed October 29, 2012, http://www.amnesty.org/en/library/info/MDE15/015/2009.

————. 2010. Palestinian Authority: Hamas Fails to Mount Credible Investigations into Gaza Conflict Violations, accessed October 29, 2012, http://www.amnesty.org/ en/library/asset/MDE21/001/2010/en/d5c82b6d-4601-469a-9e9e-adfc74e254a2/ mde210012010en.html.

Anderson, Kenneth. n.d. "Israel's View of the Application of IHL to the West Bank and Gaza Strip." *Crimes of War*, accessed October 29, 2012, http://www.crimesofwar.org/ a-z-guide/israels-views-of-the-application-of-ihl-to-the-west-bank-and-gaza-strip.

Anderson, Paul. Forthcoming. "Irony, Cynicism and Laughing Stocks: The Ethics of Bitter Self-Knowledge in Syria." *Journal of the Royal Anthropological Institute*.

An-Naʻim, Abdullahi. 1987a. "The Rights of Women and International Law in the Muslim Context." *Whittier Law Review* 9: 491–516.

———. 1987b. "Islamic Law, International Relations, and Human Rights: Challenge and Response." *Cornell International Law Journal* 20: 317–335.

———. 1999. "The Position of Islamic States Regarding the Universal Declaration of Human Rights." In *Innovation and Inspiration: Fifty Years of the Universal Declaration of Human Rights*, ed. Mignon Senders, Cees Flinterman, and Peter Baehr. Pp. 177–192. Amsterdam: Royal Netherlands Academy of Arts and Sciences.

Arendt, Hannah. (1951) 1994. *The Origins of Totalitarianism.* San Diego: Harcourt Brace Jovanovich.

Aretxaga, Begoña. 2003. "Maddening States." *Annual Review of Anthropology* 32: 393–410.

Arsanjani, Mahnoush H. 1982. "United Nations Competence in the West Bank and Gaza Strip." *International and Comparative Law Quarterly* 31 (3): 426–450.

Asad, Talal, ed. 1974. *Anthropology and the Colonial Encounter.* London: Ithaca Press.

Associated Press. 2007. "PA Security Men Open Fire at West Bank Funeral, Wounding One." *Haaretz*, November 28, accessed October 29, 2012, http://www.haaretz.com/hasen/spages/929056.html.

Associated Press and Haaretz Service. 2010. "UN Panel: Hamas, Israel Failed to Address Goldstone Gaza Report." *Haaretz*, September 21, accessed October 29, 2012, http://www.haaretz.com/news/diplomacy-defense/un-panel-hamas-israel-failed-to-address-goldstone-gaza-report-1.315005.

Association for Civil Rights in Israel (ACRI). 2011. "New Version of Boycott Prohibition Bill Approved for Final Reading." June 27, accessed October 28, 2012, http://www.acri.org.il/en/2011/06/27/new-version-of-boycott-prohibition-bill-approved-for-final-reading.

Azzam, Fatih Samih. 1998. "Update: The Palestinian Independent Commission for Citizens' Rights." *Human Rights Quarterly* 20 (2): 338–347.

———. 2005. Waiting for Justice: Al-Haq in 2004: A Twenty Five Year Prospective. In *Al-Haq: 25 Years Defending Human Rights (1979–2004): Waiting for Justice*, ed. Rouba Al-Salem. Ramallah: Al-Haq.

Bahmad, Layla. 2008. *Non-Governmental Organisations in Palestine: Last Resort of Humanitarian Aid or Stooges of Foreign Interests?* Sinzheim, Germany: Nomos Verlagsgesellschaft.

Bahour, Sam. 2010. "Economic Prison Zones." *Middle East Report Online.* November 19, accessed October 31, 2012, http://www.merip.org/mero/mero111910.

Barghouti, Iyad. 2007. *Religion and State in Palestine.* Ramallah: Ramallah Center for Human Rights.

Batrawi, Khaled. 1999. "Palestinian Human-Rights Organizations: A New Agenda." *Palestine Israel Journal of Politics, Economics and Culture* 6 (1): 25–48. http://www.pij.org/details.php?id=945.

Berlant, Lauren. 1998. "Poor Eliza." *American Literature* 70 (3): 635–668.

Bewes, Timothy. 1997. *Cynicism and Postmodernity.* London: Verso.

Bibi, Ghanem. 1995. "The NGO Phenomenon in the Arab World: An Interview with Ghanem Bibi." *Middle East Report* 193: 26–27.

Bielefeldt, Heiner. 2000. "'Western' Versus 'Islamic' Human Rights Conceptions? A Critique of Cultural Essentialism in the Discussion on Human Rights." *Political Theory* 28 (1): 90–121.

Birzeit Master's in Democracy and Human Rights (BMDHR). 1999. "Curriculum and Teaching Methods for Democracy and Human Rights: Paper Based on Discussions of Study Workshop About How to Develop the Curriculum." On file with author.

Birzeit University Institute of Law. 2006. "Informal Justice: Rule of Law and Dispute Resolution in Palestine," accessed October 31, 2012, http://lawcenter.birzeit.edu/iol/en/project/outputfile/5/a391785614.pdf.

———. 2009. "The Initiative on Judicial Independence and Human Dignity," accessed October 31, 2012, http://lawcenter.birzeit.edu/iol/en/index.php?action_id=271.

Bishara, Amahl. 2008. "Watching U.S. Television from the Palestinian Street: The Media, the State, and Representational Interventions." *Cultural Anthropology* 23 (3): 488–530.

———. 2012. *Back Stories: U.S. News Production and Palestinian Politics.* Stanford, CA: Stanford University Press.

Bishara, Ghassan. 1979. "The Human Rights Case Against Israel: The Policy of Torture." *Journal of Palestine Studies* 8 (4): 3–30.

Bisharat, George. 1995. "Courting Justice? Legitimation in Lawyering Under Israeli Occupation." *Law & Social Inquiry* 20: 349–405.

Blecher, Robert. 2005. "Citizens Without Sovereignty: Transfer and Ethnic Cleansing in Israel." *Society for Comparative Study of Society and History* 47 (4): 725–754.

Blom Hansen, Thomas. 2001. *Wages of Violence: Naming and Identity in Postcolonial Bombay.* Princeton, NJ: Princeton University Press.

———. 2005. "Sovereigns Beyond the State: On Legality and Authority in Urban India." In *Sovereign Bodies: Citizens, Migrants, and States in the Postcolonial World*, ed. Thomas Blom Hansen and Finn Stepputat. Princeton, NJ: Princeton University Press.

Blom Hansen, Thomas, and Finn Stepputat. 2006. "Sovereignty Revisited." *Annual Review of Anthropology* 35 (1): 295–315.

Bouhabib, Abdallah. 1994. "The World Bank and International Aid to Palestine: An Interview with Abdallah Bouhabib." *Journal of Palestine Studies* 23 (2): 64–74.

Bowen, Stephen, ed. 1997. *Human Rights, Self-Determination and Political Change in the Occupied Palestinian Territories.* The Hague: Martinus Nijhoff.

Boyer, Dominic, and Claudio Lomnitz. 2005. "Intellectuals and Nationalism: Anthropological Engagements." *Annual Review of Anthropology* 34 (1): 105–120.

Bradley, Grace. 2007. "Security Returns to the West Bank Town of Nablus." Bureau of International Information Programs, U.S. Department of State, November 15, accessed October 31, 2012, http://www.globalsecurity.org/military/library/news/2007/11/mil-071115-usia02.htm.

British Broadcasting Corporation (BBC). 2001a. "Transcripts: The Guerilla's Story." *BBC News*, January 1, accessed October 31, 2012, http://news.bbc.co.uk/2/hi/in_depth/uk/2000/uk_confidential/1090986.stm.

———. 2001b. "Profile: Hamas Activist Jamal Mansour." *BBC News*, July 31, accessed October 31, 2012, http://news.bbc.co.uk/1/hi/world/middle_east/1467082.stm.

Bronner, Ethan. 2009. "Six Die as Palestinian Authority Forces Clash with Hamas." *New York Times*, May 31, accessed October 31, 2012, http://www.nytimes.com/2009/06/01/world/middleeast/01mideast.html.

Browers, Michaelle. 2004. "The Civil Society Debate and New Trends on the Arab Left." *Theory & Event* 7 (2), accessed October 31, 2012, http://muse.jhu.edu/login?auth =0&type=summary&url=/journals/tae/v007/7.2browers.html.

Brown, Nathan J. 2000. "Constituting Palestine: The Effort to Write a Basic Law for the Palestinian Authority." *Middle East Journal* 54 (1): 25–43.

———. 2003. *Palestinian Politics After the Oslo Accords: Resuming Arab Palestine.* Berkeley: University of California Press.

———. 2011. Palestine: The Fire Next Time? Carnegie Endowment, July 6, accessed October 31, 2012, http://www.carnegieendowment.org/2011/07/06/palestine-fire -next-time/2sh8.

Brown, Wendy. 1995. *States of Injury: Power and Freedom in Late Modernity.* Princeton, NJ: Princeton University Press.

———. 2004. "The Most We Can Hope For: Human Rights and the Politics of Fatalism." *The South Atlantic Quarterly* 103 (2/3): 451–463.

Brubaker, Rogers. 1996. *Nationalism Reframed: Nationhood and the National Question in the New Europe.* Cambridge, UK: Cambridge University Press.

Brynen, Rex. 1996. "Buying Peace? A Critical Assessment of International Aid to the West Bank and Gaza." *Journal of Palestine Studies* 25 (3): 79–92.

———. 2000. *A Very Political Economy: Peacebuilding and Foreign Aid in the West Bank and Gaza.* Washington, DC: US Institute of Peace.

B'Tselem. 1989a. "Demolition and Sealing of Houses as a Punitive Measure in the West Bank and Gaza Strip During the Intifada." September. Jerusalem: B'Tselem.

———. 1989b. "The Military Judicial System in the West Bank." November 1, accessed October 29, 2012, http://www.btselem.org/publication/112.

———. 1996. "Human Rights in the Occupied Territories Since the Oslo Accords: Status Report." December, accessed October 29, 2012, http://www.btselem.org/sites/default/ files/human_rights_in_the_occupied_territories_since_the_oslo_accords.pdf.

———. 2002. "Policy of Destruction: House Demolition and Destruction of Agricultural Land in the Gaza Strip." February, accessed October 29, 2012, http://www.bt selem.org/publications/summaries/200202_policy_of_destruction.

———. 2004. "Forbidden Roads: The Discriminatory West Bank Road Regime." August, accessed October 29, 2012, http://www.btselem.org/publications/summaries/ 200408_forbidden_roads.

———. 2009. "Security Forces Demolish House of Family of Perpetrator of Attack in Jerusalem." April 16, accessed on October 29, 2012, http://www.btselem.org/Eng lish/Punitive_Demolitions/20090416_House_Demolition_in_East_Jerusalem.asp.

———. 2011a "Background on East Jerusalem," accessed October 29, 2012, http://www .btselem.org/jerusalem. Revised July 8, 2012.

———. 2011b. "The Separation Barrier." January 1, accessed October 29, 2012, http://www.btselem.org/separation_barrier.

———. 2011c. "Use of Firearms." January 1, accessed October 29, 2012, http://www.btselem.org/firearms.

———. 2011d. "Authorities' Handling of Complaints Regarding Settler Violence." January 1, accessed October 29, 2012, http://www.btselem.org/settler_violence/law_enforcement.

———. 2011e. "Restrictions on Movement," accessed October 29, 2012, http://www.btselem.org/freedom_of_movement. Revised July 15, 2012.

———. 2011f. "Severe Human Rights Violations in Inter-Palestinian Clashes." January 1, accessed October 29, 2012, http://www.btselem.org/English/Inter_Palestinian_Violations/Index.asp.

Buck, Tobias. 2010. "Allegations of West Bank Torture Increase." *Financial Times*, November 21, accessed October 29, 2012, http://www.ft.com/cms/s/0/c5ceda42-f58b-11df-99d6-00144feab49a.html#axzz1TJoig8Ql.

Butler, Judith. 1990. *Gender Trouble*. New York: Routledge.

———. 1992. "Contingent Foundations: Feminism and the Question of 'Postmodernism.'" In *Feminists Theorize the Political*, ed. Judith Butler and Joan Scott. Pp. 3–21. New York: Routledge.

Byrne, Aisling. 2009. "'Businessmen Posing as Revolutionaries': General Dayton and the 'New Palestinian Breed.'" *Conflicts Forum*. November, accessed on October 29, 2012, http://conflictsforum.org/wp-content/uploads/2012/03/Monograph-GeneralDayton.pdf.

———. 2011. "Building a Police State in Palestine." *Foreign Policy*, January 18, accessed on October 29, 2012, http://mideast.foreignpolicy.com/posts/2011/01/18/building_a_police_state_in_palestine.

Cabinet Secretariat. 2010. "Minister of Interior: Salafism Not a Danger to Gaza [Wazir al-Dakhiliyyah: al-Salafiyyah laysat khataran 'ala Ghazzah]." Cabinet Secretariat, March 4, accessed October 29, 2012, http://www.pmo.gov.ps/index.php?option=com_content&view=article&id=390:2010-03-04-10-35-54&catid=25:news&Itemid=67.

Caldwell, Wilbur. 2006. *Cynicism and the Evolution of the American Dream*. Dulles, VA: Potomac Books.

Calhoun, Craig J. 2007. "Sociology in America: An Introduction." In *Sociology in America: A History*. Pp. 1–38. Chicago: Chicago University Press.

Carapico, Sheila. Forthcoming. "Political Aid: The Paradoxes of Democracy Promotion in the Middle East." Cambridge, UK: Cambridge University Press.

———. 1998. *Civil Society in Yemen: The Political Economy of Activism in Modern Arabia*. Cambridge, UK: Cambridge University Press.

———. 2002. "Foreign Aid for Promoting Democracy in the Arab World." *Middle East Journal* 56 (3): 379–395.

Carbajosa, Ana. 2011. "Gazan Youth Issue Manifesto to Vent Their Anger with All Sides in the Conflict." *Observer*, January 1, accessed October 29, 2012, http://www.guardian.co.uk/world/2011/jan/02/free-gaza-youth-manifesto-palestinian.

Cardenas, Sonia. 2003. "Adaptive States: The Proliferation of National Human Rights Institutions." Carr Center for Human Rights Policy Working Paper T-01-04, accessed October 29, 2012, www.ksg.harvard.edu/cchrp/Web%20Working%20Papers/Cardenas.pdf.

Cardenas, Sonia, and Andrew Flibbert. 2005. "National Human Rights Institutions in the Middle East." *Middle East Journal* 59 (3): 411–436.

Carmichael, William D. 2001. "The Role of the Ford Foundation." In *NGOs in Human Rights: Promise and Performance*, ed. Claude E. Welch. Pp. 248–260. Philadelphia: University of Pennsylvania Press.

Catalano, Joseph. 1996. "Good and Bad Faith: Weak and Strong Notions?" In *Good Faith and Other Essays: Perspectives on a Sartrean Ethics*. New York: Rowman & Littlefield.

Chalfin, Brenda. 2010. *Neoliberal Frontiers: An Ethnography of Sovereignty in West Africa*. Chicago: University of Chicago Press.

Challand, Benoit. 2009. *Palestinian Civil Society: Foreign Donors and the Power to Promote and Exclude*. London: Routledge.

Chamberlin, Paul. 2011. "The Struggle Against Oppression Everywhere: The Global Politics of Palestinian Liberation." *Middle Eastern Studies* 47 (1): 25–41.

Chandler, David. 2001. "The Road to Military Humanitarianism: How the Human Rights NGOs Shaped a New Humanitarian Agenda." *Human Rights Quarterly* 23: 678–700.

Chatterjee, Partha. 2011. "Reflecting on 30 Years of Subaltern Studies: Conversations with Profs. Gyanendra Pandey and Partha Chatterjee." *Cultural Anthropology* Virtual Issue: Subaltern Studies, December 1, accessed October 29, 2012, http://www.culanth.org/?q=node/469.

Chomsky, Noam. 1999. *Necessary Illusions: Thought Control in Democratic Societies*. London: Pluto Press.

Christian Aid. 2009. "Failing Gaza: No Rebuilding, No Recovery, No More Excuses," accessed October 29, 2012, http://www.christianaid.org.uk/Images/failing-gaza.pdf.

Chu, Henry. 2007. "Unity Is a Gaza Casualty." *Los Angeles Times*. May 17, accessed October 29, 2012, http://articles.latimes.com/2007/may/17/world/fg-palestinians17.

Cmiel, Kenneth. 1999. "The Emergence of Human Rights Politics in the United States." *Journal of American History* 86 (3): 1231–1250.

———. 2004. "The Recent History of Human Rights." *American Historical Review* 109 (1): 117–135.

Cobain, Ian. 2009. "CIA Working with Palestinian Security Agents." *Guardian*, December 17, accessed October 29, 2012, http://www.guardian.co.uk/world/2009/dec/17/cia-palestinian-security-agents.

Cobban, Helena. 2006. "Sisterhood of Hamas: Women Fueled the Rise of the Islamist Party Through Their Work in the Schools and Hospitals That Serve the Palestinian People." *Salon*, March 14, accessed October 29, 2012, http://www.salon.com/news/feature/2006/03/14/hamaswomen/index_np.html.

Code of Conduct Coalition. 2008. "The Palestinian NGOs Code of Conduct," accessed October 29, 2012, www.ndc.ps/uploads/File/1204355297.pdf.

Cohen, Stanley, and Daphna Golan. 1991. "The Interrogation of Palestinians During the Intifada: Ill-Treatment, 'Moderate Physical Pressure' or Torture?" Jerusalem: B'Tselem.

Comaroff, Jean, and John L. Comaroff. 1999. *Civil Society and the Political Imagination in Africa: Critical Perspectives.* Chicago: University of Chicago Press.

———. 2006. *Law and Disorder in the Postcolony.* Chicago: University of Chicago Press.

———. 2009. *Ethnicity, Inc.* Chicago: University of Chicago Press.

Comaroff, John L. 1997. "Legality, Modernity, and Ethnicity in Colonial South Africa: An Excursion in the Historical Anthropology of Law." In *Law, Society, and Economy: Centenary Essays for the London School of Economics and Political Science, 1895–1995,* ed. Richard Rawlings. Pp. 247–270. Oxford, UK: Oxford University Press.

———. 2010. "The End of Anthropology, Again: On the Future of an In/Discipline." *American Anthropologist* 112 (4): 524–538.

Committee to Protect Journalists (CPJ). 2000. "Attacks on the Press 1999: Palestinian National Authority." March 22, accessed October 29, 2012, http://www.cpj .org/2000/03/attacks-on-the-press-1999-palestinian-national-aut.php.

Coombes, Sam. 2001. "Sartre's Concept of Bad Faith in Relation to the Marxist Notion of False Consciousness: Inauthenticity and Ideology Re-Examined." *Cultural Logic* 4 (2), accessed October 29, 2012, http://clogic.eserver.org/4-2/coombes.html.

Coronil, Fernando. 1997. *The Magical State: Nature, Money, and Modernity in Venezuela.* Chicago: University of Chicago Press.

Corrigan, Philip, and Derek Sayer. 1985. *The Great Arch: English State Formation as Cultural Revolution.* Oxford, UK: Blackwell.

Cowan, Jane K. 2006. "Culture and Rights After 'Culture and Rights.'" *American Anthropologist* 108 (1): 9–24.

———. 2007. "The Supervised State." *Identities: Global Studies in Culture and Power* 14 (5): 545–578.

———. 2008. "Fixing National Subjects in the 1920s Southern Balkans: Also an International Practice." *American Ethnologist* 35 (2): 338–356.

———. 2012. "Dispatches from the Field." *Sussex Anthropologist* 2 (2): 4.

Cowan, Jane K., Marie-Benedicte Dembour, and Richard Wilson, eds. 2001. *Culture and Rights: Anthropological Perspectives.* Cambridge, UK: Cambridge University Press.

Crooke, Alastair. 2008. "From Rebel Movement to Political Party: The Case of the Islamic Resistance Movement." *Conflicts Forum,* Briefing Paper 3, accessed October 29, 2012, http://conflictsforum.org/briefings/Hamas-From-rebel-movement-to-political -party.pdf.

Cruikshank, Barbara. 1999. *The Will to Empower: Democratic Citizens and Other Subjects.* Ithaca, NY: Cornell University Press.

Curtis, Jennifer. 2010. "'Profoundly Ungrateful': The Paradoxes of Thatcherism in Northern Ireland." *POLAR* 33 (2): 201–224.

Dalacoura, Katerina. 1998. "Islam and Human Rights." In *Islam, Liberalism, and Human Rights: Implications for International Relations.* London: I.B. Tauris.

Daston, Lorraine. 1992. "Objectivity and the Escape from Perspective." *Social Studies of Science* 22 (4): 597–618.

Daston, Lorraine, and Peter Galison. 2007. *Objectivity*. Cambridge, MA: Zone Books.

Davis, Rochelle A. 2010. *Palestinian Village Histories: Geographies of the Displaced*. Stanford, CA: Stanford University Press.

Dear, Peter. 1992. "From Truth to Disinterestedness in the Seventeenth Century." *Social Studies of Science* 22 (4): 619–631.

Defence for Children International–Palestine Section (DCI-Palestine). 2001. "A Generation Denied: Israeli Violations of Palestinian Children's Rights," accessed October 29, 2012, http://www.dci-pal.org/english/publ/research/2001/viol1.pdf.

Dembour, Marie-Bénédicte, and Emily Haslam. 2004. "Silencing Hearings? Victim-Witnesses at War Crimes Trials." *European Journal of International Law* 15 (1): 151–177.

Democracy and Human Rights Program. 2006. "An Analysis of the Current Situation of Human Rights Education in Palestinian Schools: A Report Prepared for the UNESCO Office." Report on file with author.

Democratic Control of Armed Forces (DCAF), Geneva Centre for the and Shams Forum. 2008. "Delivering Security to the Palestinian People: Summary Report." November 24, accessed October 29, 2012, http://www.ssronline.org/edocs/report_dcaf_shams_forum session_qalqiliya.pdf.

———. 2009. "Palestinian Security Sector Governance: The View of Security Forces in Nablus," accessed October 29, 2012, http://www.dcaf.ch/Publications/Palestinian-Security-Sector-Governance-The-View-of-Security-Forces-in-Nablus.

Dershowitz, Alan. 2003. *The Case for Israel*. New York: Wiley.

DeVoir, Joseph, and Alaa Tartir. 2009. "Tracking External Donor Funding to Palestinian Non-Governmental Organizations in the West Bank and Gaza Strip, 1999–2008." Jerusalem and Ramallah: Palestine Economic Policy Research Institute, accessed October 29, 2012, http://www.masader.ps/p/en/node/7929.

Diakonia. 2009. "Armed Struggle for Self-Determination and War of National Liberation," accessed October 29, 2012, http://www.diakonia.se/sa/node.asp?node=3144. Revised August 26, 2009.

Donohue, John L. 1983. "Islam and the Search for Identity in the Arab World." In *Voices of Resurgent Islam*, ed. John L. Esposito. Pp. 48–66. Oxford, UK: Oxford University Press.

Dorman, Sara Rich. 2005. "Studying Democratization in Africa: A Case Study of Human Rights NGOs in Zimbabwe." In *Between a Rock and a Hard Place: African NGOs, Donors, and the State*, ed. Tim Kelsall and Jim Igoe. Pp. 33–59. Durham, NC: Carolina Academic Press.

Douglass, Frederick. (1857) 1985. "The Significance of Emancipation in the West Indies." Speech, Canandaigua, New York, August 3, 1857. In *The Frederick Douglass Papers*. Series One: Speeches, Debates, and Interviews. Volume 3: 1855–1863, ed. John W. Blassingame. New Haven, CT: Yale University Press.

Doumani, Beshara B. 1992. "Rediscovering Ottoman Palestine: Writing Palestinians into History." *Journal of Palestine Studies* 21 (2): 5–28.

DPA. 2011. "Hamas Opposes 'Tactical' Palestinian Statehood Bid at UN." *Haaretz*, accessed October 29, 2012, http://www.haaretz.com/news/diplomacy-defense/hamas-opposes-tactical-palestinian-statehood-bid-at-un-1.384466.

Dubois, Laurent. 2004. *A Colony of Citizens: Revolution and Slave Emancipation in the French Caribbean, 1787–1804*. Chapel Hill: University of North Carolina Press.

———. 2006. "An Enslaved Enlightenment: Rethinking the Intellectual History of the French Atlantic." *Social History* 31 (1): 1–14.

Eagleton, Terry. 1991. *Ideology: An Introduction*. London: Verso.

Economist. 2010. "Palestinian Politics and the Mosques: The West Bank's Secular Rulers Want to Stop Preachers Backing the Islamists." February 11, accessed October 29, 2012, http://www.economist.com/node/15503327?story_id=15503327.

Eid, Haidar. 2009. "The Pitfalls of Palestinian National Consciousness." *Electronic Intifada*, August 24, accessed October 29, 2012, http://electronicintifada.net/v2/article10728.shtml.

Electronic Intifada. 2008. "Ramallah Palestinian Authority Blocks Website Reporting on Corruption." November 18, accessed October 29, 2012, http://electronicintifada.net/v2/article9972.shtml.

El Fegiery, Moataz. 2008. "The Effectiveness of Human Rights Commissions in the Arab World." *Sada* (previously *Arab Reform Bulletin*), June 12, accessed October 29, 2012, http://carnegieendowment.org/2008/08/12/effectiveness-of-human-rights-commissions-in-arab-world/6bfp.

Elshobaki, Amr, Khaled Hroub, Daniela Pioppi, and Nathalie Tocci. 2008. "Domestic Change and Conflict in the Mediterranean: The Cases of Hamas and Hezbollah." EuroMeSCo Paper 65, January, accessed October 29, 2012, http://www.euromesco.net/images/65eng.pdf.

Elyachar, Julia. 2006. "Best Practices: Research, Finance, and NGOs in Cairo." *American Ethnologist* 33 (3): 413–426.

Englund, Harri. 2006. *Prisoners of Freedom: Human Rights and the African Poor*. Berkeley: University of California Press.

Esposito, John L. 1983. "Introduction: Islam and Muslim Politics." In *Voices of Resurgent Islam*, ed. John L. Esposito. Pp. 3–16. Oxford, UK: Oxford University Press.

Euro-Mediterranean Human Rights Network. 2004. "Tightened Spaces for Human Rights—A Discussion Paper on Palestinian NGO Work," accessed October 29, 2012, http://www.euromedrights.org/en/publications-en/emhrn-publications/emhrn-publications-2004/3608.html.

European Commission (EC). 2007. "The European Union's Programme EU Partnership for Peace: Guidelines for Grant Applicants Responding to the Call for Proposals for 2007 Open Call for Proposals," accessed October 29, 2012, ec.europa.eu/europeaid/tender/data/d83/AOF80283.doc.

European Union Co-ordinating Office for Palestinian Police Support (EUPOL COPPS). n.d. Rule of Law Section, accessed October 29, 2012, http://www.eupolcopps.eu/content/rule-law-section.

———. 2009. "EUPOL COPPS Completed First Training of the Palestinian Judicial

Police Unit." *Europe in Israel Online*, August 17, accessed October 29, 2012, http://d157696.si27.siteam.co.il/eu-news/index.cfm?aId=40&eId=10.

Fabian, Johannes. 1983. *Time and the Other: How Anthropology Makes Its Object.* New York: Columbia University Press.

Falk, Richard. 2009. "The Goldstone Report and the Battle for Legitimacy." *Electronic Intifada*, September 22, accessed October 29, 2012, http://electronicintifada.net/content/goldstone-report-and-battle-legitimacy/8456.

Farraj, Khalid, Camille Mansour, and Salim Tamari. 2009. "A Palestinian State in Two Years: Interview with Salam Fayyad, Palestinian Prime Minister." *Journal of Palestine Studies* 39 (1): 58–74.

Fassin, Didier. 2008. "The Humanitarian Politics of Testimony: Subjectification Through Trauma in the Israeli–Palestinian Conflict." *Cultural Anthropology* 23 (3): 531–558.

Feldman, Allen. 2004. "Memory Theatres, Virtual Witnessing, and the Trauma-Aesthetic." *Biography* 27 (1): 163–202.

Feldman, Ilana. 2008. *Governing Gaza: Bureaucracy, Authority, and the Work of Rule, 1917–1967.* Durham, NC: Duke University Press.

Ferguson, James. 1994. *The Anti-Politics Machine: 'Development,' Depoliticization, and Bureaucratic Power in Losotho.* Minneapolis: University of Minnesota Press.

Filastin al-Muslimah. 1992a. "Facts and Background: The Dangerous Developments Between Hamas and Fateh [Haqa'iq wa-khalfiyyah: Al-tatawwurat al-khatirah bayna Hamas wa Fateh]." *Filastin al-Muslimah* 10 (8).

———. 1992b. "Hamas and Fateh: Reasons for the Clashes and Requirements for Meeting [Hamas wa Fateh: Asbab al-tasaddum wa-mutatallabat al-iltiqa']." *Filastin al-Muslimah* 10 (8).

———. 1992c. "No to the Fighting and Civil Strife [La lil-qatal wa-l-fitnah]." *Filastin al-Muslimah* 10 (8).

———. 1992d. "The Reconciliation Agreement Is Threatened with Dangerous Continuous Violations by the Brothers in the Fateh Movement [Ittifaq al-musalahah tuhaddiduhu al-khuruqat wa-l-intihakat al-khatirah wa-l-mustamirrah lil-ikhwan fi harakat Fateh]." *Filastin al-Muslimah* 10 (8).

Fisher, Ian. 2007. "In West Bank, Hamas Is Silent but Never Ignored." *New York Times*, June 28, accessed October 29, 2012, http://www.nytimes.com/2007/06/28/world/middleeast/28westbank.html.

Foundation for Middle East Peace (FMEP). n.d. "Overview of the FMEP Settlement Report." *FMEP: Foundation for Middle East Peace*, accessed October 29, 2012, http://www.fmep.org/reports.

Freed, Elizabeth. 2007. "Fatah and Hamas Human Rights Violations in the Palestinian Occupied Territories from June 2007 to December 2007." January, accessed October 29, 2012, http://www.phrmg.org/Fatah%20and%20hamas%20abuses%20since%20June%202007%20report%20_2_.pdf.

———. 2008. "Palestinian Authority Political Arrests, Illegal Detainment, and Torture." Palestinian Human Rights Monitoring Group, May, accessed October 29, 2012, http://www.phrmg.org/PA%20Political%20Arrest%20Report-May%202008.pdf.

Freire, Paulo. (1970) 1996. *Pedagogy of the Oppressed.* London: Penguin.

Frykberg, Mel. 2010. "Hamas 'Morality' Campaign Restricts Civil Liberties in Gaza." *Electronic Intifada,* August 4, accessed October 29, 2012, http://electronicintifada .net/content/hamas-morality-campaign-restricts-civil-liberties-gaza/8962.

Fujitani, Takashi. 1998. *Splendid Monarchy: Power and Pageantry in Modern Japan.* Berkeley: University of California Press.

Geertz, Clifford. 1981. *Negara: The Theatre State in Nineteenth-Century Bali.* Princeton, NJ: Princeton University Press.

Giacaman, George. 1998. "In the Throes of Oslo." In *After Oslo: New Realities, Old Problems,* ed. George Giacaman and Dag Jorund Lonning. London: Pluto.

———. 2000. "Perspectives on Civil Society in Palestine," accessed October 29, 2012, http://www.muwatin.org/george/welfare.html.

Gill, Lesley. 2000. *Teetering on the Rim: Global Restructuring, Daily Life and the Armed Retreat of the Bolivian State.* New York: Columbia University Press.

Gilsenan, Michael. 1976. "Lying, Honour and Contradiction." In *Transaction and Meaning: Directions in the Anthropology of Exchange and Symbolic Behavior,* ed. Bruce Kapferer. Pp. 191–219. Philadelphia: Institute for the Study of Humanities.

Glendon, Mary Ann. 2001. *A World Made New: Eleanor Roosevelt and the Universal Declaration of Human Rights.* New York: Random House.

Goffman, Erving. 1967. *Interaction Ritual: Essays in Face-to-Face Behavior.* Chicago, IL: Aldine.

Goldman, Michael. 2005. "Tracing the Roots/Routes of World Bank Power." *International Journal of Sociology and Social Policy* 25 (1/2): 10–29.

Goldstein, Daniel M. 2007. "Human Rights as Culprit, Human Rights as Victim, Rights and Security in the State of Exception." In *The Practice of Human Rights: Tracking Law Between the Global and the Local,* ed. Mark Goodale and Sally Engle Merry. Pp. 49–77. Cambridge, UK: Cambridge University Press.

Goodale, Mark. 2005. "Empires of Law: Discipline and Resistance Within the Transnational System." *Social and Legal Studies* 14 (4): 553–583.

———. 2007. "Introduction: Locating Rights, Envisioning Law Between the Global and the Local." In *The Practice of Human Rights: Tracking Law Between the Global and the Local,* ed. Mark Goodale and Sally Engle Merry. Pp. 1–38. Cambridge, UK: Cambridge University Press.

———. 2009. *Surrendering to Utopia: An Anthropology of Human Rights.* Stanford, CA: Stanford University Press.

Gordon, Neve. 2008. *Israel's Occupation.* Berkeley: University of California Press.

Gordon, Neve, and Nitza Berkovitch. 2007. "Human Rights Discourse in Domestic Settings: How Does It Emerge?" *Political Studies* 55 (1): 243–266.

Gorenberg, Gershom. 2006. *The Accidental Empire: Israel and the Birth of the Settlements, 1967–1977.* New York: Holt.

Green, Leslie. 2003. "Legal Positivism." *Stanford Encyclopedia of Philosophy,* ed. Edward N. Zalta. Last modified August 10, 2009, accessed October 29, 2012, http://plato .stanford.edu/archives/fall2009/entries/legal-positivism.

Guardian. 2009. "Palestinian Authority Suspends al-Jazeera in West Bank: President Mahmoud Abbas Orders Temporary Closure of Arab TV News Station Amid Allegations of Incitement and Bias." July 15, accessed October 29, 2012, http://www.guardian.co.uk/world/2009/jul/15/palestine-suspends-jazeera-west-bank.

Guest, Iain. 2007. "Defending Human Rights in the Occupied Palestinian Territory—Challenges and Opportunities: A Discussion Paper on Human Rights Work in the West Bank and Gaza." Jerusalem: Friedrich Ebert Foundation, February, accessed October 29, 2012, http://advocacynet.org/files/839.pdf.

Gunning, Jeroen. 2008. *Hamas in Politics: Democracy, Religion, Violence.* London: Hurst.

Gupta, Akhil M. 1995. "Blurred Boundaries: The Discourse of Corruption, the Culture of Politics, and the Imagined State." *American Ethnologist* 22 (2): 375–402.

Gupta, Akhil, and Aradhana Sharma. 2006. "Globalization and Postcolonial States." *Current Anthropology* 47 (2): 277–307.

Haaretz Service. 2009. "Britain: Israeli Settlements Are 'Illegal' and 'Obstacle' to Peace." *Haaretz*, November 3, accessed October 29, 2012, http://www.haaretz.com/news/britain-israeli-settlements-are-illegal-and-obstacle-to-peace-1.4858.

Haddad, Yvonne. 1983. "The Qur'anic Justification for an Islamic Revolution: The View of Sayyid Qutb." *Middle East Journal* 37 (1): 14–29.

———. 1992. "Islamists and the 'Problem of Israel': The 1967 Awakening." *Middle East Journal* 46 (2): 266–285.

Hajjar, Lisa. 1995. *Authority, Resistance, and the Law: A Study of the Israeli Military Court System in the Occupied Territories.* PhD dissertation, Department of Sociology, American University, Washington D.C.

———. 2001. "Law Against Order: Human Rights Organizations and (versus?) the Palestinian Authority." *University of Miami Law Review* 56: 59–76.

———. 2003. "Chaos as Utopia: International Criminal Prosecutions as a Challenge to State Power." *Studies in Law, Politics, and Society* 31: 3–23.

———. 2005. *Courting Conflict: The Israeli Military Court System in the West Bank and Gaza.* Berkeley: University of California Press.

Hamad, Ghazi Ahmad. 2006. "The Challenge for Hamas: Establishing Transparency and Accountability." Geneva Centre for the Democratic Control of Armed Forces, accessed October 29, 2012, http://www.dcaf.ch/content/download/3670/54819/version/1/file/hamad-challenges-for-hamas.pdf.

Hammami, Rema. 1995. "NGOs: The Professionalization of Politics." *Race & Class* 37 (2): 51–63.

———. 2000. "Palestinian NGOs Since Oslo: From NGO Politics to Social Movements?" *Middle East Report* 214: 16–19.

Hammami, Rema, Jamil Hilal, and Salim Tamari. 2001. "Civil Society and Governance in Palestine." RSC No. 2001/36, Mediterranean Programme Series. San Domenico di Fiesole, Italy: European University Institute, Robert Schuman Centre for Advanced Studies.

Hammami, Rema, and Salim Tamari. 2001. "The Second Uprising: End or New Beginning?" *Journal of Palestine Studies* 30 (2): 5–25.

Hanafi, Sari. 1999. "Profile of Donors to Palestinian NGOs: Survey and Preliminary Findings." Paper presented to Welfare Association, accessed October 29, 2012, http://staff.aub.edu.lb/sh41/dr_sarry_website/publications/145_Mazala.pdf.

Hanafi, Sari, and Linda Tabar. 2002. "NGOs, Elite Formation and the Second Intifada." *Between the Lines* 2: 18, accessed October 29, 2012, http://staff.aub.edu.lb/sh41/dr_sarry_website/publications/111_Between%20the%20Lines%20%20NGOs,%20Elite%20Formation.htm.

———. 2003. "The Intifada and the Aid Industry: The Impact of the New Liberal Agenda on the Palestinian NGOs." *Comparative Studies of South Asia, Africa and the Middle East* 23 (1–2): 205–214.

———. 2004. Donor Assistance, Rent-Seeking, and Elite Formation. In *State Formation in Palestine: Viability and Governance during a Social Transformation*, ed. Mushtaq Husain Khan, 215–238. London: Routledge.

———. 2005. "The New Palestinian Globalised Elite." *Jerusalem Quarterly* 24: 13–32, accessed October 29, 2012, http://staff.aub.edu.lb/sh41/dr_sarry_website/publications/125_Jerusalem_quarterly.pdf.

Haniyyah, Isma'il. 2007. "Mr. Isma'il Haniyyah's Khutba During the Tarawih Prayers at the Western Shati' Mosque in Gaza [Khutbat al-Ustadh Isma'il Haniyyah fi sha'ir salaah al-Tarawih min Masjid Shati' al-Gharbi bi Ghazzah]." September 13, accessed October 31, 2012, http://www.palinfo.com/site/pic/newsdetails.aspx?ItemId=70605.

———. 2009. "Text of the Sermon of Prime Minister Isma'il Haniyyah on the Occasion of the Passing of a Year After the War on Gaza [Nass khitab Ra'is al-Wuzura' Isma'il Haniyyah bi-munasibat murur 'am 'ala harb Ghazzah]." December 28, accessed October 31, 2012, http://www.dakahliaikhwan.com/viewarticle.php?id=3349&ref=search.php.

Harel, Amos, and Avi Issacharoff. 2010. "Israel and Palestinians Pass the Jericho Test: Security Cooperation Between Israel and PA Is Improving Despite Stalled Talks." *Haaretz*, February 22, accessed October 29, 2012, http://www.haaretz.com/hasen/spages/1151392.html.

Hart, H.L.A. 1994. *The Concept of Law*, 2nd ed. Oxford, UK: Clarendon Press.

Hass, Amira. 2011. "Palestinian Military Prosecutors Vow to Stop Arresting Civilians." *Haaretz*, January 19, accessed October 29, 2012, http://www.haaretz.com/print-edition/news/palestinian-military-prosecutors-vow-to-stop-arresting-civilians-1.337848.

Hasso, Frances. 2011. *Consuming Desires: Family Crisis and the State in the Middle East.* Stanford, CA: Stanford University Press.

Havel, Vaclav. 2010. "The Power of the Powerless." In *The Power of the Powerless: Citizens Against the State in Central-Eastern Europe*, ed. John Keane. Pp. 10–59. Abingdon: Routledge.

Hemment, Julie. 2007. *Empowering Women in Russia: Activism, Aid, and NGOs.* Bloomington: Indiana University Press.

Hider, James. 2009. "General Moshe Yaalon Cancels London Trip After Arrest Fear Over

Gaza Bombing." *Times.* October 6. http://www.timesonline.co.uk/tol/news/uk/article 6862322.ece.

Hilal, Jamil. 1995. "The PLO: Crisis in Legitimacy." *Race & Class* 37 (2): 1–18.

———. 2003. "Problematizing Democracy in Palestine." *Comparative Studies of South Asia, Africa and the Middle East* 23 (1/2): 163–172.

Hillier, Timothy. 1983. "The Reply of Law in the Service of Man / Al-Haq to the US Report on Human Rights Practices in the Occupied Territories by Israel for 1982." Al-Haq, accessed October 29, 2012, http://www.alhaq.org/publications/publications -index/item/the-reply-of-al-haq-to-the-us-report-on-human-rights.

Hiltermann, Joost. 1988. "Human Rights and the Politics of Computer Software." *Middle East Report* 150: 8–9.

———. 1989a. "Human Rights and the Palestinian Struggle for National Liberation." *Journal of Palestine Studies* 18 (2): 109–118.

———. 1989b. "Human Rights and Mass Movement: The First Year of the Intifadah." *Journal of Palestine Studies* 18 (3): 126–33.

———. 1990. "Deaths in Israeli Prisons." *Journal of Palestine Studies* 19 (3): 101–110.

———. 1991. *Behind the Intifada: Labor and Women's Movements in the Occupied Territories.* Princeton, NJ: Princeton University Press.

———. 2000. "Al-Haq: The First Twenty Years." *MERIP* 214 (30): 42–44.

Hiss, J., T. Kahana, and B. Arensburg. 1997. "Forensic Medicine in Israel." *American Journal of Forensic Medicine and Pathology* 18 (2): 154–157.

Høigilt, Jacob. 2010. "Raising Extremists? Islamism and Education in the Palestinian Territories." Oslo, Norway: Fafo, accessed October 29, 2012, http://www.fafo.no/ pub/rapp/20149/index.html.

House of Commons, International Development Committee. 2004. "Development Assistance and the Occupied Palestinian Territories." Second Report of Session 2003– 04, vol. 1. London: Stationery Office, February 5, accessed October 29, 2012, http:// www.publications.parliament.uk/pa/cm200304/cmselect/cmintdev/230/230.pdf.

Hovannisian, Richard G., ed. 1985. *Ethics in Islam.* Malibu, CA: Undena.

Hroub, Khaled. 2000. *Hamas: Political Thought and Practice.* Washington DC: Institute for Palestine Studies.

Hudson, Michael C. 1972. "Developments and Setbacks in the Palestinian Resistance Movement, 1967–1971." *Journal of Palestine Studies* 1 (3): 64–84.

Hull, M. S. 2008. "Ruled by Records: The Expropriation of Land and the Misappropriation of Lists in Islamabad." *American Ethnologist* 35(4): 501–518.

Human Rights Watch (HRW). 1991. "Prison Conditions in Israel and Israeli-Occupied West Bank and Gaza Strip." April 1, accessed October 29, 2012, http://www.hrw.org/ en/reports/1991/04/01/prison-conditions-israel-and-israeli-occupied-west-bank -and-gaza-strip.

———. 2008. "Occupied Palestinian Territories: New Arrests Highlight Abuses by Hamas, Fatah." July 30, accessed October 29, 2012, http://www.hrw.org/en/ news/2008/07/29/occupied-palestinian-territories-new-arrests-highlight-abuses -hamas-fatah.

———. 2009. "Internal Fight." July 30, accessed October 29, 2012, http://www.hrw.org/reports/2008/07/29/internal-fight.

———. 2010. "Gaza: Hamas Report Whitewashes War Crimes." January 28, accessed October 29, 2012, http://www.hrw.org/en/news/2010/01/28/gaza-hamas-report-whitewashes-war-crimes.

———. 2011. "Palestinian Authority: No Justice for Torture Death in Custody." February 16, accessed October 29, 2012, http://www.hrw.org/en/news/2011/02/16/palestinian-authority-no-justice-torture-death-custody.

Human Rights Watch/Middle East. 1994. "Torture and Ill-Treatment: Israel's Interrogation of Palestinians from the Occupied Territories." New York: HRW.

Humphrey, Caroline. 1995. "Creating a Culture of Disillusionment: Consumption in Moscow: A Chronicle of Changing Times." In *Worlds Apart: Modernity Through the Prism of the Local*, ed. Daniel Miller. Pp.43–68. New York: Routledge.

Independent Commission for Human Rights (ICHR). n.d.a. "Donors," accessed October 29, 2012, http://www.ichr.ps/en/2/2/258/Donors-Donors.htm.

———. n.d.b. "About Us," accessed October 29, 2012, http://www.ichr.ps/en/2/2/251/About-Us-About-Us.htm.

———. n.d.c. "2008 Is Witness to Most Violations of Civil Institutions and Societies' Rights in Gaza and the West Bank [2008 akthar intihakan li-huquq al-mu'assasat wa-a-jam'iyyat al-ahliyyah fi Ghazzah wa-l-Daffah]." May 4, accessed October 31, 2012, http://www.ichr.ps.

———. n.d.d. "Report on the Freedom of Association in the Palestinian Controlled Territory," accessed October 29, 2012, www.ichr.ps/pdfs/eFreedomofassociation.pdf.

———. 2008. "Follow Up on Complaints and Oversight of Detention Centers in the Palestinian-Controlled Territory Throughout 2008," accessed October 29, 2012, http://www.ichr.ps/pdfs/ecomplaint-report-08.pdf.

———. 2009a. "A Legal Review of Provisions on Torture in the Palestinian Legal System." *Legal Reports* 69, accessed October 29, 2012, http://www.ichr.ps/en/2/12/319/ICHR-issues-a-legal-report-entitled-A-Legal-Review-of-Provisions-on-Torture-in-the-Palestinian-Legal-System-ICHR-issues-a-legal-report-entitled-A-Legal-Review-of-Provisions-on-Torture-in-the-Palestinian-Legal-System.htm?d=2009.

———. 2009b. "ICHR Demands That a Fact-Finding Mission Be Established for an Investigation into the Death of Mohammed al Hajj in the Preventive Security Detention Centre of Jordan," accessed October 29, 2012, http://www.ichr.ps/en/2/4/389/ICHR-Demands-that-a-Fact-Finding-Mission-Be-Established-for-an-Investigation-into-the-Death-of-Mohammed-al-Hajj-in-the-Preventive-Security-D-ICHR-Demands-that-a-Fact-Finding-Mission-Be-Established-for-an-Investigation-into-the-Death-of-Mohammed-al-Hajj-in-the-Preventive-Security-Detention-Centre-of-Jenin.htm?d=2009.

———. 2009c. "ICHR Forewarns the Gravity of the Recurrent Cases of Death at Detention Centers Operated by the Palestinian Security Agencies," accessed October 29, 2012, http://www.ichr.ps/en/2/4/375/ICHR-forewarns-the-gravity-of-the-recurrent-cases-of-death-at-detenion-centers-operated-by-the-Palestinian-Security-agencies

-ICHR-forewarns-the-gravity-of-the-recurrent-cases-of-death-at-detenion-centers
-operated-by-the-Palestinian-Security-agencies.htm?d=2009.

———. 2009d. "ICHR Judicially Challenges the Validity of the Security Clearance Pre-
requisites for Assuming Public Office," accessed October 29, 2012, http://www.ichr
.ps/en/2/12/311/ICHR-Judicially-Challenges-the-Validity-of-the-Security-Clearance
-Prerequisites-for-Assuming-Public-Office-ICHR-Judicially-Challenges-the-Validity
-of-the-Security-Clearance-Prerequisites-for-Assuming-Public-Office.htm?d=2009.

———. 2009e. "ICHR Receives Accreditation with the International Coordinating
Committee of National Institutions for the Promotion and Protection of Human
Rights," accessed October 29, 2012, http://www.ichr.ps/en/2/12/329/ICHR-receives
-Accreditation-with-the-International-Coordinating-Committee-of-National
-Institutions-for-the-Promotion-and-Protection-of-Human-ICHR-receives
-Accreditation-with-the-International-Coordinating-Committee-of-National
-Institutions-for-the-Promotion-and-Protection-of-Human-Rights-%28ICC%29
.htm?d=2009.

———. 2009f. "Violations of Human Rights and Public Freedoms in the Palestinian-
Controlled Territory." November, accessed October 29, 2012, http://www.ichr.ps/
pdfs/eMRV-11-09.pdf.

———. 2010a. "ICHR Denounces the Banning of Its Workshop in Gaza City," May 24,
2010, accessed October 29, 2012, http://www.ichr.ps/en/2/4/362/ICHR-Denounces
-the-Banning-of-its-Workshop-in-Gaza-City-ICHR-Denounces-the-Banning-of
-its-Workshop-in-Gaza-City.htm?d=2010.

———. 2010b. "ICHR Condemns the Obstruction of Its Staff While on Duty." May
30, accessed October 29, 2012, http://www.ichr.ps/en/2/4/361/ICHR-condemns-the
-obstruction-of-its-staff-while-on-duty-ICHR-condemns-the-obstruction-of-its
-staff-while-on-duty.htm?d=2010.

———. 2011a. "Strategic Plan 2011–2013," accessed October 29, 2012, http://www.ichr
.ps/en/2/2/256/Strategic-Document-Strategic-Document.htm.

———. 2011b. "Monthly Report on Violations of Human Rights and Public Freedoms
in the Palestinian Controlled Territory." February, accessed October 29, 2012, http://
www.humanrights.ps/ar/node/736.

International Commission of Jurists (ICJ). n.d. "Overview," accessed October 29, 2012,
http://old.icj.org/rubrique.php3?id_rubrique=11&lang=en.

International Committee of the Red Cross. 2011. "Gaza: No End in Sight to Hard-
ship and Despair." May 20, accessed October 29, 2012, http://www.icrc.org/eng/
resources/documents/interview/2011/palestine-israel-interview-2011-05-19.htm.

International Council on Human Rights Policy. 2005. "National Human Rights Institutions: Measuring Effectiveness." Versoix, Switzerland: International Council on Human Rights Policy and The Office of the United Nations High Commissioner for
Human Rights, accessed October 29, 2012, http://www.ichrp.org/en/projects/125.

International Crisis Group (ICG). 2003. "Islamic Social Welfare Activism in the Occupied Territories: A Legitimate Target?" *Middle East Report* 13, accessed October
29, 2012, http://www.crisisgroup.org/en/regions/middle-east-north-africa/israel

-palestine/013-islamic-social-welfare-activism-in-the-occupied-palestinian-terri
tories-a-legitimate-target.aspx.
———. 2008. "Ruling Palestine II: The West Bank Model." *Middle East Report* 79, accessed October 29, 2012, http://www.crisisgroup.org/en/regions/middle-east-north
-africa/israel-palestine/079-ruling-palestine-II-the-west-bank-model.aspx.
———. 2009. Ending the War in Gaza. *Middle East Briefing* 26, accessed October 29,
2012, http://www.crisisgroup.org/en/regions/middle-east-north-africa/israel-pale
stine/B026-ending-the-war-in-gaza.aspx.
———. 2010. "Squaring the Circle: Palestinian Security Reform under Occupation."
Middle East Report 98, accessed October 29, 2012, http://www.crisisgroup.org/en/
regions/middle-east-north-africa/israel-palestine/98-squaring-the-circle-palestinian
-security-reform-under-occupation.aspx.
———. 2011. "Radical Islam in Gaza." *Middle East Report* 104, accessed October 29,
2012, http://www.crisisgroup.org/en/regions/middle-east-north-africa/israel-pales
tine/104-radical-islam-in-gaza.aspx.
Isaac, Jeffrey C. 1996. "A New Guarantee on Earth: Hannah Arendt on Human Dignity
and the Politics of Human Rights." *American Political Science Review* 90 (1): 61–73.
Ishkanian, Armine. 2003. "Is the Personal Political? The Development of Armenia's
NGO Sector During the Post-Soviet Period." Berkeley Program in Soviet and Post-
Soviet Studies, University of California, accessed October 29, 2012, http://escholar
ship.org/uc/item/2j57b1h5.
Isin, Engin F., and Bryan S. Turner. 2002. "Citizenship Studies: An Introduction." In
Handbook of Citizenship Studies, ed. Engin F. Isin and Bryan S. Turner. Pp. 1–10.
London: Sage.
Israel National Section of the International Commission of Jurists. 1981. *The Rule of Law
in the Areas Administered by Israel.* Tel Aviv: International Commission of Jurists.
Israeli Committee Against Home Demolitions (ICAHD). 2012. "Displacement Trends,"
accessed October 29, 2012, http://www.icahd.org/displacement-trends.
Issacharoff, Avi. 2010. "Palestinian Police Chief Knows 'the Secret of the Correct Use
of Force.'" *Haaretz*, March 11, accessed October 29, 2012, http://www.haaretz.com/
palestinian-police-chief-knows-the-secret-of-the-correct-use-of-force-1.264682.
Jad, Islah. 2004. "The NGO-isation of Arab Women's Movement." *IDS Bulletin* 35 (4):
34–42.
———. 2005. "Islamist Women of Hamas: A New Women's Movement?" In *On Shifting Ground: Muslim Women in the Global Era*, ed. Fereshteh Nouraie-Simone. Pp.
172–202. New York: Feminist Press.
Jamal, Amaney A. 2007. *Barriers to Democracy: The Other Side of Social Capital in Palestine and the Arab World.* Princeton, NJ: Princeton University Press.
Jarrar, Allam. 2005. "The Palestinian NGO Sector: Development Perspectives." *Palestine
Israel Journal of Politics, Economics, and Culture* 12 (1), accessed October 29, 2012,
http://www.pij.org/details.php?id=324.
Johnson, Penny. 1988. "The Routine of Repression." *Middle East Report* 150: 3–7+10–11.

Kanaaneh, Rhoda Ann. 2002. *Birthing the Nation: Strategies of Palestinian Women in Israel.* Berkeley: University of California Press.

Kassem, Sattar. 2009. "The Role of US Trained Palestinian Security Forces." June 11, accessed October 29, 2012, http://www.silviacattori.net/article853.html.

Kassis, Mudar. 2006. "The Effect of Human Rights and Democracy Education on the Nature of Involvement in Political Life: A Case Study of the Human Rights and Democracy Program at Birzeit [Athr taʿlim al-dimuqratiyyah wa huquq al-insan ʿala tabiʿat al-inkhirat fi al-hayaat al-siyasiyyah: dirasah hawl barnamij al-dimuqratiyyah wa huquq al-insan fi Jamiʿat Birzeit]." On file with author.

Kates, Robert W. 1978. "Human Issues in Human Rights: The Experience of the Committee on Human Rights of the National Academy of Sciences." *Science* 201 (4355): 502–506.

Kaviraj, Sudipta. 2010. *The Imaginary Institution of India: Politics and Ideas.* New York: Columbia University Press.

Keane, Webb. 2007. *Christian Moderns: Freedom and Fetish in the Mission Encounter.* Berkeley: University of California Press.

———. 2010. "Minds, Surfaces, and Reasons in the Anthropology of Ethics." In *Ordinary Ethics: Anthropology, Language, and Action*, ed. Michael Lambek. Pp. 64–83. New York: Fordham University Press.

Keating, Michael, Anne Le More, and Robert Lowe. 2005. *Aid, Diplomacy, and Facts on the Ground: The Case of Palestine.* London: Chatham House.

Keenan, Alan. 1998. "The Twilight of the Political? A Contribution to the Democratic Critique of Cynicism." *Theory & Event* 2 (1), accessed October 29, 2012, http://muse.jhu.edu/login?auth=0&type=summary&url=/journals/theory_and_event/v002/2.1keenan.html.

Kelly, Tobias. 2006. *Law, Violence and Sovereignty Among West Bank Palestinians.* Cambridge, UK: Cambridge University Press.

———. 2010. "In a Treacherous State: The Fear of Collaboration among West Bank Palestinians." In *Traitors: Suspicion, Intimacy and the Ethics of State-Building*, eds. Sharika Thiranagama and Tobias Kelly. Pp. 169–187. Philadelphia: University of Pennsylvania Press.

———. 2012. *This Side of Silence: Human Rights, Torture, and the Recognition of Cruelty.* Philadelphia: University of Pennsylvania Press.

Kennedy, Duncan. 2002a. "The Critique of Rights in Critical Legal Studies." In *Left Legalism/Left Critique*, ed. Wendy Brown and Janet Halley. Pp. 178–228. Durham, NC: Duke University Press.

———. 2002b. "The International Human Rights Movement: Part of the Problem?" *Harvard Human Rights Journal* 15: 101–126.

Kershner, Isabel. 2009. "Israeli Military Says Actions in Gaza War Did Not Violate International Law." *New York Times*, April 22, accessed October 29, 2012, http://www.nytimes.com/2009/04/23/world/middleeast/23gaza.html.

Khadduri, Majid. 2001. *The Islamic Conception of Justice.* Baltimore: Johns Hopkins University Press.

Khalidi, Rashid. 1998. *Palestinian Identity: The Construction of Modern National Consciousness.* New York: Columbia University Press.

Khan, Mushtaq Husain. 2004. *State Formation in Palestine: Viability and Governance During a Social Transformation.* New York: Routledge.

Khashan, Ali. 2006. "Hamas, Islam, and Authority: The Implications of the Participation of an Islamic Movement in a Secular System." *Palestine Israel Journal of Politics, Economics, and Culture* 13 (3), accessed October 29, 2012, http://www.pij.org/details.php?id=864.

Klein, Menachem. 2009. "Against the Consensus: Oppositionist Voices in Hamas." *Middle Eastern Studies* 45 (6): 881–892.

Konrad-Adenauer-Stiftung. 2007a. "Strengthening NGOs: Guide to Public Hearings for NGOs." *Palestinian Territories,* accessed October 29, 2012, http://www.kas.de/palaestinensische-gebiete/en/publications/12297.

———. 2007b. "Large Number of Palestinian NGOs Sign Code of Conduct." July 19, 2007, accessed October 29, 2012, http://www.kas.de/palaestinensische-gebiete/en/publications/11459.

Kracke, Waud, and Gilbert Herdt. 1987. "Introduction: Interpretation in Psychoanalytic Anthropology." *Ethos* 15 (1): 3–7.

Kretzmer, David. 2002. *The Occupation of Justice: The Supreme Court of Israel and the Occupied Territories.* Albany: State University of New York Press.

Kuttab, Jonathan. 1992. "Avenues Open for Defence of Human Rights in the Israeli-Occupied Territories." In *International Law and the Administration of Occupied Territories: Two Decades of Israeli Occupation of the West Bank and Gaza Strip,* ed. Emma Playfair. Pp. 489–504. Oxford, UK: Oxford University Press.

Kuttab, Jonathan, and Raja Shehadeh. 1980. *The West Bank and the Rule of Law.* Geneva: International Commission of Jurists, accessed October 29, 2012, http://www.alhaq.org/publications/publications-index/item/the-west-bank-and-the-rule-of-law.

Lambek, Michael. 2010. "Introduction." In *Ordinary Ethics: Anthropology, Language, and Action,* ed. Michael Lambek. Pp. 1–38. New York: Fordham University Press.

Langer, Felicia. 1995. "The History of the Legal Struggle Against Torture in Israel." In *Torture: Human Rights, Medical Ethics, and the Case of Israel,* ed. Neve Gordon and Ruchama Marton. Pp. 75–80. London: Zed Books.

Lasensky, Scott. 2004. "Paying for Peace: The Oslo Process and the Limits of American Foreign Aid." *Middle East Journal* 58 (2): 210–234.

Lasensky, Scott, and Robert Grace. 2006. "Dollars and Diplomacy: Foreign Aid and the Palestinian Question." USIP Briefing, August. Washington, DC: United States Institute of Peace, accessed October 29, 2012, http://www.usip.org/files/resources/palestinian_aid.pdf.

Latour, Bruno. 2004. "Scientific Objects and Legal Objectivity." In *Law, Anthropology, and the Constitution of the Social: Making Persons and Things,* ed. Alain Pottage and Martha Mundy. Pp. 73–114. Cambridge, UK: Cambridge University Press.

Lauren, Paul Gordon. 2003. *The Evolution of International Human Rights: Visions Seen,* 2nd ed. Philadelphia: University of Pennsylvania Press.

Law in the Service of Man (LSM). 1984. "Jnaid, The New Israeli Prison in Nablus: An Appraisal. January 1, accessed October 29, 2012, http://www.alhaq.org/publications/publications-index/item/jnaid-the-new-israeli-prison-in-nablus.

———. 1986. "Torture and Intimidation in the West Bank: The Case of al-Fara'a Prison." January 1, accessed October 29, 2012, http://www.alhaq.org/publications/publications-index/item/torture-and-intimidation-in-the-west-bank-the-case-of-al-fara-a-prison.

Lazar, Sian. 2010. "Schooling and Critical Citizenship: Pedagogies of Political Agency in El Alto, Bolivia." *Anthropology and Education Quarterly* 41 (2): 181–205.

Le More, Anne. 2005. "Killing with Kindness: Funding the Demise of a Palestinian State." *International Affairs* 81 (5): 981–999.

———. 2008. *International Assistance to the Palestinians After Oslo: Political Guilt, Wasted Money*. London: Routledge.

Li, Tania. 2007. *The Will to Improve: Governmentality, Development, and the Practice of Politics*. Durham, NC: Duke University Press.

Luhrmann, T. M. 1994. "The Good Parsi: The Postcolonial 'Feminization' of a Colonial Elite." *Man*, New Series 29 (2): 333–357.

Lybarger, Loren D. 2007. *Identity and Religion in Palestine: The Struggle Between Islamism and Secularism in the Occupied Territories*. Princeton, NJ: Princeton University Press.

Lynch, Marc. 2009. "Khaled Meshaal, Keith Dayton, and the Future of Palestinian Security Forces." *Foreign Policy*, June 26, accessed October 29, 2012, http://lynch.foreignpolicy.com/posts/2009/06/25/hamas_offers_a_cautious_welcome_and_a_warning.

Macintyre, Donald. 2007. "Hamas Vows to Continue Campaign of Resistance." *Independent*, November, 28, accessed October 29, 2012, http://www.independent.co.uk/news/world/middle-east/hamas-vows-to-continue-campaign-of-resistance-760754.html.

Mansour, Jamal. 2000. *The Palestinian Transition to Democracy: An Islamist Perspective*. Trans. Alyce Abdalla. Papers in Contemporary Palestinian Islamic Thought and Politics. Center for Palestine Research and Studies.

Maurer, Bill. 2006. "The Anthropology of Money." *Annual Review of Anthropology* 35: 15–36.

Mawdudi, Abul Ala. 1980. *Human Rights in Islam*. Leicester, UK: Islamic Foundation.

Mayer, Ann Elizabeth. 2007. "Restrictions on the Rights and Freedoms of Women." In *Islam and Human Rights: Tradition and Politics*. Pp. 109–142. Boulder, CO: Westview Press.

Mazower, Mark. 2004. "The Strange Triumph of Human Rights, 1933–1950." *Historical Journal* 47: 379–398.

———. 2009. *No Enchanted Palace: The End of Empire and the Ideological Origins of the United Nations*. Princeton, NJ: Princeton University Press.

Mazzarella, William. 2008. "Affect: What Is It Good for?" In *Enchantments of Modernity: Empire, Nation, Globalization*, ed. Saurab Dhube. Pp. 291–309. London: Routledge.

Mazzawi, Reem, and Hazem Jamjoum. 2009. "In Search of a Courtroom: Who Will Try Israeli Perpetrators?" *Al-Majdal: Litigating Palestine* 41 (Spring-Summer): 4–7. Badil

Resource Center for Palestinian Residency and Refugee Rights, accessed October 29, 2012, http://www.badil.org/en/component/k2/item/10-commentary.

McAlister, Melani. 2001. *Epic Encounters: Culture, Media, and U.S. Interests in the Middle East, 1945–2000.* Berkeley: University of California Press.

McCarthy, Rory. 2007. "Israeli Minister Cancels UK Trip in Fear of Arrest." *Guardian,* December, 6, accessed October 29, 2012, http://www.guardian.co.uk/world/2007/dec/07/israelandthepalestinians.foreignpolicy?INTCMP=SRCH.

———. 2010. "British Government Will Fight Legal Attempts to Indict Israeli Leaders in UK." *Guardian,* January 5, accessed October 29, 2012, http://www.guardian.co.uk/world/2010/jan/05/israel-war-crimes-warrants-britain.

Mearsheimer, John J., and Stephen M. Walt. 2007. *The Israel Lobby and U.S. Foreign Policy.* New York: Farrar, Straus and Giroux.

Mehta, Uday S. 1990. "Liberal Strategies of Exclusion." *Politics & Society* 18 (4): 427–454.

Merry, Sally Engle. 2003. "Rights Talk and the Experience of Law: Implementing Women's Human Rights to Protection from Violence." *Human Rights Quarterly* 25 (2): 343–381.

———. 2006. *Human Rights and Gender Violence: Translating International Law into Local Justice.* Chicago: University of Chicago Press.

———. 2011. "Measuring the World: Indicators, Human Rights, and Global Governance, with Comment by John M. Conley." *Current Anthropology* 52 (Supplement 3): S83–S95, accessed October 29, 2012, http://www.iilj.org/documents/MeasuringtheWorldCA.pdf.

Mertus, Julie A. 2009. *Human Rights Matters: Local Politics and National Human Rights Institutions.* Stanford, CA: Stanford University Press.

Middle East Report. 2000. "From the Editor." *Middle East Report* 214, accessed October 29, 2012, http://www.merip.org/mer/mer214/editor.

Miller, Peter, and Nikolas Rose. 1992. "Political Power beyond the State: Problematics of Government." *British Journal of Sociology* 43 (2): 173–205.

Milton-Edwards, Beverley. 1996. *Islamic Politics in Palestine.* London: I.B. Tauris.

———. 2007. "Hamas: Victory with Ballots and Bullets." *Global Change, Peace, and Security* 19 (3): 301–316.

———. 2008. "The Ascendance of Political Islam: Hamas and Consolidation in the Gaza Strip." *Third World Quarterly* 29 (8): 1585–1599.

Milton-Edwards, Beverley, and Stephen Farrell. 2010. *Hamas: The Islamic Resistance Movement.* Cambridge, UK: Polity Press.

Ministry of Interior. 2010. "Human Rights Unit in the Ministry of Interior Visits Turkish Humanitarian Relief I.H.H. June 16 [Wahdat huquq al-insan bi-Wizarat al-Dakhiliyyah tazur Hay'at al-Ighathah al-Insaniyyah al-Turkiyyah]," accessed March 25, 2012, http://www.moi.gov.ps/Page.aspx?page=details&nid=17450.

———. 2011. "During Visit of the Human Rights Unit to His Office, Brig. Al-Batsh: All Rehabilitation Centers Are Open to Human Rights [Khilal ziyarat wahdat huquq al-insan li-maktabihi, al-'Amid al-Batsh: jami' marakiz al-ta'-hil maftuha imam al-huquqiyyin]." September 18, accessed October 31, 2012, http://www.moi.gov.ps.

Mish'al, Khalid. 2006. "We Will Not Sell Our People or Principles for Foreign Aid." *Guardian*, January 31, accessed October 29, 2012, http://www.guardian.co.uk/world/2006/jan/31/comment.israelandthepalestinians.

Mitchell, Richard P. 1993. *The Society of the Muslim Brothers*. New York: Oxford University Press.

Mitchell, Timothy. 1991. "The Limits of the State: Beyond Statist Approaches and Their Critics." *American Political Science Review* 85 (1): 77–96.

———. 1999. "Society, Economy, and the State Effect." In *State/Culture: State Formation After the Cultural Turn*, ed. George Steinmetz. Pp. 76–97. Ithaca, NY: Cornell University Press.

Mitnick, Joshua. 2009. "War Crimes Accusations Rattle Israel." *Christian Science Monitor*, February 4, accessed October 29, 2012, http://www.csmonitor.com/World/Middle-East/2009/0204/p06s01-wome.html.

Mohamedou, Mohammad-Mahmoud Ould. 2002. "Accuracy and Consistency: Establishing National Human Rights Institutions as Trusted Sources of Information." International Council on Human Rights Policy, July 15–16, accessed October 29, 2012, http://www.ichrp.org/files/papers/48/106_waif_paper_-_Accuracy_and_Consistency_-_Establishing_NHRIs_Mohamedou__Mohammad-Mahmoud_Ould___2002__staff.pdf.

Moodie, Ellen. 2006. "Microbus Crashes and Coca-Cola Cash: The Value of Death in 'Free-Market' El Salvador." *American Ethnologist* 33 (1): 63–80.

Moosa, Ebrahim. 2000. "The Dilemma of Islamic Rights Schemes." *Journal of Law and Religion* 15 (1): 185–215.

———. 2001–2002. "The Poetics and Politics of Law After Empire: Reading Women's Rights in the Contestations of Law." *Journal for Islamic and Near Eastern Law* 1 (1): 1–46.

Morris, Benny. 1999. *Righteous Victims: A History of the Zionist-Arab Conflict, 1881-2001*. London: John Murray.

Morris, Rosalind C. 1995. "All Made Up: Performance Theory and the New Anthropology of Sex and Gender." *Annual Review of Anthropology* 24: 567–592.

Moussalli, Ahmad S. 1992. *Radical Islamic Fundamentalism: The Ideological and Political Discourse of Sayyd Qutb*. Beirut: American University of Beirut.

Moyn, Samuel. 2010. *The Last Utopia: Human Rights in History*. Cambridge, MA: Belknap Press of Harvard University Press.

———. 2012. "Human Rights, Not So Pure Anymore." *New York Times, Sunday Review*, May 12, accessed October 29, 2012, http://www.nytimes.com/2012/05/13/opinion/sunday/human-rights-not-so-pure-anymore.html?pagewanted=all.

Muhsin, Samih. Ed. 2005. *Religious Sacrifice Is a Reformist View* [Al-fida' al-dini nathrah islahiyyah]. Ramallah: Ramallah Center for Human Rights.

Murdock, Donna F. 2008. *When Women Have Wings: Feminism and Development in Medellin, Colombia*. Ann Arbor: University of Michigan Press.

Muslih, Muhamad Y. 1987. "Arab Politics and the Rise of Palestinian Nationalism." *Journal of Palestine Studies* 16 (4): 77–94.

Mutua, Makau. 2009. "Human Rights NGOs in East Africa: Defining the Challenges." In *Human Rights NGOs in East Africa Political and Normative Tensions*, ed. Makau Mutua. Pp. 13–36. Kampala, Uganda: Fountain.

Nakhleh, Khalil. 2004. *The Myth of Palestinian Development: Political Aid and Sustainable Deceit.* Jerusalem: Palestinian Academic Society for the Study of International Affairs.

Nassali, Maria. 2011. "Mainstreaming Human Rights into All NGO Work." *East African Journal of Peace and Human Rights* 17 (1): 18–52.

Navaro-Yashin, Yael. 2002. *Faces of the State: Secularism and Public Life in Turkey.* Princeton, NJ: Princeton University Press.

Nazaha. 2006. "Public Opinion Poll on the State of Palestinian NGOs." June 15–18, accessed October 29, 2012, http://www.kas.de/palaestinensische-gebiete/en/publications/8798.

Nelson, Diane M. 2010. *Reckoning: The Ends of War in Guatemala.* Durham, NC: Duke University Press.

NGO Development Center (NDC). 2009a. "Good Governance as a Centre of Gravity for Democracy." *This Week in Palestine* 138, accessed October 29, 2012, http://www.thisweekinpalestine.com/details.php?id=2891&ed=174&edid=174.

———. 2009b. "Annual Report 2009," accessed October 29, 2012, http://www.ndc.ps/uploads/File/AR%202009%20for%20website.pdf.

Obeid, Michelle. 2010. "Searching for the 'Ideal Face of the State' in a Lebanese Border Town." *Journal of the Royal Anthropological Institute* 16 (2): 330–346.

Office of the High Commissioner for Human Rights (OHCHR). 2004. "World Programme for Human Rights Education," accessed October 29, 2012, http://www2.ohchr.org/english/issues/education/training/programme.htm.

Okafor, Obiora Chinedu, and Shedrack C. Agbakwa. 2002. "On Legalism, Popular Agency and 'Voices of Suffering': The Nigerian National Human Rights Commission in Context." *Human Rights Quarterly* 24 (3): 662–720.

Omar, Mohammed. 2008. "Gaza Teachers Trapped Between Fatah and Hamas." *Electronic Intifada*, September 15, accessed October 29, 2012, http://electronicintifada.net/v2/article9829.shtml.

Ong, Aihwa. 1996. "Cultural Citizenship as Subject-Making: Immigrants Negotiate Racial and Cultural Boundaries in the United States." *Current Anthropology* 37 (5): 737–762.

———. 2000. "Graduated Sovereignty in South-East Asia." *Theory, Culture & Society* 17 (4): 55–75.

Orentlicher, Diane F. 1990. "Bearing Witness: The Art and Science of Human Rights Fact-Finding." *Harvard Human Rights Journal* 3: 83–135.

Osanloo, Arzoo. 2009. *The Politics of Women's Rights in Iran.* Princeton, NJ: Princeton University Press.

Osborne, Thomas. 1994. "Bureaucracy as a Vocation: Governmentality and Administration in Nineteenth-Century Britain." *Journal of Historical Sociology* 7 (3): 289–313.

Oxfam. 2007. "Poverty in Palestine: The Human Cost of the Financial Boycott." Oxfam

International, April, accessed October 29, 2012, http://www.oxfam.org/sites/www
.oxfam.org/files/poverty%20in%20palestine.pdf.

———. 2008. "The Middle East Quartet: A Progress Report." September 25, accessed
October 29, 2012, http://www.oxfam.org/sites/www.oxfam.org/files/middle-east
-quartet-progress-report-25-sept08.pdf.

Palestinian Center for Human Rights (PCHR). 2002. "Annual Report 2002," accessed
October 29, 2012, http://www.pchrgaza.org/portal/en/index.php?option=com_con
tent&view=article&id=2389:annual-report-2002&catid=40:pchrannualreports&Ite
mid=172.

———. 2007a. "Black Pages in the Absence of Justice: Report on Bloody Fighting in
the Gaza Strip from 7 to 14 June 2007," accessed October 29, 2012, http://www
.pchrgaza.org/portal/en/index.php?option=com_content&view=article&id=2862:
black-pages-in-the-absence-of-justice-report-on-bloody-fighting-in-the-gaza-strip
-from-7-to-14-june-2007&catid=47:special-reports&Itemid=191.

———. 2007b. "The Center Condemns the Threats Against the Independent Commission for Citizen's Rights [Al-Markaz yudin al-tahdidat allati tata'arrad laha al-
Hay'ah al-Mustaqillah li-Huquq al-Insan]," accessed October 29, 2012, http://www
.pchrgaza.org/files/PressR/arabic/2007/150-2007.html.

———. 2009a. "Annual Report 2009," accessed October 29, 2012, http://www.pchrgaza
.org/files/Reports/English/pdf_annual/PCHR%20Annual-Eng-09.pdf.

———. 2009b. "Confirmed Figures Reveal the True Extent of the Destruction Inflicted
upon the Gaza Strip." March 12, accessed October 29, 2012, http://www.pchrgaza
.org/portal/en/index.php?option=com_content&view=article&id=1073:confirmed
-figures-reveal-the-true-extent-of-the-destructioninflicted-upon-the-gaza-strip
-israels-offensive-resulted-in-1417-dead-including-926-civilians-255-police-officers
-and-236-fighters&catid=36:pchrpressreleases&Itemid=194.

———. 2010a. "Translation of Appeal to Spanish Supreme Court." February 28, accessed
on October 29, 2012, http://www.pchrgaza.org/portal/en/index.php?option=com
_content&view=article&id=6198:translation-of-appeal-to-spanish-supreme-court
-&catid=73:universal-jurisdiction-other-info&Itemid=216.

———. 2010b. "PCHR Condemns Continued Campaign Against Non-Governmental
Organizations." June 15, accessed October 29, 2012, http://www.pchrgaza.org/por
tal/en/index.php?option=com_content&view=article&id=6757:pchr-condemns
-continued-campaign-against-non-governmental-organizations-&catid=36:pchrp
ressreleases&Itemid=194.

———. 2011. "PCHR Calls for an Investigation into a Suspicious Death in a Police Station in al-Nussairat Refugee Camp." June 26, accessed on October 29, 2012, http://
www.pchrgaza.org/portal/en/index.php?option=com_content&view=article&id=7
522:pchr-calls-for-an-investigation-into-a-suspicious-death-in-a-police-station-in
-al-nussairat-refugee-camp&catid=36:pchrpressreleases&Itemid=194.

Palestinian Central Bureau of Statistics (PCBS). 2011. "On the Eve of International Population Day." http://www.pcbs.gov.ps/Portals/_pcbs/PressRelease/int_Pop_2012e
.pdf.

Palestinian Government, Gaza. 2010. "The Implementation of the Recommendations of the UN Fact-Finding Mission Report on the Israeli Aggression Against Gaza 12/2008–1/2009. January [Halat tatbiq tawsiyat taqrir bʻatha taqassi al-haqaʼiq al-Umamiyyah al-mutaʻlliqah bil-ʻadwan al-Israʼili ʻala Ghazzah 12/2008–1/2009. Kanun al-thani]." On file with author.

Palestinian Independent Commission for Citizens' Rights (PICCR). 2007. *Facts' Finding Report on the Events of al-Najah National University.* Series of Fact-Finding Reports no. 5, accessed October 29, 2012, http://www.ichr.ps/pdfs/eTSR5.pdf.

Palestinian Information Center (PIC). n.d. "Hamas's Election Campaign: Astounding Success Through Organization, Publication, Activities, and Impact Without Expenditure [Al-hamlah al-intikhabiyyah li-ʻHamas' najah bahir fi al-tanzim wa-l-intishar wa-l-faʻaliyyah wa al-taʼthir dun ayy israf maddi]," accessed October 31, 2012, http://www.palestine-info.com/arabic/palestoday/reports/report2006_1/entkhabat06/entkhabat_tashre3i_06/24_1_06.htm.

———. 2007a. "Fateh Threatens Palestinian Independent Commission for Human Rights That Revealed the Truth of the Crime of Execution of the Student Radad at ʻAn-Najah' [Fateh tuhaddid hayʼah huquqiyyah al-mustaqillah baʻd kashafat haqiqat jarimat iʻdam al-talib Radad fi ʻal-Najah']," accessed October 31, 2012, http://www.alrepat.com/vb/archive/index.php/t-13648.html.

———. 2007b. "Bahar Praises the Performance of the Police and Confirms the Focus on Their National Role in Preserving Security." November 30, accessed October 29, 2012, http://www.palestine-info.co.uk/en/default.aspx?xyz=U6Qq7k%2bcOd87M DI46m9rUxJEpMO%2bi1s7uxNI1DKN5W7TUrgE0egs%2fphHCzvcNqwCH5HF miiPPPSLPwseNPwBKZ9cbBdZWTtsXPTWKxcmFPQTx1MUDeZA%2fCmu4jeL o14cER1qf9Vjj14%3d.

———. 2007c. "Haneyya: We Are Advocating National Dialogue, Keen on Preserving Human Rights." June 26. http://www.vtjp.org/news/elections0707.php.

———. 2009. "While Accusing Its Director in Gaza of Working for a Partisan Agenda, the Ministry of Interior Contends the Involvement of ICHR in a Political and Security Escalation Against the Haniyyah Government [Ittahamat mudiraha fi Ghazzah bi-l-ʻamal wifqa ajindah hizbiyyah, al-dakhiliyyah tuʻakkid ʻal-Mustaqillah li-Huquq al-Insan' fi tasʻid amani siyasi didd hukumat Haniyyah]," accessed October 29, 2012, http://www.palinfo.com/site/pic/newsdetails.aspx?itemid=16928.

Palestinian National Authority (PNA). 2009. "Palestine: Ending the Occupation, Establishing the State." August, accessed October 29, 2012, http://www.americantaskforce.org/palestinian_national_authority_ending_occupation_establishing_state.

Palestinian Police [Al-Shurtah al-Filastiniyyah]. 2010. "Brigadier Abu ʻUbaydah Met with a Delegation of the International Committee of the Red Cross [ʻAmid Abu ʻUbaydah yustaqbal wafd min al-Salib al-Ahmar al-Dowli]," accessed October 29, 2012, http://www.police.ps/ar/news-action-show-id-1992.htm.

Parker, Kunal. 2003. "Response: History, Law, and Regime Change." *PoLAR: Political and Legal Anthropology Review* 26 (1): 43–48.

Paul, Robert A. 1989. "Psychoanalytic Anthropology." *Annual Review of Anthropology* 18: 177–202.

Peacebuilding Initiative. n.d. "Human Rights Promotion and Protection: Actors and Activities," accessed October 29, 2012, http://peacebuildinginitiative.org/index .cfm?pageId=1849#_ftn90.

Peteet, Julie. 1991. *Gender in Crisis: Women and the Palestinian Resistance Movement.* New York: Columbia University Press.

———. 1994. "Male Gender and Rituals of Resistance in the Palestinian 'Intifada': A Cultural Politics of Violence." *American Ethnologist* 21 (1): 31–49.

———. 1996. "The Writing on the Walls: The Graffiti of the Intifada." *Cultural Anthropology* 11 (2): 139–159.

———. 1997. "Icons and Militants: Mothering in the Danger Zone." *Signs* 23 (1): 103–129.

Phillips, Sarah D. 2008. *Women's Social Activism in the New Ukraine: Development and the Politics of Differentiation.* Bloomington: Indiana University Press.

Piot, Charles. 2010. *Nostalgia for the Future: West Africa After the Cold War.* Chicago: University of Chicago Press.

Pitner, Julia. 2000. "NGOs' Dilemmas." *Middle East Report* 214: 34–37.

Playfair, Emma. 1992. *International Law and the Administration of Occupied Territories: Two Decades of Israeli Occupation of the West Bank and Gaza Strip.* Oxford, UK: Oxford University Press.

Pohjolainen, Anna-Elina. 2006. "The Evolution of National Human Rights Institutions: The Role of the United Nations." Denmark: Danish Institute for Human Rights, January, accessed October 29, 2012, http://www.nhri.net/pdf/Evolution_of_NHRIs.pdf.

Pollis, Adamantia. 1987. "The State, the Law, and Human Rights in Modern Greece." *Human Rights Quarterly* 9 (4): 587–614.

Postero, Nancy Grey. 2007. *Now We Are Citizens: Indigenous Politics in Post-Multicultural Bolivia.* Stanford, CA: Stanford University Press.

Postone, Moishe. 1996. *Time, Labor, and Social Domination: A Reinterpretation of Marx's Critical Theory.* Cambridge, UK: University of Cambridge Press.

Public Committee Against Torture in Israel (PCATI). n.d., accessed October 29, 2012. http://www.stoptorture.org.il/en.

Qutb, Sayyid. 2000. *Social Justice in Islam.* Trans. John B. Hardie. New York: Islamic Publications International.

Rabbani, Mouin. 1994. "Palestinian Human Rights Activism Under Israeli Occupation: The Case of Al-Haq." *Arab Studies Quarterly* 16 (2): 27–52.

———. 1996. "Palestinian Authority, Israeli Rule: From Transitional to Permanent Arrangement." *Middle East Report* 201: 2–22.

———. 2009a. "Human Rights Watch's Double Standard on Israel and Palestine: A New Low on Gaza?" *Counterpunch*, February 6–8, accessed October 29, 2012, http:// www.counterpunch.org/rabbani02062009.html.

———. 2009b. "Israel's Assault on Gaza: A Transformational Moment? An Interview with Azmi Bishara." *Journal of Palestine Studies* 38 (3): 38–53.

Rabie', Ghandi. 2008. "The Detention of Civilians by Palestinian Security Agencies with a

Stamp of Approval by the Military Judicial Commission [Ihtijaz al-madaniyyin lada al-ajhizah al-amniyyah al-Filastiniyyah bi-qirar min hay'ah al-qada' al-'askari]," accessed October 30, 2012, www.ichr.ps/pdfs/SP64.pdf.

Ramadan, Ahmad. 1992. "The Central Council Was in Labor, So What Did They Give Birth To? [Tamakhkhad al-majlis al-markazi, fa-madha walad?]," *Filastin al-Muslimah* 10 (6).

Rangwala, Glen. 2002. "Historical Justification and the Portrayal of Palestinian Political Identity, 1967–1977." PhD dissertation, Department of Social and Political Science, Cambridge University.

Rass, Michael. 2009. "Gaza Conflict." *PRI's The World*, October 16, accessed October 30, 2012, http://www.theworld.org/2009/10/gaza-conflict.

Reuters. 2007. "Palestinian Killed as Israel Raids West Bank Camp." June 26, accessed October 30, 2012, http://www.reuters.com/article/idUSL26340127.

Richard, Analiese M. 2009. "Mediating Dilemmas: Local NGOs and Rural Development in Neoliberal Mexico." *PoLAR: Political and Legal Anthropology Review* 32 (2): 166–194.

Rieff, David. 2002. *A Bed for the Night: Humanitarianism in Crisis.* New York: Simon and Schuster.

Rizek, Mira, and Chris Sidoti. 2010. "Al-Haq, Part of Palestine's Heritage, Strategic Assessment and Planning Report, Final Report." Accessed October 30, 2012, http://www.alhaq.org/about-al-haq/transparency.

Roberts, Hugh. 2002. "Moral Economy or Moral Polity? The Political Anthropology of Algerian Riots." Crisis States Programme, Development Research Centre Working paper no. 17. London: Crisis States Programme, Development Research Centre, London School of Economics, accessed October 30, 2012, http://eprints.lse.ac.uk/28292.

Rose, David. 2008. "The Gaza Bombshell." *Vanity Fair*, March 10, accessed October 30, 2012, http://www.vanityfair.com/politics/features/2008/04/gaza200804.

Rose, Nikolas. 1996. *Inventing Our Selves.* Cambridge, UK: Cambridge University Press.

———. 1999. *Powers of Freedom: Reframing Political Thought.* Cambridge, UK: University of Cambridge Press.

Roy, Arundhati. 2004. *Public Power in the Age of Empire.* New York: Seven Stories Press.

Roy, Sara. 1996. "US Economic Aid to the West Bank and Gaza Strip: The Politics of Peace." *Middle East Policy* 4 (4): 50–76.

———. 2000. "The Transformation of Islamist NGOs in Palestine." *Middle East Report* 214, accessed October 30, 2012, http://www.merip.org/mer/mer214/transformation-islamist-ngos-palestine.

———. 2010. "Gaza: Treading on Shards." *Nation*, March 1, accessed October 30, 2012, http://www.thenation.com/article/gaza-treading-shards.

———. 2011. *Hamas and Civil Society in Gaza: Engaging the Islamist Social Sector.* Princeton, NJ: Princeton University Press.

Sahiliyah, Sanad. 2004. "Palestinian Poll: Higher Confidence in Services, NGOs, Lower in Leadership." *Al-Quds*, June 29, p .13, accessed October 31, 2012, http://www.access mylibrary.com/coms2/summary_0286-21818427_ITM.

Sahlins, Marshall. 1999. "Two or Three Things That I Know About Culture." *Journal of the Royal Anthropological Institute* 5 (3): 399–421.

Said, Abdul Aziz. 1979. "Precept and Practice of Human Rights in Islam." *Universal Human Rights* 1 (1): 63–79.

Said, Edward W. 1979. *The Question of Palestine*. New York: Times Books.

———. 2000. "America's Last Taboo." *New Left Review* 6: 45–53.

———. 2001. *The End of the Peace Process: Oslo and After*. London: Vintage.

Samaha, Nour. 2011. "Palestinian Statehood Opinion Causes Uproar." Last modified September 1, accessed on October 30, 2012, http://www.aljazeera.com/indepth/features/2011/08/20118291464077832.html.

Sassen, Saskia. 1996. *Losing Control? Sovereignty in an Age of Globalization*. University Seminars/Leonard Hastings Schoff Memorial Lectures. New York: Columbia University Press.

Sayigh, Rosemary. 1998. "Palestinian Camp Women as Tellers of History." *Journal of Palestine Studies* 27 (2): 42–58.

Sayigh, Yezid. 1997. *Armed Struggle and the Search for State: The Palestinian National Movement, 1949–1993*. Oxford, UK: Oxford University Press.

———. 2009. "'Fixing Broken Windows': Security Sector Reform in Palestine, Lebanon, and Yemen." Washington, DC: Carnegie Endowment for International Peace, accessed October 30, 2012, http://www.carnegieendowment.org/files/security_sector_reform.pdf.

———. 2010. "Hamas Rule in Gaza: Three Years On." Crown Center for Middle East Studies, Brandeis University, March, accessed October 30, 2012, http://www.brandeis.edu/crown/publications/meb/meb41.html.

———. 2011. "'We Serve the People': Hamas Policing in Gaza." Crown Center for Middle East Studies, Brandeis University, April, accessed October 30, 2012, http://www.brandeis.edu/crown/publications/cp/cp5.html.

Schielke, Samuli. 2009. "Ambivalent Commitments: Troubles of Morality, Religiosity and Aspiration Among Young Egyptians." *Journal of Religion in Africa* 39 (2): 158–185.

Scott, James C. 1977. *Moral Economy of the Peasant: Rebellion and Subsistence in South East Asia*. New Haven, CT: Yale University Press.

———. 1998. *Seeing Like a State: How Certain Schemes to Improve the Human Condition Have Failed*. New Haven, CT: Yale University Press.

Sewell, William H. 1996. "Historical Events as Transformation of Structures: Inventing Revolution at the Bastille." *Theory and Society* 25: 841–881.

Shah, Alpa. 2010. *In the Shadows of the State: Indigenous Politics, Environmentalism, and Insurgency in Jharkhand, India*. Durham, NC: Duke University Press.

Shaheen, Jack G. 2001. *Reel Bad Arabs: How Hollywood Vilifies a People*. Northampton, MA: Interlink.

Shamir, Ronen. 1990. "'Landmark Cases' and the Reproduction of Legitimacy: The Case of Israel's High Court of Justice." *Law and Society Review* 24 (3): 781–805.

Shammakh, 'Amr, ed. 2004. *Memoirs of the Martyr Doctor 'Abd al-'Aziz al-Rantisi* [Mudhakkirat al-shahid al-Duktur 'Abd al-'Aziz al-Rantisi]. Dar al-Tawzi' wa-l-Nashr al-Islamiyyah.

Shapin, Steven. 1984. "Pump and Circumstance: Robert Boyle's Literary Technology." *Social Studies of Science* 14 (4): 481–520.

Shapiro, Barbara J. 1969. "Law and Science in Seventeenth-Century England." *Stanford Law Review* 21 (4): 727–766.

Sharma, Aradhana, and Akhil Gupta. 2006. "Introduction: Rethinking Theories of the State in an Age of Globalization." In *The Anthropology of the State: A Reader*, ed. Aradhana Sharma and Akhil Gupta. Malden, MA: Blackwell.

Shehadeh, Aziz, Fuad Shehadeh, and Raja Shehadeh. 1984. *Israeli Proposed Road Plan for the West Bank: A Question for the International Court of Justice*. Ramallah: Law in the Service of Man, accessed October 30, 2012, http://www.alhaq.org/publications/publications-index/item/israeli-proposed-road-plan-for-the-west-bank-a-question -for-the-international-court-of-justice?category_id=9.

Shehadeh, Raja. 1984. *Samed: Journal of a West Bank Palestinian*. New York: Adama Books.

———. 1988. *Occupier's Law: Israel and the West Bank*. Washington, DC: Institute for Palestine Studies.

———. 1997. *From Occupation to Interim Accords: Israel and the Palestinian Territories*. London: Kluwer Law International.

———. 2002. *Strangers in the House: Coming of Age in Occupied Palestine*. South Royalton, VT: Steerforth Press.

———. 2008. "Human Rights and the Israeli Occupation." *New Centennial Review* 8 (1): 33–55.

Sheizaf, Noam. 2011. "Everything You (Never) Wanted to Know About Israel's Anti-Boycott Law: A Reader's Guide to Democracy's Dark Hour." *+972*, July 13, accessed October 30, 2012, http://972mag.com/boycott2325-7132011.

Shestack, Jerome. 1998. "The Philosophic Foundations of Human Rights." *Human Rights Quarterly* 20 (2): 201–234.

Shlaim, Avi. 1994. "The Oslo Accord." *Journal of Palestine Studies* 23 (3): 24–40.

Shohat, Ella. 2003. "Rupture and Return: Zionist Discourse and the Study of Arab Jews." *Social Text* 21 (2): 49–74.

Sidoti, Chris, and Fadia Daibes-Murad. 2004. "Mapping of Palestinian, Israeli and International Human Rights, Good Governance and Public Participation Sector Non-Government Organizations Relating to the Occupied Palestinian Territories: Final Report." November 5, Accessed on October 30, 2012, http://www.multaqa.org/pdfs/FinalReportNGOMappin5Nov04.pdf.

Sloterdijk, Peter. 1988. *Critique of Cynical Reason*. London: Verso.

Smith, Helena. 2004. "Human Rights Record Haunts Turkey's EU Ambitions." *Guardian*, December 12, accessed October 30, 2012, http://www.guardian.co.uk/world/2004/dec/13/eu.turkey1.

Smith, James Howard. 2008. *Bewitching Development: Witchcraft and the Reinvention of Development in Neoliberal Kenya*. Chicago: University of Chicago Press.

Speed, Shannon. 2007. *Rights in Rebellion: Indigenous Struggle and Human Rights in Chiapas*. Stanford, CA: Stanford University Press.

Spencer, Jonathan. 2007. *Anthropology, Politics, and the State: Democracy and Violence in South Asia*. Cambridge, UK: Cambridge University Press.

Spyer, Patricia. 2006. "Some Notes on Disorder in the Indonesian Postcolony." In *Law and Disorder in the Postcolony*, ed. Jean Comaroff and John L. Comaroff. Chicago: Chicago University Press.

Steinmüller, Hans. 2010. "Communities of Complicity: Notes on State Formation and Local Sociality in Rural China." *American Ethnologist* 37 (3): 539–549.

Stern, Yoav. 2007. "US Chides Israel for Curbing Palestinian Security Forces." *Haaretz*, November 7, accessed October 30, 2012, http://www.haaretz.com/hasen/spages/921527.html.

Subramanian, Ajantha. 2009. *Shorelines: Space and Rights in South India*. Stanford, CA: Stanford University Press.

Sullivan, Denis J. 1996. "NGOs in Palestine: Agents of Development and Foundation of Civil Society." *Journal of Palestine Studies* 25 (3): 93–100.

Sunday Times (London). 1977. "Israel and Torture: An Insight Inquiry." June 19.

Swiss Agency for Development and Cooperation (SDC). 2010. "The Cooperation Strategy 2010-2014." Accessed October 30, 2012, http://www.swiss-cooperation.admin.ch/gazaandwestbank/en/Home/The_Cooperation_Strategy_2010_2014.

Tamari, Salim. 1988. "What the Uprising Means." *Middle East Report* 152: 24–30.

Tamimi, Azzam. 2007a. *Hamas: Unwritten Chapters*. London: Hurst.

———. 2007b. *Hamas: A History from Within*. New York: Olive Branch Press.

Tanabe, Akio. 2007. "Toward Vernacular Democracy: Moral Society and Post-postcolonial Transformation in Rural Orissa, India." *American Ethnologist* 34 (3): 558–574.

Taraki, Lisa. ed. 2006. *Living Palestine: Family Survival, Resistance, and Mobility Under Occupation*. Syracuse, NY: Syracuse University Press.

———. 2008. "Urban Modernity on the Periphery: A New Middle Class Reinvents the Palestinian City." *Social Text* 26 (2): 61–81.

Tate, Winifred. 2007. *Counting the Dead: The Culture and Politics of Human Rights Activism in Colombia*. Berkeley: University of California Press.

Taylor, Diana. 1997. *Disappearing Acts: Spectacles of Gender and Nationalism in Argentina's "Dirty War."* Durham, NC: Duke University Press.

Tetta, Alberto. 2009. "Spanish Judge Pursues Israel for 'Crimes Against Humanity.'" *Bianet*, January 30, accessed October 30, 2012, http://bianet.org/english/english/112243-spanish-judge-pursues-israel-for-crimes-against-humanity.

Thompson, Edward P. 1971. "The Moral Economy of the English Crowd in the Eighteenth Century." *Past and Present* 50: 76–136.

Tolley, Howard B., Jr. 1994. *The International Commission of Jurists: Global Advocates for Human Rights*. Philadelphia: University of Pennsylvania Press.

Tsing, Anna Lowenhaupt. 2005. *Friction: An Ethnography of Global Connection.* Princeton, NJ: Princeton University Press.

United Nations. n.d. "The Universal Declaration of Human Rights: An Historical Record of the Drafting Process," accessed October 30, 2012, http://www.ohchr.org/EN/UDHR/Pages/Language.aspx?LangID=eng.

———. 2005. "The Milennium Development Goals Report," accessed October 30, 2012, http://unstats.un.org/unsd/mi/pdf/mdg%20book.pdf.

United Nations Convention Against Torture and Other Cruel, Inhuman, or Degrading Treatment or Punishment (UNCAT). 1997. "Summary Record of the First Part (Public) of the 295th Meeting: Israel" [CAT/C/SR.295], accessed October 30, 2012, http://www.unhchr.ch/tbs/doc.nsf/0/87b2a1733266b4ca80256515005915a3?Open document.

United Nations Educational, Scientific and Cultural Organization (UNESCO). 2006. "Plan of Action: World Programme for Human Rights Education—First Phase," accessed October 30, 2012, http://unesdoc.unesco.org/images/0014/001478/147853e.pdf.

———. 2003. "World Directory of Human Rights Research and Training Institutions," 6th ed., accessed October 30, 2012, http://unesdoc.unesco.org/images/0013/001321/132133m.pdf.

United Nations General Assembly (UNGA). 1971. "Report of the Special Committee to Investigate Israeli Practices Affecting the Human Rights of the Population of the Occupied Territories." Twenty-Sixth Session of the General Assembly [A/8389]. October 5, accessed July 27, 2011, http://unispal.un.org/UNISPAL.NSF/0/858C88EB973847F4802564B5003D1083.

———. 1974. "Twenty-Ninth Session, Official Records." 2282nd Plenary Meeting [A/PV.2282 and Corr.1]. November 13, accessed July 27, 2011, http://unispal.un.org/UNISPAL.NSF/0/A238EC7A3E13EED18525624A007697EC.

———. 1976. "Report of the Special Committee to Investigate Israeli Practices Affecting the Human Rights of the Population of the Occupied Territories." Thirty-First Session of the General Assembly" [A/31/218]. October 1.

———. 1977. "Recent Illegal Israeli Measures in the Occupied Arab Territories Designed to Change the Legal Status, Geographical Nature and Demographic Composition of Those Territories in Contravention of the Principles of the Charter of the United Nations, of Israel's International Obligations Under the Fourth Geneva Convention of 1949 and of the United Nations Resolutions, and Obstruction of Efforts Aimed at Achieving a Just and Lasting Peace in the Middle East." Thirty-Second Session of the General Assembly [32/5], October 28.

———. 1988. "Report of the Special Committee to Investigate Israeli Practices Affecting the Human Rights of the Population of the Occupied Territories." Forty-Third Session of the General Assembly [A/43/904]. December 2.

———. 1993. "National Institutions for the Promotion and Protection of Human Rights." 85th Plenary Meeting [A/RES/48/134]. December 20, accessed July 27, 2011, http://www.un.org/documents/ga/res/48/a48r134.htm.

———. 2005. "The Issue of Palestinian Women Giving Birth at Israeli Checkpoints." 60th Session [A/60/324]. August 31, accessed July 27, 2011, http://unispal.un.org/UNISPAL.NSF/0/7ACAC141D3593CCE85257085004DD6C5.

United Nations Information System on the Question of Palestine (UNISPAL). n.d. "The Question of Palestine," accessed July 27, 2011, http://unispal.un.org/unispal.nsf/home.htm.

United Nations Office for the Coordination of Humanitarian Affairs (OCHA). n.d. Gaza Update, accessed October 30, 2012, http://www.ochaopt.org/gazacrisis.aspx?id=1000.

———. 2009. *Humanitarian Monitor*. December, accessed October 30, 2012, http://www.ochaopt.org/documents/ocha_opt_the_humanitarian_monitor_2010_01_18_english.pdf.

———. 2012. *Monthly Humanitarian Monitor*. January, accessed October 30, 2012, http://www.ochaopt.org/reports.aspx?id=118.

United Nations Office for the Coordination of Humanitarian Affairs—Occupied Palestinian Territories (OCHA oPt). 2009. "Locked In: The Humanitarian Impact of Two Years of Blockade on the Gaza Strip," accessed October 30, 2012, http://www.ochaopt.org/documents/Ocha_opt_Gaza_impact_of_two_years_of_blockade_August_2009_english.pdf.

U.S. Department of State, Diplomacy in Action. 2009. *2008 Human Rights Report: Preface*. US Department of State, Diplomacy in Action, February 25, accessed October 30, 2012, http://www.state.gov/g/drl/rls/hrrpt/2008/frontmatter/118982.htm.

USA Today. 2007. "Israeli Troops Crack Down on West Bank City." February 25, accessed October 30, 2012, http://www.usatoday.com/news/world/2007-02-25-west-bank_x.htm.

Usher, Graham. 1993. "Why Gaza Mostly Says Yes." *Middle East International* 459: 19–20.

———. 1995. *Palestine in Crisis: The Struggle for Peace and Political Independence After Oslo.* London: Pluto Press.

Wallace, Tim, and Daniela N. Diamente. 2005. "Keeping the People in the Parks: A Case Study from Guatemala." *NAPA Bulletin* 23: 191–218.

Waltz, Susan Eileen. 2004. "Universal Human Rights: The Contribution of Muslim States." *Human Rights Quarterly* 26 (4): 799–844.

Washington Institute for Near East Policy. 2009. "Program of the Soref Symposium. Michael Stein Address on U.S. Middle East Policy: Lieutenant General Keith Dayton, US Security Coordinator, Israel and the Palestinian Authority." May 7, accessed October 30, 2012, http://www.washingtoninstitute.org/html/pdf/DaytonKeynote.pdf.

Weber, Max. 1978. *Economy and Society: An Outline of Interpretive Sociology,* ed. Guenther Roth and Claus Wittich. Berkeley: University of California Press.

Wedeen, Lisa. 1998. "Acting 'As If': Symbolic Politics and Social Control in Syria." *Comparative Studies in Society and History* 40 (03): 503–523.

———. 1999. *Ambiguities of Domination: Politics, Rhetoric, and Symbols in Contemporary Syria.* Chicago: University of Chicago Press.

———. 2003. "Seeing Like a Citizen, Acting Like a State: Exemplary Events in Unified Yemen." *Comparative Studies in Society and History* 45 (04): 680–713.

———. 2008. *Peripheral Visions: Publics, Power, and Performances in Yemen.* Chicago: Chicago University Press.

Weill, Sharon. 2007. "The Judicial Arm of the Occupation: The Israeli Military Courts in the Occupied Territories." *International Review of the Red Cross* 89 (866): 395–419.

———. 2009. "The Targeted Killing of Salah Shehadeh." *Journal of International Criminal Justice* 7 (3): 617–631.

Welchman, Lynn. 2008. "The Bedouin Judge, the Mufti, and the Chief Islamic Justice: Competing Legal Regimes in the Occupied Palestinian Territories." *Journal of Palestine Studies* 38 (1): 6–23.

Welsh, James. 2000. "Documenting Human Rights Violations: The Example of Torture." Amnesty International, August, accessed October 30, 2012, http://www.amnesty.org/es/library/asset/ACT75/004/2000/es/39b04d03-de9d-11dd-b378-99b26579b978/act750042000en.pdf.

Williams, Raymond. 1977. *Marxism and Literature.* Oxford, UK: Oxford University Press.

Wilson, Richard A. 2001. *The Politics of Truth and Reconciliation in South Africa: Legitimizing the Post-Apartheid State.* Cambridge, UK: Cambridge University Press.

Winegar, Jessica. 2006. *Creative Reckonings: The Politics of Art and Culture in Contemporary Egypt.* Stanford, CA: Stanford University Press.

World Bank. 2004a. "Deep Palestinian Poverty in the Midst of Economic Crisis." October, accessed October 30, 2012, http://web.worldbank.org/WBSITE/EXTERNAL/TOPICS/EXTPOVERTY/EXTPA/0,,contentMDK:20689641menuPK:435735pagePK:148956piPK:216618theSitePK:430367isCURL:YisCURL:Y,00.html.

World Bank. 2004b. "Disengagement, the Palestinian Economy and the Settlements." Jerusalem: World Bank, June 23, accessed October 30, 2012, http://domino.un.org/UNISPAL.NSF/eed216406b50bf6485256ce10072f637/cdf4f0f82b8205ec85256ebd0075d859/$FILE/ATTZWN7S/DisengagementIssuesPaper.pdf.

———. 2009. "A Palestinian State in Two Years: Institutions for Economic Revival." September 22, accessed October 30, 2012, http://siteresources.worldbank.org/INTWESTBANKGAZA/Resources/AHLCSept09WBreportfinal.pdf.

Ynet News. 2009. "Spain Court Drops Gaza Probe into Israeli Air Raid." June 30, accessed October 30, 2012, http://www.ynet.co.il/english/articles/0,7340,L-3739264,00.html.

Yousef, Ahmad. 2007. "Hamas Is the Key." *Haaretz,* September 21, accessed October 30, 2012, http://www.haaretz.com/print-edition/opinion/hamas-is-the-key-1.229802.

———. 2010. "Hamas Does Not Oppress Women." *Palestine Chronicle.* December 13, accessed October 30, 2012, http://palestinechronicle.com/view_article_details.php?id=16482.

Zizek, Slavoj. n.d. "Against Human Rights." *libcom,* October 9, accessed October 30, 2012, http://libcom.org/library/against-human-rights-zizek.

———. 1989. *The Sublime Object of Ideology.* London: Verso.

Index

Stones of Hope: How African Activists Reclaim Human Rights to Challenge Global Poverty
Edited by Lucie E. White and Jeremy Perelman
2011

Judging War, Judging History: Behind Truth and Reconciliation
Pierre Hazan
2010

Localizing Transitional Justice: Interventions and Priorities after Mass Violence
Edited by Rosalind Shaw and Lars Waldorf, with Pierre Hazan
2010

Surrendering to Utopia: An Anthropology of Human Rights
Mark Goodale
2009

Human Rights for the 21st Century: Sovereignty, Civil Society, Culture
Helen M. Stacy
2009

Human Rights Matters: Local Politics and National Human Rights Institutions
Julie A. Mertus
2009